Urban Inequality

Urban Inequality

Special Issue Editor

Jesús Manuel González Pérez

MDPI • Basel • Beijing • Wuhan • Barcelona • Belgrade

MDPI

Special Issue Editor
Jesús Manuel González Pérez
University of the Balearic Island
Spain

Editorial Office
MDPI
St. Alban-Anlage 66
Basel, Switzerland

This is a reprint of articles from the Special Issue published online in the open access journal *Urban Science* (ISSN 2413-8851) from 2017 to 2018 (available at: http://www.mdpi.com/journal/urbansci/special_issues/urban_inequality)

For citation purposes, cite each article independently as indicated on the article page online and as indicated below:

LastName, A.A.; LastName, B.B.; LastName, C.C. Article Title. *Journal Name* **Year**, *Article Number*, Page Range.

ISBN 978-3-03897-200-6 (Pbk)
ISBN 978-3-03897-201-3 (PDF)

This special issue is inscribed in the research project:
'Crisis and social vulnerability in Spanish island cities Changes in the social reproduction spaces'
CSO2015-68738-P (MINECO/FEDER).

Contents

About the Special Issue Editor

Jesús Manuel González Pérez has a PhD in Geography and has been an Associate Professor at the University of the Balearic Islands (Spain), Assistant Professor in the Master of Spatial Planning and Environmental Management of the University of Barcelona (Spain), and Visiting Scholar (2015) and Visiting Professor (2016) at Stanford University. He has also been a visiting researcher at thirteen European and American universities. He has contributed as author to more than 150 national and international publications. He was a member of a research team that has undertaken a total of 30 funded research projects. Dr. González is currently Chairman of the Urban Geography Group of the Association of Spanish Geographers and a member of the Urban Geography Commission of the International Geographical Union. Professor González is an expert evaluator for different Spanish scientific agencies. He is also a member of the scientific or editorial committees of eight international journals, one as editor-in-chief and another as Advisory Board member, and a reviewer for another thirty-five.

urban science

MDPI

Editorial

Urban Inequality: The City after the 2007 Crisis

Jesús M. González-Pérez

Department of Geography, Guillem Colom building, University of the Balearic Islands (Spain),
Cra. de Valldemossa km 7.5, 07122 Palma, Spain; jesus.gonzalez@uib.es; Tel.: +34-690-051586

Received: 24 July 2018; Accepted: 30 July 2018; Published: 31 July 2018

Abstract: After the impact of the 2007 crisis and post-crisis austerity policies, cities are being reconfigured under the auspices of inequality. Social divides are widening, and there is a growing population of excluded and poor people. The urban and welfare state crises of the 1980s are currently being replicated, albeit even more acutely, given that the welfare state in many countries is very weak and there are worrying signs of a crisis of democracy. In the present urban order of globalization, new players have emerged from the financial sector, including investment funds and the so-called vulture funds. Our contribution to this Special Issue is an analysis of urban inequality today based on theoretical and empirical research. The issue includes articles on social movements and resistance in Latin American cities, vulnerability in crisis-hit Spanish cities, and the segregation and quality of basic services in US cities.

Keywords: urban inequality; vulnerability; segregation; crisis; urban governance; social movements

---

"Any city, however small, is in fact divided into two, one the city of the poor, the other of the rich; these are at war with one another" (Plato, *The Republic* IV, 422B, 380 BC). [1]

One of the main problems of the recent process of urbanization is the increase of the polarization and the social inequalities in the inner city. In the first decade of the 21st century, Michael Pacione (2001) [2] characterized the post-industrial city by the coexistence of four main processes. One of them is the increase of the inequalities, the social and spatial segregation, the privatization of the urban space and increase of the defensible spaces. From an urbanistic point of view, the fragmentation of the urban form is a consequence of many of these processes and an increasingly palpable reality of the city of the 21st century. A growing interest can currently be seen in analysing social polarization, the impact of post-crisis policies and the new social order that have come about from the processes of impoverishment, the risk of declining social mobility, and greater vulnerability and social segregation [3,4]. Over the last 50 years, there have been two key dates linked to greater inequality in cities, and both are related to periods of crisis of capitalism and changes in economic cycles: 1973 and 2007.

The city product of the crisis of 1973 is urbanistically extensive and socially unequal. In the early 21st century, Hammett (2001) [5] stated that most urban inequality between rich and poor came about in the 1980s. Dual cities [6] and divided cities [7] are some of the terms coined from the urban crisis from the 1980s onwards to analyze inequality in late capitalist cities. Nonetheless, Hammett's affirmation should be reviewed in the face of the socio-urban transformations being seen in cities since the 2007 crisis. Initially the crisis and then the neoliberal policies of austerity have not only widened the chasm between social classes and are configuring new urban spaces characterised by segregation and exclusion but have also collectively led to a new stage in investigating urban inequalities. The crisis has dragged a large section of society down into a situation of unprecedented precariousness and social unrest. Alongside this, the current, fragile, and uncertain recovery is spatially imbalanced and socially polarizing. In short, we find ourselves in a new period for analysing urban inequality where globalization, in its different analytical perspectives and especially those linked to the world of finance, have brought new agents into the analysis of inequality and opened up new lines of research. In this context, the capitalism–welfare state–democracy trifecta is crumbling. Many of the processes that lead to inequality are common around the world, albeit at different intensities based not only on each country's level of economic development but also, and especially, on the state's protective role and the strength of the welfare state. In this sense and on a large scale, the main differences can be seen between two types of countries: those with high levels of economic development, and a highly developed social safety net and welfare state; and those who have committed to privatized services and the market economy which, in Europe, includes countries in the south and the most recent member states of the European Union.

The analysis of urban inequalities needs new analyzes and interpretations in recent years. The socio-urban consequences of the economic crisis and policies called post-crisis, or austerity, are transforming everyday life in cities around the world. There are processes of impoverishment, increased vulnerability and social segregation, which is producing a new space order. The first public responses to the crisis were dominated by the impulse of neoliberal policies, which are aggravating socio-urban inequalities. The current real estate-financial cycle is producing a new stage of accumulation, albeit without abandoning the processes of dispossession (mortgage foreclosures and repossessions, insecure employment and lower wages, the privatization of social housing, expanding new forms of poverty...). The recession and austerity have had a negative impact on most cities [8]. Authors such as Harvey (2012) and Peck (2012) [9,10] point out that the financial crisis is a particularly urban one. In this way, the consequences of the economic crisis and neoliberal strategies introduced for the recovery have led to fundamental changes in cities: lower investment in public spaces, a halt to urban regeneration, abandoning sustainable mobility policies, the introduction of privatization measures in urban management and planning, etc. Nevertheless, and above all these, we would spotlight the impoverishment of many urban spaces and higher inequality within cities.

Cities are therefore ever more unequal and polarized [11–13]. Even those with the highest economic growth rates have seen increases in the number of people at the risk of exclusion [14]. Societies have fractured into seven or even eight levels, with worryingly large increases among those in precarious circumstances or exclusion. A precariat comprising diverse socio-professional groups in terms of education levels or the type of job they have, but who share a collective experience of precariousness [15]. In this new stage of research into inequality, special focus is placed, on the one hand, on intraurban analysis. Studies into gentrification, vulnerability, or evictions at the neighbourhood level are examples of this trend. On the other, focus is placed on new types of urban agents, mainly those from the world of finance. Investment funds are the main purchasers of land and property in the new property cycle. The so-called vulture funds moved strongly into real estate during the crisis, especially in those countries who most suffered from the bursting of a property bubble.

In this context, the objective of this Special Issue is to study inequalities in the city at different scales and in all territories, from informal settlements and the "urbanization of poverty" in the countries of the South to the fragmentation of the city or urban segregation as global phenomena in the city of the 21st century. In line with this, we have proposed introducing new debates on the city and inequality linked to social movements, urban governance, and access to and quality of drinking water, among other topics.

A total of seven articles have been published in this Special Issue looking at the problems of urban inequality from different perspectives and methodologies. The multi-scale and -sector analysis perspectives contribute to understanding the problems of inequality in cities today. Three articles [16–18] look at cities in countries that were most seriously affected by the Great Recession (Bolivia, Mexico, Argentina, and Brazil in Latin America and Spain as an example from southern Europe). Two articles offer a more theoretical approach [19,20], and a further two are focused on US cities [21,22].

The two articles that look as the problem from a more global theoretical scale analyze urban inequality from two different perspectives. In his article "Urbanization and Inequality/Poverty" [19],

Brantley Liddle uses different indicators to show the relationship between urbanization and poverty and inequality. The article pays particular attention to urban and rural comparisons, without looking at the socio-urban inequalities within cities. Although increases in GDP per capita unambiguously lower poverty and narrow rural-urban gaps, this paper has confirmed that rapid and excessive urbanization can lead to greater poverty and inequality. In turn, Vojislava Filipcevic ("City Sovereignty: Urban Resistance and RebelCities Reconsidered") [20] includes a major theoretical component in her reflections on the city, inequality, urban commons, and city power from a critical and committed approach. The article argues for an increase in de facto already claimed city sovereignty. If cities are to assume greater capacity to govern and to ensure life, liberty, and the sustainability of their populations, they have to overcome serious constraints in the four domains: surveillance and control of urban space, privatization of public space, the rise of the luxury city, large-scale developments, megaprojects, and homelessness. The article highlights the role played by sanctuary cities that represent "bottom-up sovereignty" and rebel cities, which are similar to rebel governance in the sense that both seek legitimacy that the state has been unable to provide.

Two articles look at cities in Latin America: Brazil, Argentina, Mexico, and Bolivia. Although they use different methodologies and have different objectives, both analyze socio-urban processes linked to the lowest social strata, including the so-called precariat, mainly from the standpoint of social movements and resistance. The paper "Counter Land-Grabbing by the Precariat: Housing Movements and Restorative Justice in Brazil" [16] reflects on Brazilian social housing movements' courageous response to the grave and growing land and housing crisis in Brazil. Professor Irazábal offers an extraordinary paper on social housing movements and the role of Brazil's precariat or lowest-income class in claiming their rights to the city mainly through restorative justice practices. Land occupations by the *Movimento dos Trabalhadores Sen Teto* and other social housing movements in Rio de Janeiro and São Paulo serve as the basis for the article. In turn, Chryssanthi Petropoulou ("Social Resistances and the Creation of Another Way of Thinking in the Peripheral 'Self-Constructed Popular Neighborhoods': Examples from Mexico, Argentina, and Bolivia" [17]) offers an interesting counterpart to the debates opened up in the previous article. In looking at urban movements, Petropoulou adds an analysis of self-constructed popular neighbourhoods. The article refers to urban social movements, creative social resistances (refers to all those collectivities that offer not only an anti-systemic logic but, also, that express creative action in everyday life), and the collectives that are emerging today in "self-constructed popular neighborhoods." The research is based on the use of qualitative techniques, including interviews and thorough fieldwork in *villas* in South Greater Buenos Aires, *barrios* of Ciudad Nezahualcóyotl in the Metropolitan Area of Mexico City, and *barrios* of El Alto in the Metropolitan Area of La Paz.

The real estate-financial crisis and post-crisis policies introduced since 2007 are having serious socio-urban impacts in countries in southern Europe, especially those who had large property markets. Supported by an interesting mapping, Piñeira, Durán, and Taboada analyze the impacts of the crisis from two points of view. First, to what extent the crisis has impacted the different urban sectors through the analysis of degree of vulnerability. Second, through urban governance, they analyze the proposals to combat vulnerability presented by the ruling parties in their programs for the 2015 municipal elections. Although the case study looks at two medium-sized cities in Spain (Vigo and A Coruña), the first sections analyze urban vulnerability in Spain through different indicators. The article prioritizes research at an intraurban level. In this sense, the authors highlight the need to take action in historical centres, where the loss of centrality and the predominance of an aging population has led to degradation, and in working-class neighbourhoods and the outskirts, where social unrest is increasing.

Two articles look at US cities. Walter, Foote, Cordoba, and Sparks ("Historic Roots of Modern Residential Segregation in a Southwestern Metropolis: San Antonio, Texas in 1910 and 2010") [22] analyze residential segregation in San Antonio (Texas) based on racial patterns. The methodology used and the historical analysis are particularly interesting aspects. The article reveals a consistent residential racial pattern as the city core expands over the last century. By 1910, San Antonio was already a remarkably segregated city and the original patterns of residential segregation resemble contemporary San Antonio. Particularly, residential racial segregation in the Hispanic concentrated southwestern portion of the city has increased over time resulting in an exceptionally racially divided metropolis. Finally, in the article "Pipe Dreams: Urban Wastewater Treatment for Biodiversity Protection" [21], Cunningham and Gharipour, inequality is approached from a new variable: the different treatment of wastewater in cities in the United States and its environmental impact, and how this treatment mainly prejudices the poorest urban areas. After a detailed analysis based on case studies, the authors underline three main conclusions: (a) wastewater treatment systems in urban areas of the US are in a state of disrepair leading to significant negative outcomes affecting human and non-human habitats, (b) green wastewater infrastructure strategies that support native hydrology with positive environmental impacts are integral to the protection of the clean water humans and other species rely on for survival, and (c) the use of constructed wetlands in green wastewater infrastructure has great potential to ameliorate biodiversity losses in urban ecosystems while supporting and enhancing densely populated anthropogenic environments with multiple benefits to human health.

In short, in the decade after the start of the last great crisis of capitalism inequality has risen in cities. Three final reflections on the issue: (i) Inequality needs to be mapped; (ii) The territorial spread of the different expressions of inequality and the characterization of the subsequent urban shaping have become increasingly important in the context of the most recent real estate-financial crisis; and (iii) Inequality needs to be confronted by ideas of spatial justice (Soja, 2010) [23], as some governance models are beginning to incorporate. The challenges for the academic and scientific communities are extraordinary. Urban studies must maintain a critical, non-conformist stance in light of the increasing social divisions and urban fragmentation being seen in our cities.

Acknowledgments: This research has been funded by the research project "Crisis and social vulnerability in Spanish island cities. Changes in the social reproduction spaces" CSO2015-68738-P (MINECO/FEDER).

Conflicts of Interest: The author declares no conflicts of interest.

References

1. Plato. *The Republic IV*; 380 BC; Alianza Editorial: Madrid, Spain, 2005; ISBN 9788420636733.
2. Pacione, M. *Urban Geography. A Global Perspective*, 1st ed.; Routledge: London, UK; New York, NY, USA, 2001; ISBN 0-415-34305-4.
3. Koutrolikou, P. Governmentalities of Urban Crises in Inner-City Athens, Greece. *Antipode* **2015**, *48*, 172–192. Available online: https://onlinelibrary.wiley.com/doi/pdf/10.1111/anti.12163 (accessed on 2 July 2018). [CrossRef]
4. Vale, M. Economic crisis and the Southern European regions: Towards alternative territorial development policies. In *Identity and Territorial Character. Re-Interpreting Local-Spatial Development*; Salom, J., Farinós, J., Eds.; University of Valencia: Valencia, Spain, 2014; pp. 37–48, ISBN 978-84-370-9463-2.
5. Hammet, C. Social Segregation and Social Polarization. In *Handbook of Urban Studies*; Paddison, R., Ed.; SAGE Publications: London, UK, 2001; pp. 162–176, ISBN 0 8039 7695 X.
6. Mollenkopf, J.H.; Castells, M. (Eds.) *Dual City: Restructuring New York*; Russell Sage: New York, NY, USA, 1991; ISBN 978-0871546081.
7. Fainstein, S.S.; Gordon, I.; Harloe, M. (Eds.) *Divided Cities: New York & London in the Contemporary World*; Blackwell: Oxford, UK, 1992; ISBN 978-0631181811.
8. URBACT. *Cities Facing the Crisis: Impact and Responses*; European Union: Saint-Denis La Plaine, France, November 2010; Manuscript of Work. Available online: http://urbact.eu/sites/default/files/import/general_library/Crise_urbact__16-11_web.pdf (accessed on 26 July 2018).
9. Harvey, D. The urban roots of financial crises: Reclaiming the city fir anti-capitalist struggle. *Soc. Regist.* **2012**, *48*, 1–35. Available online: https://socialistregister.com/index.php/srv/article/view/15644 (accessed on 28 June 2018).

10. Peck, J. Austerity Urbanism. *City* **2012**, *16*, 626–655. Available online: https://www.tandfonline.com/doi/abs/10.1080/13604813.2012.734071 (accessed on 7 July 2018). [CrossRef]

11. Dorling, D.; Ballas, D. Spatial Divisions of Poverty and Wealth. In *Understanding Poverty, Wealth and Inequality: Policies and Prospects*; Ridge, T., Wright, S., Eds.; Bristol University Press: Bristol, UK, 2008; pp. 103–134, ISBN 978-1861349149.

12. Lemoy, R.; Raux, C.; Jensen, P. Where in Cities Do 'Rich' and 'Poor' People Live? The Urban Economics Model Revisited. Manuscript of Work, HAL. Available online: https://hal.archives-ouvertes.fr/hal-00805116/ (accessed on 26 July 2018).

13. Lennert, M.; van Hamme, G.; Patris, C.; Smetkowski, C.; Ploszaj, A.; Gorzelak, G.; Kozak, M.; Olechnicka, A.; Wojnar, K.; Hryniewicz, J.; et al. *FOTI Future Orientations for Cities*; ESPON: Brussels, Belgium, 2010. Available online: https://hal.archives-ouvertes.fr/hal-00734406 (accessed on 26 July 2018).

14. EC. *Employment and Social Developments in Europe 2012*; Publications Office of the European Union: Luxemburg, 2012.

15. Méndez, R. Economías alternativas ¿para una sociedad postcapitalista? Algunas experiencias en Madrid. In *XV Coloquio Internacional de Geocrítica*; University of Barcelona: Barcelona, Spain, 2018. Available online: http://www.ub.edu/geocrit/XV-Coloquio/RicardoMendez.pdf (accessed on 26 July 2018).

16. Irazábal, C. Counter Land-Grabbing by the Precariat: Housing Movements and Restorative Justice in Brazil. *Urban Sci.* **2018**, *2*, 49. [CrossRef]

17. Petropoulou, C.C. Social Resistances and the Creation of Another Way of Thinking in the Peripheral "Self-Constructed Popular Neighborhoods": Examples from Mexico, Argentina, and Bolivia. *Urban Sci.* **2018**, *2*, 27. [CrossRef]

18. Piñeira-Mantiñán, M.J.; Durán-Villa, F.R.; Taboada-Failde, J. Urban Vulnerability in Spanish Medium-Sized Cities during the Post-Crisis Period (2009–2016). The Cases of A Coruña and Vigo (Spain). *Urban Sci.* **2018**, *2*, 37. [CrossRef]

19. Liddle, B. Urbanization and Inequality/Poverty. *Urban Sci.* **2017**, *1*, 35. [CrossRef]

20. Filipcevic Cordes, V. City Sovereignty: Urban Resistance and Rebel Cities Reconsidered. *Urban Sci.* **2017**, *1*, 22. [CrossRef]

21. Cunningham, C.; Gharipour, M. Pipe Dreams: Urban Wastewater Treatment for Biodiversity Protection. *Urban Sci.* **2018**, *2*, 10. [CrossRef]

22. Walter, R.J.; Foote, N.; Cordoba, H.A.; Sparks, C. Historic Roots of Modern Residential Segregation in a Southwestern Metropolis: San Antonio, Texas in 1910 and 2010. *Urban Sci.* **2017**, *1*, 19. [CrossRef]

23. Soja, E. *Seeking Spatial Justice*; University of Minnesota Press: Minneapolis, MN, USA, 2010; ISBN 9780816666683.

urban science

MDPI

Article

Historic Roots of Modern Residential Segregation in a Southwestern Metropolis: San Antonio, Texas in 1910 and 2010

Rebecca J. Walter [1,*], Nathan Foote [2], Hilton A. Cordoba [3] and Corey Sparks [4]

[1] Urban and Regional Planning Program, College of Architecture, Construction and Planning, The University of Texas at San Antonio, One UTSA Circle, San Antonio, TX 78249, USA

[2] Edward J. Bloustein School of Planning and Public Policy, Rutgers, The State University of New Jersey, 33 Livingston Ave., New Brunswick, NJ 08901, USA; nathan.foote@rutgers.edu

[3] Department of History, Geography and Philosophy, College of Liberal Arts, University of Louisiana at Lafayette, P.O. Box 43605, Lafayette, LA 70504, USA; hac9361@louisiana.edu

[4] Department of Demography, College of Public Policy, The University of Texas at San Antonio, One UTSA Circle, San Antonio, TX 78249, USA; corey.sparks@utsa.edu

* Correspondence: Rebecca.Walter@utsa.edu; Tel.: +1-210-458-3013

Academic Editor: Jesús Manuel González Pérez
Received: 19 April 2017; Accepted: 27 May 2017; Published: 1 June 2017

Abstract: This study seeks to understand the historic roots of modern segregation by comparing residential racial patterns in the city of San Antonio over time. The year 1910 is recreated for San Antonio by georeferencing and digitizing historic Sanborn maps and aligning residential structures with historical census and city directory race data for the head of household. The historical point data are aggregated to the census block level and compared to 2010 householder race data by calculating the two most common dimensions of residential segregation: evenness (dissimilarity and Theil's index) and exposure (isolation and interaction). The findings reveal that by 1910 San Antonio was already a remarkably segregated city and the original patterns of residential segregation resemble contemporary San Antonio. Particularly, residential racial segregation in the Hispanic concentrated southwestern portion of the city has increased over time resulting in an exceptionally racially divided metropolis.

Keywords: residential segregation; race; San Antonio; Hispanic

---

1. Introduction

Residential segregation, the degree to which two or more groups live apart from one another [1], is a dominant feature of the urban landscape in America. The rise of residential segregation, by both race and income, over the last several decades has been frequently highlighted by scholars. A wealth of research exists examining the determinants and consequences of residential segregation [2–7] and policies over the last century have resulted in the perpetuation of poor minority distressed neighborhoods in inner cities across the nation [8–11].

What about the origins of residential segregation prior to twentieth century factors and policies that have perpetuated it? The historic roots of this topic are important. Although the factors that perpetuate segregation may be different than those that initially generated it, an understanding of original segregation patterns compared to contemporary patterns can help guide effective strategies to combat residential segregation [12]. Furthermore, while the segregation of other minority groups has not received as much attention, due perhaps to the "hypersegregation" of Black neighborhoods compared to other groups [13], varying degrees of segregation of various minority groups have been documented [13–18]. More recently, the segregation of Hispanics from Whites and Blacks has become of increasing interest as individuals of Hispanic descent make up more of the population in the United States, and as the Hispanic population moves into a variety of urban areas [15,17,19,20]. One urban area that has been a consistent destination for individuals of many ethnic groups is the southwestern city of San Antonio. These influxes have led to a pattern of segregation in San Antonio in which immigrants from Latin America, Korea, and Vietnam, as well as Blacks, live in central city enclaves, while those of European descent live in suburban areas [16]. This situation raises the question of how long these patterns have existed.

This study seeks to understand the historic roots of modern segregation in the southwestern cosmopolis of San Antonio by examining the two most common dimensions of residential segregation in the city of San Antonio, one of the most residentially segregated cities in the nation [13,16,21]. Historical residential neighborhoods around the city core are reconstructed digitally by georeferencing and digitizing historic Sanborn maps which are aligned with historic city directory and census data to address the following research questions: (1) What was the pattern of residential segregation in San Antonio's city core in 1910 and how has this configuration changed over the last century?; and (2) Is the spatial distribution of residential segregation in the original 1910 city core similar to the central city in 2010? It is important to note that the first question only compares the urban core, the original two square miles of historic San Antonio which is centered on Main Plaza and San Fernando Cathedral. The second research question compares the central city of 1910 to 2010, which is a much larger area in 2010 (181 square miles defined by the Interstate 410 loop).

This study contributes to the existing literature by uncovering the patterns of residential segregation over one hundred years ago by using historical data to create a unique geodatabase. This database allows for detailed analysis of residential settlement patterns that provide insight into the past to establish the foundation for answering research questions about the perpetuation of residential segregation over time. Only a few studies have examined residential segregation patterns in the early twentieth century [22,23] and comparing patterns over a century is unique to the literature. Furthermore, the growing importance of non-Black minorities in the urban landscape of the United States makes the historical analysis in San Antonio useful to future scholarship on the segregation of Hispanics, the largest and fastest growing minority group in America.

2. Theoretical Background

Chung and Brown [24] discuss four major theories, or frameworks, for understanding why residential segregation occurs and how it propagates. The spatial assimilation framework has the earliest roots of the four theories, since it rests on Chicago School ideas about neighborhood change and segregation. Assimilation theory posits that residential patterns, including segregation, are the result of economic, human, and cultural capital accumulation, or the lack thereof. Increasing capital leads families to find housing in more up-scale neighborhoods, while stagnant capital accumulation keeps families in neighborhoods with fewer amenities. Segregation in the spatial assimilation model is based on the economic choices made by individuals. The fact that this leads to segregation is a consequence of the differing socioeconomic status among minority racial and ethnic groups [25–28]. In contrast, segregation in the place stratification framework is based on choices made for or against these minority groups by majority groups because of their race or ethnicity. Segregation is propagated through the household-level choices of the majority group (the white-flight phenomenon), direct actions (block-busting), or government policy (mortgage underwriting policy) [29]. While assimilation is based on economics, stratification is based on racial and ethnic prejudice. This keeps minority groups of lower socioeconomic standing in segregated neighborhoods that then become more distressed over time since these areas often experience disinvestment and the residents do not have the means to maintain the neighborhoods [24,30].

The third framework identified by Chung and Brown is the Ethnic Resurgence theory, which shares traits with the two frameworks just discussed. Like the Spatial Assimilation model, Ethnic Resurgence suggests that some segregation is the result of choices made by households in the segregated group, but like Place Stratification theory, these choices are based more on race and ethnicity. These choices lead to "ethnic communities" of different socioeconomic levels [24]. The fourth framework proposed by Chung and Brown is Market-Led Pluralism, which suggests that the spatial distribution and intensity of segregated areas is dependent on five types of actors in the residential market: developers, lenders, real estate agents, consumers, and local communities. These market-makers in different cities or metropolitan areas interact in different ways to create the mosaic of segregated space across the urban area.

Although these four theories help explain why residential segregation occurs, few studies have applied and examined the prevalence, let alone the causes, of segregation in American cities of the late nineteenth and early twentieth centuries. Gilliland and Olson [31] demonstrate that American cities of this timeframe have not been as well-studied as their English counterparts. Their study of segregation in 1880 Montreal shows that there were high levels of segregation by both ethnicity and occupation. Railway workers clustered near their places of work, while White Protestants and French Canadians showed high levels of segregation from each other at both the block and street-level. Interestingly, Irish Catholics were more integrated with the other two groups, likely a result of their shared heritage with both groups. In their sweeping work on segregation, Massey and Denton [4] include a survey of White/Black segregation within selected Northern and Southern cities over the course of the late nineteenth through the mid-twentieth century at the ward-level, and found generally increasing levels of segregation over time. A study using a finer level of geographic analysis conducted by Logan and colleagues [23] found that isolation and dissimilarity in ten Northern cities increased between 1880 and 1940. The authors of that study further suggest that the origins of segregation in those cities pre-date the Great Migration of Southern Blacks to the North.

These studies mostly focus on the segregation of ethnic White groups from each other, or White/Black segregation in Northern cities. Examining the historical incidence of residential segregation in an American city with three races: Whites, Blacks, and Hispanics is unique. Given the increasing importance of the Hispanic population in the United States, the origins of segregation in cities with various minority-concentrated races is an important topic that needs further analysis. Since San Antonio has been an important city in the Hispanic and specifically, the Mexican American, experience since Texas joined the United States [32], it provides an excellent study area for examining segregation in the multi-racial city. This research does so, and adds another layer to the analysis by examining the durability of segregation one hundred years after the historical year being studied (1910).

3. Materials and Methods

3.1. Historical San Antonio (1910)

In 1910, the City of San Antonio was home to 96,614 people and covered approximately 36 square miles [33]. San Antonio was the wealthiest city in Texas and ranked first in terms of population, trade, and taxable value. The economic drivers in the city included the wool district, horse market, and cattle industry. Seventy miles of electric street railways and 130 cars provided transit throughout the city [34]. Although the city covered a large land area in 1910, the built environment for downtown was only recreated for the core of the city, an approximately two square mile area where one-third of the residents lived. Historical data and Sanborn maps outside of this area are sparse, which made it difficult to recreate the urban form for the entire city in 1910. However, since the purpose of this study was to focus on the central city, and in 1910 the central city was represented by the two-square mile core that was used for the study area, the data outside of this area were not included. The year 1910 was selected as the base year to recreate San Antonio for two primary reasons. First, it is believed that ethnic and racial segregation patterns of contemporary San Antonio were established by 1910. Prior to the twentieth century, segregation by income and race was limited and Mexicans and Americans intermingled until the 1880s; however, contemporary San Antonio represents spatial ethnic and racial patterns of 1910 [35]. The data used in this study allows for this hypothesis to be tested. Second, all the data sources used to build the dataset aligned for this timeframe, allowing for the historical geodatabase to be created to test this hypothesis. The 1910 Jules A. Appler's General Directory and Blue Book of the City of San Antonio, also known as the city directory, was used to identify the names and addresses of residents in the city. Even though the first city directory was published in 1861, it wasn't until 1903 that the directory listed businesses and head of household by street address. To properly identify the occupant of each residential structure, a year after 1903 was the most realistic to use. Since the census data are only available every 10 years, 1910 was the first year available after the 1903 date. The city directory was used as the primary resource to identify heads of households, followed by the census since local historians use the city directory as the principal guide to determine where households lived at the time. Census data were used as a secondary resource to verify, supplement, and complete any missing city directory data. In addition, a complete set of Sanborn maps was completed in 1911–1912, which corresponds well with the 1910 census and city directory data.

The geodatabase for 1910 was created by first georeferencing the Sanborn maps to the 2014 streets and parcel shapefiles provided by the Bexar County Property Appraiser using ESRI's world imagery basemap that was updated December 2014 and provides a 0.3 m resolution imagery in the United States. To measure configured space and evaluate the urban form, building footprints are commonly used and the Sanborn maps provide this information. The Sanborn maps were originally developed for fire insurance purposes and are accepted as the most accurate and detailed set of maps representing the built environment in the early 1900s. Special attention was given to areas where street names or the street network changed over time and where blocks have been vacated. Once the Sanborn maps were georeferenced and projected using the NAD 1983 State Plane Texas South Central coordinate system, the Sanborns were digitized at a scale of 1:200. Separate feature classes were created for the following attributes: streets (line feature class), building footprints (polygon feature class), and blocks (polygon feature class).

The building footprints were digitized by outlining the actual living or occupied space, and porches were not included in the outline. Structures detached from the occupied spaces were not digitized, leaving out stables, outhouses, storage spaces, and any other independent structures that were not occupied living or working spaces. The land use for each building was assigned to one of the following categories: commercial, industrial, mixed use, public/institutional, and residential. Vacant structures listed in the city directory were classified according to the surrounding land uses identified on the Sanborn maps.

The city directory was used to identify the head of household for each residential property digitized on the Sanborn maps. Only the head of household for each residential unit was included in the dataset since limited information exists for each household member and head of household was a consistent unit of analysis that could be compared across all data sources. The city directory identifies Black residents and the 1910 census data were used to supplement the city directory data to identify the race of every householder. At the time, Hispanic households were not consistently identified so Hispanics were identified using Census data such as the county of origin, last name, birthplace, and ethnicity of the parents. For instance, the head of household is labeled as Hispanic if the last name is Hispanic, both parents were born in Mexico, and county of origin was listed as Mexico. There were a total of 7130 head of households identified in the study area in 1910 and race was identified for over 85 percent of the head of households.

3.2. San Antonio 100 Years Later (2010)

In 2010, San Antonio was home to 1,327,407 people and covered approximately 461 square miles. San Antonio is a minority-majority city with over 63 percent of the population identifying as Hispanic. The median household income of $46,317 is more than $7000 below the national average, and the number of persons living in poverty is slightly above 20 percent [36]. San Antonio has been ranked as one of the most residentially segregated cities in the nation [21] and spatial segregation among Hispanics is particularly high [13,16]. Kirwan Institute's Child Opportunity Index communicates a parallel story.

Child opportunity, measured by health, environmental, educational, social, and economic variables, demonstrates the greatest opportunity in primarily the northern portions of San Antonio where there is a concentration of Whites and the lowest levels of opportunity for children in areas concentrated by Hispanics and Blacks [37]. In a majority-minority city of Hispanics, the nation's second largest Hispanic share of population only trailing Miami [38], addressing residential segregation becomes critical.

To answer the first research question that compares the change over time, the same approximately two square mile core of downtown San Antonio is used in 2010. However, since the central city today is much larger than a century ago, the second research question addresses how the original pattern of residential segregation is represented within today's central city. This area is defined by and contained within the Interstate 410 loop. This results in a much larger land area covering approximately 181 square miles and is home to 224,546 households.

Unfortunately, since household point data is not available for 2010, race data for the head of household were collected at the next smallest geographic scale, the census block. The 1910 data were aggregated to the 2010 census blocks to allow for a comparable unit of analysis across time periods. In the southeastern portion of the city core, the blocks were vacated for the 1968 World's Fair. The 1910 block shapefile was used to recreate the blocks in this area to represent the original built environment in 1910. The number of Whites, Blacks, and Hispanics were calculated for each block along with the percent share for each timeframe. No other races, such as Asian, were included in the analysis because of the small number of households that identify as other races.

3.3. Residential Racial Segregation Metrics

Residential racial segregation is multidimensional and has been measured using a variety of metrics with the most common being residential evenness by the index of dissimilarity [39]. Dissimilarity is the proportion of a race that would have to move for that race to be completely integrated with another race. This index is represented on a scale from zero to one with zero representing complete integration and one representing complete segregation [1,19].

Exposure is another dimension of segregation. Both isolation, the likelihood of a race to encounter another member of their own race, and interaction, the probability that one race is in contact to another race, are two common indices used to measure exposure. Isolation is measured on a scale of zero to one with one representing the greatest isolation. Interaction consists of the same range and is interpreted as the probability that one race interacts within an area with another race. Higher values of isolation and lower values of interaction imply more residential segregation [1]. Although not as common, other studies have incorporated metrics of centralization, which is the distance from the city center, concentration, the density of one race across the study area, and clustering, the degree to which minorities adjoin in the study area.

For this paper, the two most common degrees of residential racial segregation, evenness and exposure, were analyzed. To calculate evenness, the dissimilarly index was used in addition to the Theil's Information Theory Index (H) since Theil's index considers multigroup calculations, all three races analyzed in this study (Black, White, and Hispanic) can be accounted for simultaneously. Theil's H reveals how diverse neighborhoods are compared to the overall diversity of the study area. The scale is consistent with the dissimilarity index with one representing no diversity and zero representing complete diversity. For exposure, both the most widely used isolation and interaction indices were used. To address the first research question, a statistic for each of the four indices (dissimilarity, interaction, isolation, and the Theil's index) were calculated for each of the five city core sections (refer to Figure 1) and compared between 1910 and 2010. These metrics were also repeated to address the second research question but a global score was first calculated for the entire central city and then a local score for each central city section in 2010. The reason the city was divided in sections is because as a very divided and segregated city, areas in San Antonio are commonly referred to directionally from the urban core. For instance, west of downtown is an area commonly known as Hispanic with distressed neighborhoods. The city sections allow for a local analysis to better understand how residential segregation has changed in specific areas of the city.

4. Results

To address the first research question comparing the patterns of residential segregation in the city core from 1910 to 2010, the spatial distribution of the three races (White, Hispanic, and Black) are first mapped and displayed in Figure 1. The 1910 map exhibits the point data by householder race and the 2010 data are symbolized by the dot density method of the three races in each block. One dot is equal to one head of household. Point data are displayed instead of aggregated block data because the data mapped by blocks in this case are visually distracting since the blocks are laid out in a disorderly pattern. The city core is split into five sections (north, northeastern, southeastern, southwestern, and northwestern) by the five major historical streets that converge in the historical core (Fredericksburg Road, Broadway Street, East Commerce Street, South Flores Street, and West Commerce Street). This division allows for a finer level of analysis for residential racial segregation to be compared across time periods along historically important corridors and city sections.

In 1910, the city represents the monocentric model with commercial land uses and jobs concentrated in the central business district. Residential, primarily single-family homes, surround the central business district in all the city sections. The railroad creates divisions in the urban form within residential neighborhoods located in the northwestern and southwestern sections of the city. Figure 1 reveals that in 1910 White householders were distributed throughout the city but primarily resided in neighborhoods away from the railroad in the north, northeastern, and southeastern sections of the city. Hispanics are primarily confined to the southwestern and northwestern portions of the city and Blacks are concentrated near East Commerce Street in the eastern sections of the city near the railroad.

By 2010, there was a substantial population loss (a decline of 29.27 percent) in the city core; 7130 households in 1910 compared to 5043 households in 2010. By this time, the city has reorganized and represents the polycentric model with several major centers throughout the city and the concentration of jobs along major highway corridors. The population that remains is much more concentrated in the neighborhoods to the south and north of downtown. There is also a concentration of households in downtown that reside in multifamily developments. In the southeastern section, there is more integration of White and Hispanic households in 2010 but in the northwestern section there is a much greater concentration of Hispanic households today than in 1910. The other sections of the city are difficult to interpret due to the lack of residential population; however, it is interesting to note that the southwestern section of the city that was heavily concentrated by Hispanics in 1910 is almost entirely vacated of residential buildings and is primarily commercial. Also, Interstates 35 and 10, the two most significant highways in San Antonio that connect the city to Austin and Houston, now divide this section of the city.

Race distribution is also analyzed in the entire central city of San Antonio in 2010 due to the population loss in the city core. This larger study area helps address the second research question about how the patterns of segregation have spread over time. Although this area is much larger than the original center of the city (181 square miles compared to two square miles), it is suitable to use to analyze how segregation has changed over time since each area is a representation of the center of the city for each given timeframe. About one third of the city population resides in this area today which is approximately the same proportion in the study area used for 1910. The central city is split into the same five sections as the core using identical major roadways as boundaries but each section expands further away from the center of the city.

Figure 2 represents the centroid of each block and are classified by the dominant householder race within that block. Point data were used again instead of polygon blocks because of the visual distraction created by the data mapped by blocks. The gaps in residential population throughout the central city are primarily due to military bases, parks, and commercial areas. There are areas in the southern portion of the central city that still have undeveloped parcels as this area has seen less investment compared to the northern portion of the city. Whites are still dominant in the north and northeastern sections and in the urban core of the southeastern section, but there appears to be substantially more concentration today than in 1910. Hispanic householders are disproportionally concentrated in the northwestern, southwestern, and southeastern sections of the city. One noticeable difference from 1910 is that Hispanic householders are currently dispersed throughout all the other portions of the city as well but the two original Hispanic sections could likely be classified as hypersegregated today. In 1910, Black householders were predominantly located along the dividing line in the two eastern sections, which is consistent with today, the only difference is that the concentration is located further east of downtown. In summary, there is not much difference in the distribution of householder race in the city sections a century later besides the fact that the population has moved away from the city core and the racial patterns established in 1910 appear to be preserved throughout the central city in 2010.

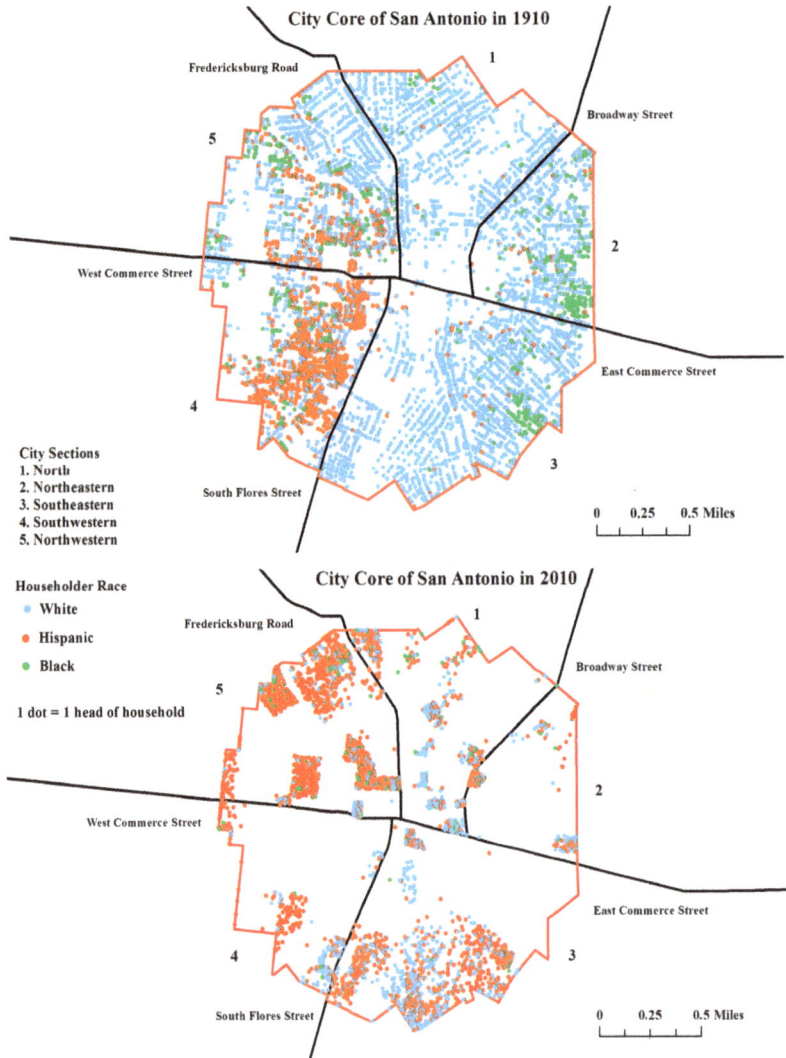

Figure 1. San Antonio's city core in 1910 and 2010 by householder race.

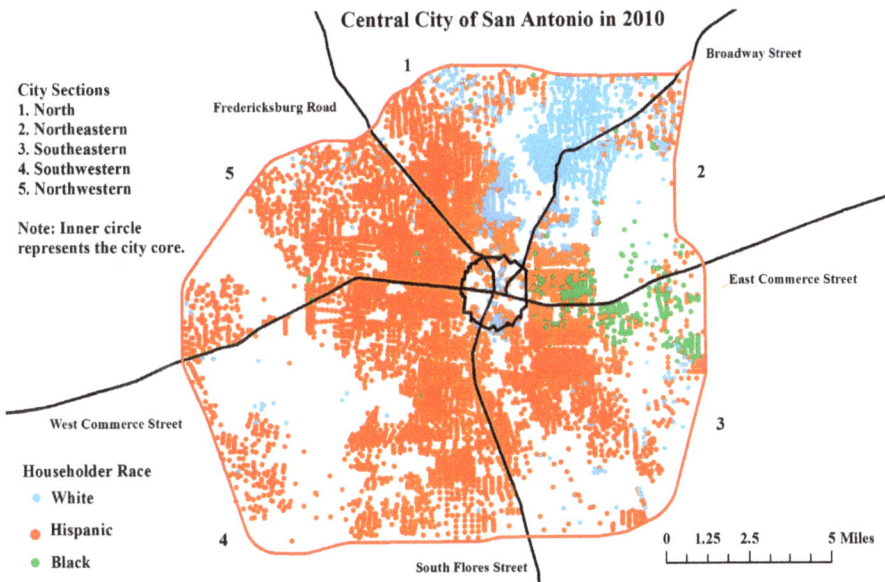

Figure 2. San Antonio's central city in 2010 by householder race.

Although there appears to be consistency in the patterns of racial distribution from 1910 to 2010, the residential racial segregation metrics are used to assess this hypothesis. The first research question is addressed by comparing the four segregation indices in the city core for 1910 and 2010. As shown in Figure 3, the dissimilarity index for each section in the city core for 1910 and 2010 reveals a higher level of segregation for every section of the city for Whites versus Black, Whites versus Hispanics, and Blacks versus Hispanics with one exception. In the southwestern section of the city, there is a higher level of segregation in 2010 of Whites compared to Hispanics. There is a small residential population in this area today, only about 257 households, and approximately 60 percent of these households are Hispanic. Although the level of segregation is overall higher in 1910, there are consistent patterns. For example, White/Black dissimilarity is relatively high in both the southeastern and northwestern sections of the city and have remained high over time; a difference of only 0.0531 and 0.0484, respectively. These two sections also have high segregation among Whites and Hispanics and Blacks and Hispanics. The northern section of the city is the only area where segregation has declined substantially; White/Black dissimilarity has decreased by 0.2207, White/Hispanic by 0.4413, and Black/Hispanic by 0.5023. The difference may be contributed to the fact that in 1910, the northern section was predominantly American and Texan born Whites with very few Hispanic and Black households. The north was buffered by White European settlers segregating American born Whites from Hispanic immigrants that settled in the west and Black households that traditionally lived closer to the central business district and service oriented occupations.

(a) White/Black Dissimilarity

● 1910 City Core   ● 2010 City Core

(b) White/Hispanic Dissimilarity

● 1910 City Core   ● 2010 City Core

(c) Black/Hispanic Dissimilarity

● 1910 City Core   ● 2010 City Core

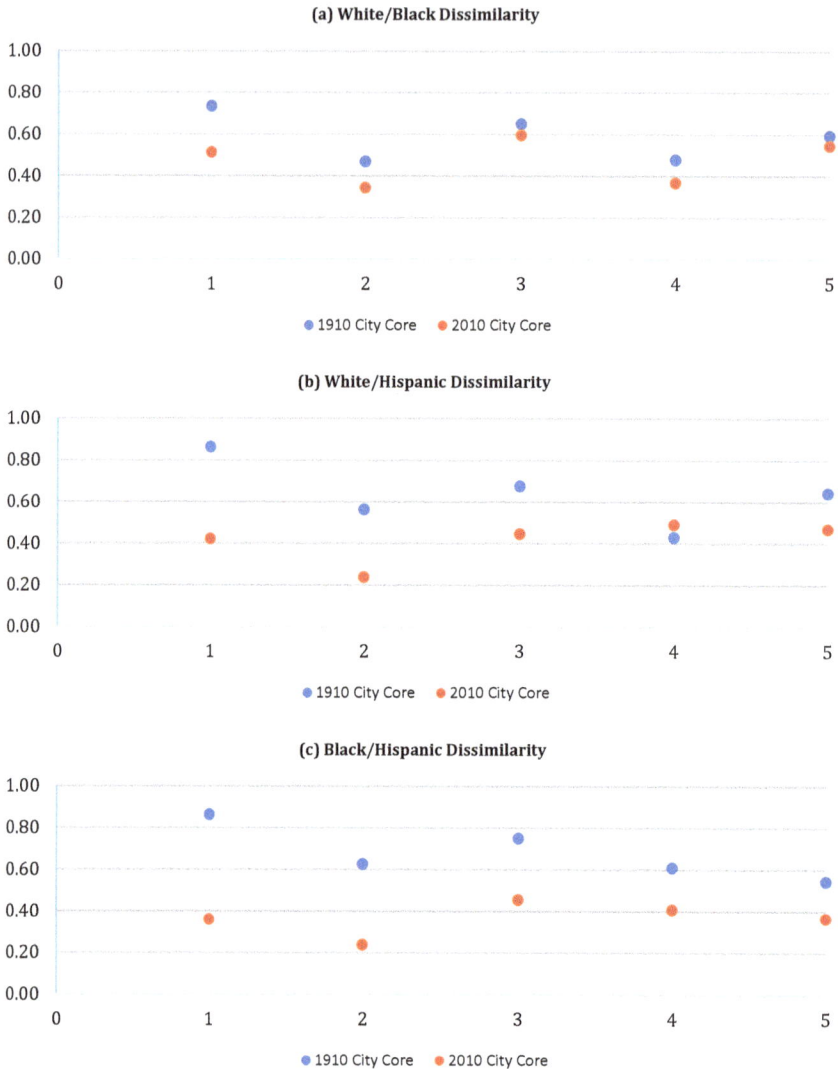

Figure 3. Dissimilarity index values for the city core sections in 1910 and 2010; (**a**) Description of White/Black Dissimilarity is contained in the first panel; (**b**) Description of White/Hispanic Dissimilarity is contained in the second panel; (**c**) Description of Black/Hispanic Dissimilarity is contained in the third panel.

Interaction reveals a slightly different story. As shown in Figure 4, White/Black and White/Hispanic interaction is higher in 1910 except for the southwestern section again where there is more interaction today among Whites and Blacks and Whites and Hispanics. This finding may be because many residents that live in the central core of the city today are clustered in a few neighborhoods and within multifamily developments in downtown whereas in 1910, single family residential dwellings were disbursed evenly throughout the city core (refer again to Figure 1). Conversely, Black and Hispanic interaction is much higher today in the city core than it was in 1910. Except for the southwestern section, all the remaining portions of the city have seen a substantial increase in interaction among Black and Hispanics over time. This finding may be due to the growing Hispanic population since 1910 in areas where Blacks were historically concentrated.

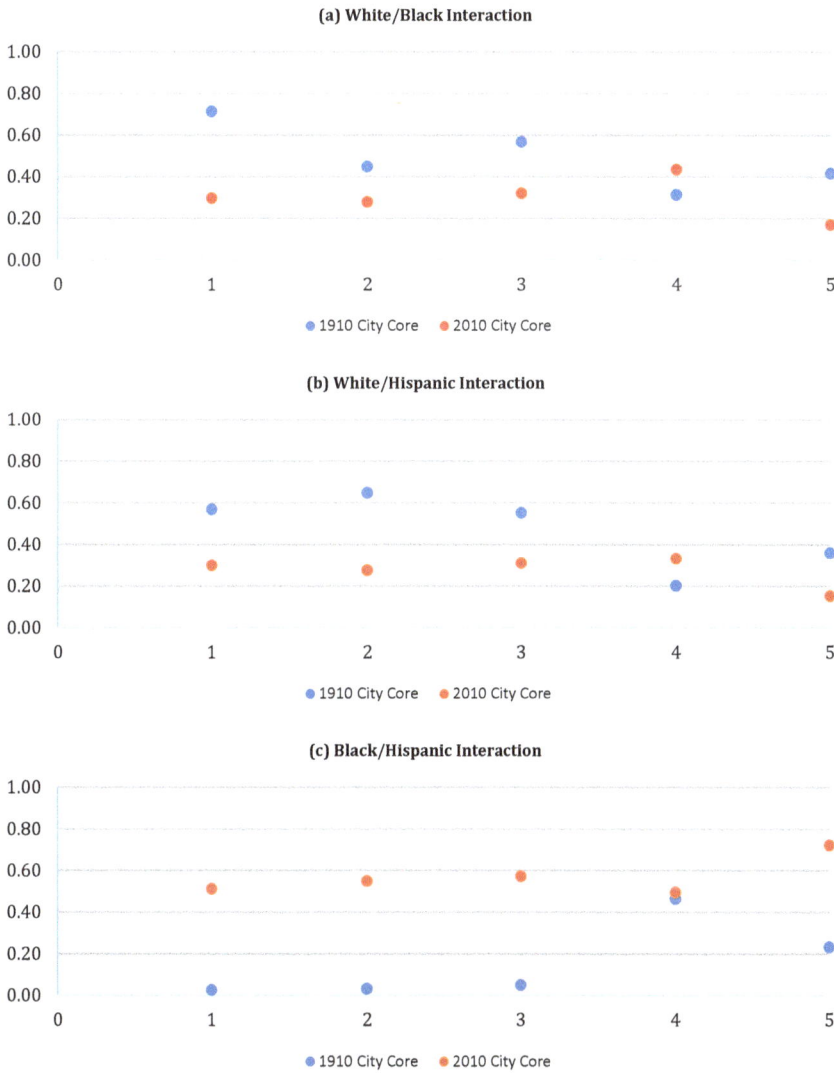

(a) White/Black Interaction

(b) White/Hispanic Interaction

(c) Black/Hispanic Interaction

Figure 4. Interaction index values for the city core sections in 1910 and 2010; (**a**) Description of White/Black Interaction is contained in the first panel; (**b**) Description of White/Hispanic Interaction is contained in the second panel; (**c**) Description of Black/Hispanic Interaction is contained in the third panel.

Taking a closer look at isolation in Figure 5, Whites are more isolated than Blacks and Hispanics in both 1910 and 2010, and almost completely isolated to the northern and southeastern sections of the city in 1910 (0.9554 and 0.9002, respectively). Although Whites are the most isolated, over time this has decreased except for the southwestern portion of the city core. Blacks are the least likely to be isolated in all portions of the city and have become even less isolated over time but this may be because Blacks only account for approximately ten percent of all households in 1910 and 14 percent of all households in 2010. Hispanic households have become more isolated in 2010, especially in the northeastern section of the city. Again, the only exception to this pattern is the southwestern section.

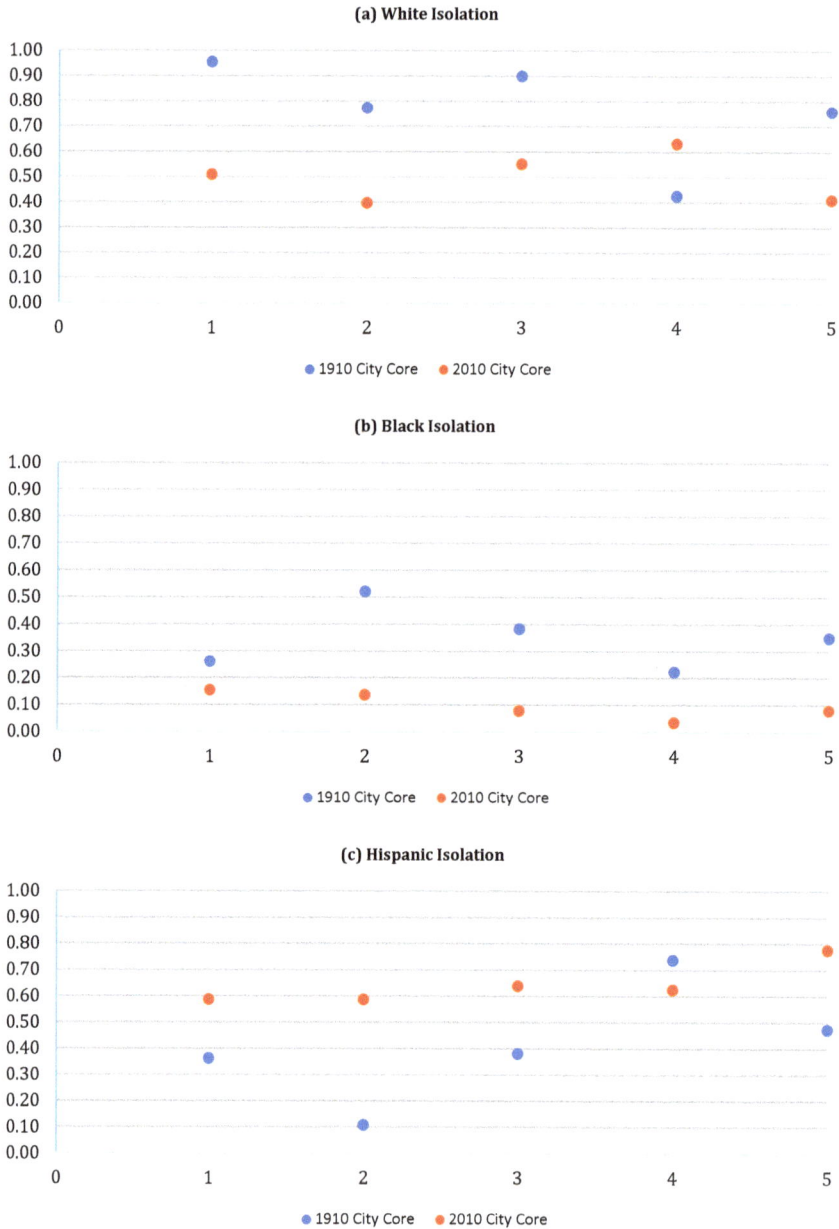

Figure 5. Isolation index values for the city core sections in 1910 and 2010; (**a**) Description of White Isolation is contained in the first panel; (**b**) Description of Black Isolation is contained in the second panel; (**c**) Description of Hispanic Isolation is contained in the third panel.

The Theil's index conveys a pattern of greater diversity in 2010 than 1910 across all sections in the city core as shown in Figure 6. In fact, the north and northeastern portions of the city have become substantially more diverse over time (decreases of 0.6991 and 0.4769, respectively). In 1910, the north and southeastern sections of the city, where Whites were the most isolated, had the least diversity. Today, the southeastern section remains the least diverse but the northern section has become one of the most diverse. The only section in the city that has seen almost no change in terms of diversity is again the southwestern section.

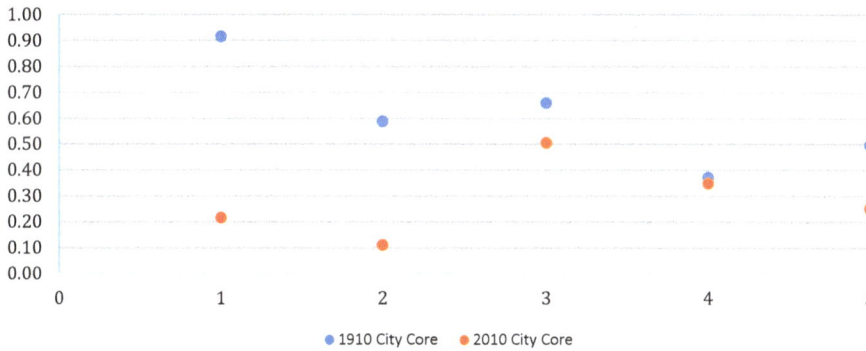

Figure 6. Theil's index values for the city core sections in 1910 and 2010.

To address the second research question regarding how the original patterns of segregation are resembled throughout today's central city, the four indices were calculated for the entire central city for 2010 (the 181 square mile area) and compared to the two square mile core in 1910. Table 1 reveals, in terms of dissimilarity, White versus Blacks have become more segregated over time but Whites versus Hispanics and Blacks versus Hispanics have become less segregated over time although the segregation levels for all three are still considerably high and consistent with other literature classifying San Antonio as an extremely residentially segregated city. Consistent with the dissimilarity index, interaction among Whites and Blacks and Whites and Hispanics has fallen over time and is noticeably low. Black and Hispanic interaction has increased but was considerably low in 1910. In terms of isolation, Whites were the most isolated in 1910 but by 2010 Hispanics have become the most isolated group. There has been relatively little change, a slight decrease, among Black isolation over the last century. The Theil's index has remained fairly stable with diversity improving only slightly over time.

Table 1. Residential racial segregation scores for the central city in 1910 and 2010.

	1910	2010
Dissimilarity		
White/Black	0.6799	0.7169
White/Hispanic	0.7744	0.5408
Black/Hispanic	0.7231	0.6926
Interaction		
White/Black	0.4207	0.1422
White/Hispanic	0.2613	0.1355
Black/Hispanic	0.1680	0.4758
Isolation		
White	0.8259	0.4646
Black	0.4113	0.3614
Hispanic	0.6590	0.8092
Theil's Index	0.6677	0.6003

Taking a closer look at how segregation patterns have spread throughout the city sections, Table 2 reveals that segregation has declined since 1910 in the northern section of the city when considering White/Black, White/Hispanic, and Black/Hispanic dissimilarity. Conversely, interaction has decreased among Whites and Blacks and Whites and Hispanics; however, Black and Hispanic interaction has increased over time. In 1910, Whites were the most isolated in the north but by 2010 Hispanics have become more isolated. The most dramatic change is revealed in the Theil's index with the level of diversity substantially improving in this area over time. Although there is more diversity in the northern section of the central city compared to a century ago, segregation is still high and is perpetuated throughout this area.

Table 2. Residential racial segregation scores for the northern section.

Section 1 (North)	1910	2010
Dissimilarity		
White/Black	0.7327	0.6794
White/Hispanic	0.8626	0.5211
Black/Hispanic	0.8628	0.6100
Interaction		
White/Black	0.7147	0.3347
White/Hispanic	0.5679	0.2682
Black/Hispanic	0.0246	0.4779
Isolation		
White	0.9554	0.6022
Black	0.2608	0.1493
Hispanic	0.3637	0.6787
Theil's Index	0.9165	0.5668

As shown in Table 3, the northeastern section, which was much less segregated than the northern section in 1910, has become more segregated over time in terms of White/Black dissimilarity but less in terms of White/Hispanic and Black/Hispanic dissimilarity. Isolation and interaction are also mixed depending on what race is considered. White/Black and White/Hispanic interaction has decreased over time while Black/Hispanic interaction has slightly improved. Whites were the most isolated in the northeast in 1910 and remain the most isolated today although Hispanic isolation has substantially increased. Again, diversity has improved although the Theil's index shows only a slight improvement a century later.

Table 3. Residential racial segregation scores for the northeastern section.

Section 2 (Northeastern)	1910	2010
Dissimilarity		
White/Black	0.4687	0.6992
White/Hispanic	0.5622	0.4800
Black/Hispanic	0.6272	0.4685
Interaction		
White/Black	0.4481	0.1654
White/Hispanic	0.6480	0.2686
Black/Hispanic	0.0310	0.3732
Isolation		
White	0.7734	0.5932
Black	0.5209	0.4304
Hispanic	0.1089	0.5158
Theil's Index	0.5889	0.4424

Moving on to the southeastern section of the city, Table 4 reveals White/Black dissimilarity is perpetuated through this area and has become slightly more segregated over time. Black/Hispanic and White/Hispanic dissimilarity was very high in 1910 and have become less segregated for Blacks/Hispanics and Whites/Hispanics. Interaction has only improved among Blacks and Hispanics with White/Black and White/Hispanic interaction decreasing substantially. In 1910, Whites were extremely isolated in this area but by 2010 Hispanics have become the most isolated race. Once again, the Theil's index reveals diversity has improved over time in the central city but only slightly.

Table 4. Residential racial segregation scores for the southeastern section.

Section 3 (Southeastern)	1910	2010
Dissimilarity		
White/Black	0.6492	0.6929
White/Hispanic	0.6762	0.3935
Black/Hispanic	0.7503	0.6585
Interaction		
White/Black	0.5683	0.1006
White/Hispanic	0.5521	0.1460
Black/Hispanic	0.0490	0.4259
Isolation		
White	0.9002	0.2905
Black	0.3827	0.4600
Hispanic	0.3822	0.7557
Theil's Index	0.6605	0.5217

Table 5 indicates that the southwestern section of the central city, the outlier of the city core analysis, is also quite different than the other sections of the central city. Segregation has increased since 1910, with higher White/Black, White/Hispanic, and Black/Hispanic dissimilarity values in 2010. Interaction among races has decreased with the expectation of Black/Hispanic interaction which has substantially risen. In 1910, Hispanics were the most isolated in this area of the city and this has remained consistent with Hispanics becoming almost entirely isolated by 2010 (an index score of 0.9095). This is the only section of the city that the Theil's index indicates less diversity over time.

Table 5. Residential racial segregation scores for the southwestern section.

Section 4 (Southwestern)	1910	2010
Dissimilarity		
White/Black	0.4777	0.6665
White/Hispanic	0.4298	0.4733
Black/Hispanic	0.6102	0.7488
Interaction		
White/Black	0.3134	0.1232
White/Hispanic	0.2018	0.0695
Black/Hispanic	0.4635	0.7570
Isolation		
White	0.4262	0.2102
Black	0.2231	0.1011
Hispanic	0.7383	0.9095
Theil's Index	0.3714	0.6352

The northwestern section of the central city, as shown in Table 6, has become slightly less segregated in terms of White/Black and White/Hispanic dissimilarity, with the index score for Black/Hispanic dissimilarity only slightly increasing by 2010. Interaction has decreased since 1910 between Whites and Blacks and Whites and Hispanics in this area, but Black/Hispanic interaction has improved substantially. Whites were the most isolated race in the northwest in 1910 and today Hispanics have become the most isolated. The Theil's index reveals a slight increase in diversity over time.

Table 6. Residential racial segregation scores for the northwestern section.

Section 5 (Northwestern)	1910	2010
Dissimilarity		
White/Black	0.5939	0.5789
White/Hispanic	0.6437	0.4409
Black/Hispanic	0.5442	0.5599
Interaction		
White/Black	0.4168	0.1175
White/Hispanic	0.3601	0.1067
Black/Hispanic	0.2328	0.7265
Isolation		
White	0.7592	0.2546
Black	0.3504	0.1383
Hispanic	0.4743	0.8461
Theil's Index	0.4966	0.4663

5. Discussion

In summary, the findings reveal a consistent residential racial pattern as the city core expands over the last century. By 1910, San Antonio is already a very segregated city and this pattern has been perpetuated throughout the last century. The approximately two square mile city core has become slightly less segregated and more diverse over time with lower dissimilarity and Theil's index scores. Although the interaction index scores are lower in 2010, this may be a result of population loss and reconfiguration of residential households over the last one hundred years. In 1910, households were very evenly distributed in predominantly single family homes throughout the city core whereas today there are only a few residential neighborhoods and large multifamily buildings disbursed throughout primarily commercial uses. Whites were the most isolated in 1910, especially in the northern section of the city core, and over time, even though White isolation remains high, Hispanic isolation has noticeably increased. The southwestern section of the city core is an exception; not only is there more segregation today but very little change in diversity has occurred since 1910 in this portion of the city core.

The historical patterns of segregation in the city core are resembled throughout today's central city. Although there is less segregation and slightly more diversity, the overall residential racial segregation metrics are still high. Hispanics have become more isolated than Whites over time. The most notable results are in the southwestern portion of the city that has become less diverse and significantly more segregated over time. Over 89 percent of the households in this section of the central city are Hispanic. This area has been commonly recognized for having very poor socioeconomic conditions and decades of disinvestment.

Historical documentation can help provide insight on the factors that created the original patterns of Hispanic segregation in southwestern San Antonio. The existence of a Spanish caste system where Canary Islanders saw Native Americans, Spaniards born in Mexico, and Spaniards of mixed heritage as less Spaniard, led to the segregation among Hispanic groups and to the creation of Villa de San Fernando on the western side of the city [40–42]. The decline in socioeconomic standing of Hispanics after the transition of Texas into the Union, and the emancipation of African Americans in the South, provide the context necessary to explain it. Both groups were in the lower ranks of society after the Civil

War, which meant that they held low paying occupations and unstable employment, limiting them to areas that they could afford or were considered undesirable by wealthier White residents [40,43].

The arrival of the railroad in the late 1870s and early 1880s from Galveston was instrumental in transforming the urban morphology of San Antonio and increasing its status as a population center. Despite its late and slow arrival, it completely changed the viability of the city and positioned it at the center of the east to west traffic of the southern half of the country, and later as the gateway for all rail traffic coming from Mexico. This created opportunities for farmers who could now haul their harvest to other markets, but also for ranchers who could carry their cattle to railheads in Kansas [32]. This was a strong factor that contributed to the end of the cattle drives in Texas, but at the same time, it helped lure the army back into the city. With the destruction of Galveston during the hurricane of 1900, the railroad turned San Antonio into a true urban center with reliable transportation [44].

However, the railroad also reshaped the urban landscape and influenced the direction of suburbanization, land values, location of industries, and therefore the spatial assortment of residents. Nineteenth century railroads were dangerous coal fired vehicles that were dirty and noisy. Only the poor resided near the railroads which created two long corridors of undesirable land uses on the west and east sides of downtown and divided the city. The wealthy elites migrated north of town on Broadway towards Fort Sam Houston enticed by advertisements for northern neighborhoods as the only place in the city where one could make it home from downtown without crossing a railroad [35].

The streetcar system benefited from the growth of economic activity in the downtown area from the arrival of new residents and tourists created by the railroad. The early lines ran in a north to south direction, causing property values where the lines were constructed to increase, and for new housing developments, that at the time were on the outskirt of town, to become accessible. With the creation of new desirable areas in the northern portions of the city, and the hustle and bustle of the downtown and businesses along the east/west corridors brought on by the railroad, the newly built communities became desirable places for wealthier families, while the surrounding neighborhoods of the core were now affordable for working class residents. This urban transformation opened the door for early African American communities such as Newcombville and the Baptist settlement to locate near downtown [40].

Local politics reordered the urban space and the southwest side became an area for Mexican immigrants to settle. The first ordinance that reinforced emerging land use patterns was adopted in 1889 which moved vice related activities such as brothels and gambling to the west side of downtown. This caused vice activities to no longer be intermingled with other downtown activities and this clustering branded the west side as a less desirable area. Large homes were turned into brothels and wealthy residents moved north. This was reinforced by another ordinance established in the early twentieth century that required all slaughter houses to be moved to the southwest side of town. Logically, these businesses clustered close to the railroad since it was their lifeline, which further contributed to undesirable uses [35].

To understand the perpetuation of segregation in southwestern San Antonio, it is vital to consider the immigration patterns between the United States and Latin America throughout the twentieth century. The Mexican Revolution of 1910 led to internal displacement of Mexicans and their arrival in San Antonio and many other cities in the Southwest. Labor shortages during both World Wars also meant that United States farmers and manufacturers needed to rely on Mexican labor and often recruited directly from Mexico or by passing temporary work authorization arrangements such as the Bracero Program [45]. With the continued flow of Mexicans and other immigrant groups from Latin America, especially from Central American countries in the 1980s and 1990s, like northern cities that saw the formation of ethnic neighborhoods with the arrival of European immigrants, the southwestern sector of San Antonio, also known as the West Side Barrio or Mexican Quarter, developed into a place of employment, social networking, a cultural heaven, and a transnational place. Consequently, ethno-racial communities are a safety net for groups in society that have been intentionally excluded or are seeking a transition into the dominant host society.

segregation including the Federal Housing Administration and New Deal [9,46], public housing [8,47],

Both past and current federal housing policies have been linked to the perpetuation of residential segregation including the Federal Housing Administration and New Deal [9,46], public housing [8,47], Housing Choice Voucher program [48,49], and the Low-Income Housing Tax Credit program [50,51] and this is seen in San Antonio. Until recently, federally assisted housing has been built in high poverty minority concentrated neighborhoods to the east of downtown where Blacks have historically settled and currently reside, and in Hispanic neighborhoods south and west of downtown. Steering and predatory lending has also been found to contribute to residential segregation [11] as well as land use and zoning practices [10,52]. Lending practices and federally supported policies have specifically perpetuated segregation in minority-concentrated communities in the southwestern and southeastern sections of San Antonio. The Home Owners' Loan Corporation city surveys of San Antonio during 1935 and 1936 are coded based on levels of security for real estate investment. The entire west side that is primarily occupied by Hispanics and east side where Blacks are concentrated is coded as red which represented a lending hazard and led to years of disinvestment in these neighborhoods.

This study provides insight on the historic roots of modern segregation in the southwestern cosmopolis of San Antonio, currently one of the most residentially segregated cities in the nation. It contributes to the literature by uncovering the patterns of residential segregation in 1910 in a city that has limited historical data and information on how decisions of the past have had long-term consequences on the urban landscape and has led to an entire quadrant of the city suffering from blight and disinvestment a century later. As a next step, the historical geodatabase and findings produced by this study present an opportunity to conduct a richer historical and sociological analysis on the origins of Hispanic segregation in San Antonio and the factors that have contributed to its perpetuation over time. With the increasing dispersion of the Latino community away from the Southwest U.S. into states such as North Carolina, Georgia, and Louisiana, and especially for future generations who are growing up in Latino enclaves, more research on the formation, perpetuation, and evolution of these communities is called for.

Acknowledgments: This project was funded in-part by the University of Texas at San Antonio, Office of the Vice President for Research.

Author Contributions: Rebecca J. Walter, Nathan Foote, and Hilton A. Cordoba conceived and designed the experiments; Corey Sparks performed the experiments; Rebecca J. Walter and Corey Sparks analyzed the data; and Rebecca J. Walter, Nathan Foote, and Hilton A. Cordoba wrote the paper.

Conflicts of Interest: The authors declare no conflict of interest. The founding sponsors had no role in the design of the study; in the collection, analyses, or interpretation of data; in the writing of the manuscript, and in the decision to publish the results.

References

1. Massey, D.; Denton, N. The Dimensions of Residential Segregation. *Soc. Forces* **1988**, *67*, 281–315. [CrossRef]
2. Charles, C.Z. The Dynamics of Racial Residential Segregation. *Ann. Rev. Sociol.* **2003**, *29*, 167–207. [CrossRef]
3. Galster, G. Residential Segregation and Interracial Economic Disparities: Simultaneous-Equations Approach. *J. Urban Econ.* **1987**, *21*, 22–44. [CrossRef]
4. Massey, D.; Denton, N. *American Apartheid: Segregation and the Making of the Underclass*; Harvard University Press: Cambridge, MA, USA, 1993.
5. Ovadia, S. The Dimensions of Racial Inequality: Occupational and Residential Segregation across Metropolitan Areas in the United States. *City Community* **2003**, *2*, 313–333. [CrossRef]
6. Von Lockette, N.D. The Impact of Metropolitan Residential Segregation on the Employment Chances of Blacks and Whites in the United States. *City Community* **2010**, *9*, 256–273. [CrossRef]
7. Wilson, W.J. *The Truly Disadvantaged: The Inner City, the Underclass, and Public Policy*; University of Chicago Press: Chicago, IL, USA, 1987.
8. Goering, J. *Housing Desegregation and Federal Policy*; UNC Press: Chapel Hill, NC, USA, 1986.
9. Jackson, K. *Crabgrass Frontier: The Suburbanization of the United States*; Oxford University Press: New York, NY, USA, 1985.

10. Resseger, M. *The Impact of Land Use Regulation on Racial Segregation: Evidence from Massachusetts Zoning Borders*; Harvard University: Boston, MA, USA, 2013.
11. Turner, M.A.; Ross, S.; Galster, G.; Yinger, J. *Discrimination in Metropolitan Housing Markets: National Results from Phase I HDS 2000*; U.S. Department of Housing and Urban Development: Washington, DC, USA, 2002.
12. Logan, J.; Zhang, W.; Turner, R.; Shertzer, A. Creating the Black Ghetto: Black Residential Patterns before and during the Great Migration. *Ann. Am. Acad. Political Soc. Sci.* **2015**, *660*, 18–35. [CrossRef] [PubMed]
13. Massey, D.; Denton, N. Hypersegregation in US Metropolitan Areas: Black and Hispanic Segregation along Five Dimensions. *Demography* **1989**, *26*, 373–391. [CrossRef] [PubMed]
14. Ellen, I.G.; Steil, J.P.; De la Roca, J. The Significance of Segregation in the 21st Century. *City Community* **2016**, *15*, 8–13. [CrossRef]
15. Flippen, C.A. The More Things Change the More They Stay the Same: The Future of Residential Segregation in America. *City Community* **2016**, *15*, 14–17. [CrossRef]
16. Jones, R. The Segregation of Ancestry Groups in San Antonio. *Soc. Sci. J.* **2003**, *40*, 213–232. [CrossRef]
17. Logan, J.R. The Persistence of Segregation in the 21st Century Metropolis. *City Community* **2013**, *12*, 160–168. [CrossRef] [PubMed]
18. Timberlake, J.M.; Iceland, J. Change in Racial and Ethnic Residential Inequality in American Cities, 1970–2000. *City Community* **2007**, *6*, 335–365. [CrossRef]
19. Denton, N. Interpreting U.S. Segregation Trends: Two Perspectives. *City Community* **2013**, *12*, 156–159. [CrossRef]
20. Lichter, D.; Parisi, D.; Taquino, M. Spatial Assimilation in U.S. Cities and Communities? Emerging Patterns of Hispanic segregation from Blacks and Whites. *Ann. Am. Acad. Political Soc. Sci.* **2015**, *660*, 36–56. [CrossRef]
21. Fry, R.; Taylor, P. *The Rise of Residential Segregation by Income*; Pew Research Center: Washington, DC, USA, 2012.
22. Gotham, K.F. Urban Space, Restrictive Covenants and the Origins of Racial Residential Segregation in a US City, 1900–50. *Int. J. Urban Reg. Res.* **2000**, *24*, 616–633. [CrossRef]
23. Logan, J.; Zhang, W.; Chunyu, M. Emergent Ghettos: Black neighborhoods in New York and Chicago, 1880–1940. *Am. J. Sociol.* **2015**, *120*, 1055–1094. [CrossRef] [PubMed]
24. Chung, S.; Brown, L. Racial/Ethnic Residential Sorting in Spatial Context: Testing the Explanatory Frameworks. *Urban Geogr.* **2007**, *28*, 312–339. [CrossRef]
25. Massey, D. Ethnic Residential Segregation: A Theoretical Synthesis and Empirical Review. *Sociol. Soc. Res.* **1985**, *69*, 315–350.
26. Massey, D. Segregation and Stratification. A Biosocial Perspective. *DuBois Rev. Soc. Sci. Res. Race* **2004**, *1*, 1–19. [CrossRef]
27. Massey, D.; Denton, N. Spatial Assimilation as a Socioeconomic Process. *Am. Sociol. Rev.* **1985**, *50*, 94–105. [CrossRef]
28. Massey, D.; Mullan, B. Processes of Hispanic and Black Spatial Assimilation. *Am. J. Sociol.* **1984**, *89*, 836–873. [CrossRef]
29. Alba, R.D.; Logan, J.R. Minority Proximity to Whites in Suburbs: An Individual-Level Analysis of Segregation. *Am. J. Sociol.* **1983**, *98*, 1388–1427. [CrossRef]
30. Goldsmith, P.R. Perpetuation Theory and the Racial Segregation of Young Adults. *Soc. Sci. Res.* **2016**, *56*, 1–15. [CrossRef] [PubMed]
31. Gilliland, J.; Olson, S. Residential Segregation in the Industrializing City: A Closer Look. *Urban Geogr.* **2010**, *31*, 29–58. [CrossRef]
32. Arreola, D. The Mexican American Cultural Capital. *Geogr. Rev.* **1987**, *77*, 17–34. [CrossRef]
33. *Population of the 100 Largest Urban. Places: 1910*; U.S. Census Bureau: Washington, DC, USA, 1910.
34. Appler, J. *San Antonio City Directory*; Jules, A., Ed.; Appler Directory: San Antonio, TX, USA, 1910.
35. Johnson, D.; The University of Texas at San Antonio, San Antonio, TX, USA. Personal interview, 7 February 2017.
36. QuickFacts, San Antonio City, TexasU.S. Census Bureau: Washington, DC, USA, 2010. Available online: https://www.census.gov/quickfacts/table/PST045214/4865000/embed/accessible (accessed on 31 May 2017).
37. Kirwan Institute for the Study of Race and Ethnicity. *San Antonio-New Braunfels, TX (Metro Area) Child. Opportunity Index*; Institute for Child, Youth and Family Policy, Brandeis University: Waltham, MA, USA, 2015.

38. Brown, A.; Lopez, M.H. *Ranking Latino Population's in the Nation's Metropolitan Areas*; Pew Research Center: Washington, DC, USA, 2013.
39. Fischer, M. The Relative Importance of Income and Race in Determining Residential Outcomes in U.S. Urban Areas, 1970–2000. *Urban Aff. Rev.* **2003**, *38*, 669–696. [CrossRef]
40. Mason, K. *African Americans and Race Relations in San Antonio Texas, 1867–1937*; Garland Publishing, Inc.: New York, NY, USA, 1998.
41. Diaz, D.R. *Barrio Urbanism: Chicanos, Planning, and American Cities*; Routledge: New York, NY, USA, 2015.
42. Diaz, D.R.; Torres, R.D. *Latino Urbanism: The Politics of Planning, and Redevelopment*; University Press: New York, NY, USA, 2012.
43. Montejano, D. *Anglos and Mexicans in the Making of Texas, 1836–1896*; University of Texas Press: Austin, TX, USA, 1987.
44. Boryczka, R. The busiest man in town: John Hermann Kampmann and the urbanization of San Antonio, Texas, 1848–1885. *Southwest. Hist. Q.* **2012**, *115*, 329–363. [CrossRef]
45. Henderson, T.J. *Beyond Borders: A History of Mexican Migration to the United States*; Wiley-Blackwell: West Sussex, UK, 2011.
46. Katznelson, I. *When Affirmative Action Was White: An Untold History of Racial Inequality in the Twentieth Century America*; W.W. Norton: New York, NY, USA, 2005.
47. Solomon, R. *Public Housing Reform and Voucher Success: Progress and Challenges*; The Brookings Institute: Washington, DC, USA, 2005.
48. Hartung, J.; Henig, J. Housing Vouchers and Certificates as a Vehicle for Deconcentrating the Poor: Evidence from the Washington, D.C., Metropolitan Area. *Urban Aff. Rev.* **1997**, *32*, 403–419. [CrossRef]
49. Pendall, R. Why Voucher and Certificate Users Live in Distressed Neighborhoods. *Hous. Policy Debate* **2000**, *11*, 881–910. [CrossRef]
50. Cummings, J.; DiPasquale, D. The Low-Income Housing Tax Credit: An Analysis of the First Ten Years. *Hous. Policy Debate* **1999**, *10*, 251–307. [CrossRef]
51. Van Zandt, S.; Mhatre, P. Growing Pains: Perpetuating Inequality through the Production of Low-Income Housing in the Dallas/Fort Worth Metroplex. *Urban Geogr.* **2009**, *30*, 490–513. [CrossRef]
52. Lens, M.; Monkkonen, P. Do Strict Land Use Regulations Make Metropolitan Areas More Segregated by Income? *J. Am. Plan. Assoc.* **2016**, *82*, 6–21. [CrossRef]

urban science

MDPI

Article

City Sovereignty: Urban Resistance and Rebel Cities Reconsidered

Vojislava Filipcevic Cordes

Urban Studies Program, Fordham University, Lincoln Center, 33 W. 60th Street, New York, NY 10023, USA; vcordes@fordham.edu

Received: 17 February 2017; Accepted: 21 June 2017; Published: 23 June 2017

Abstract: The article argues for an increase in de facto already claimed city sovereignty. It situates the discussion, first in the historical context of city-state relationships, and second, in the current urban crises in the United States tied to the sanctuary city movement, then examines legal grounds for devolution of power to cities, before discussing the legal concepts of "urban commons" and "city power", finally outlining constraints facing increasingly sovereign cities. The article argues that current legal literature on "urban commons" and "city power" needs a stronger normative lens and better conceptualization of urban inequality, redistribution, and publicness. Moreover, if cities are to assume greater capacity to govern and to ensure life, liberty, and the sustainability of their populations, they have to overcome serious constraints in the four domains outlined in the article: (1) surveillance and control of urban space, (2) privatization of public space, (3) the rise of the luxury city, large-scale developments, megaprojects, and (4) homelessness.

Keywords: city sovereignty; urban inequality; sanctuary cities

1. Introduction

Cities are schoolhouses of democracy, argued Tocqueville and "can retain their ability to enable people to learn the skills of self-government only if they are given sufficient power to make decisions that have tangible consequences for the quality of local life" [1] (p. 50). Benjamin Barber argues that cities should be empowered "to secure human sustainability, especially when nations fail to do so" [2] (p. 7). In *If Mayors Ruled the World*, Barber emphasized that "politics cannot be found in (or rescued from) increasingly dysfunctional nation-states or rigidly ideological national parties" (cited [2] (p. 10); "[t]he crisis in national governance is a crisis in sovereignty, in the capacity of the nation-state to make good on the terms of social contract on which their founding legitimacy turns" [2] (p. 17).

It is critical that today's protest movements have assumed an urban dimension with cities emerging as chief locations of political action and progressive policies ranging from minimum wage to immigration. This can most poignantly be seen in the example of sanctuary cities in the United States that have posed a challenge to federal rule in the domain of immigration. Cities—their resources, capacities, and institutional infrastructures, by which I mean especially the urban legal apparatus—are becoming "the most important, constructive alternative to a Trump agenda", noted Benjamin Barber most recently (cited in [3]) arguing further for "the necessity for intercity cooperation and networking" in an interdependent cosmopolitan world [2] (p. 22). "A national government may think it simple to defeat one city's policies on climate or immigration, but let it try to defeat six hundred cities working together nationally, or six thousand acting together globally" [2] (p. 27).

This article argues for an increase in de facto already claimed city sovereignty. While Barber's argument is global, this article focuses on the United States, arguing that in the face of a hostile sovereign, cities have a significant role to play—a role that shows signs of claiming increasing powers and enfranchising substantive governance [4]. While cities cannot replace the state's capacity in military, taxation, redistribution, infrastructure or public services, international relations, trade and migration policies, they are nevertheless showing signs of leadership in the arenas of land use and development, minimum wage, regional tax sharing, sustainable development planning and climate change, and, especially, as will be emphasized in this article, in the case of sanctuary practices in the area of immigrant inclusion. Sanctuary cities in the United States can be defined as places where a local government or police department have passed a resolution, a city ordinance, an executive order, or a departmental policy expressly forbidding city or law enforcement officials from inquiring into immigration status and/or cooperation with the Department of Homeland Security's Immigration and Customs Enforcement (ICE) Agency.

The article situates the discussion, first in the historical context of city-state relationships, and second, in the current urban crises in the United States tied to the sanctuary city movement, then examines legal grounds for devolution of power to cities, before discussing the legal concepts of "urban commons" [5,6] (see also [7]) and "city power" [8], finally outlining constraints facing increasingly sovereign cities. While mayors may not "rule the world", as Barber's forceful argument would have it, this article argues instead that cities are not utilizing the powers that they increasingly do possess to sufficiently and substantively address urban inequalities and to expand urban citizenship into a fundamentally inclusive category. Barber is arguing that expanded city sovereignty ought to be a normative goal given the crises of the nation state, while this article argues that the noted normative goal should be approached with caution given the persistence of urban inequalities. The current context of the state hostile to redistributive urban policies, however, opens up a social and political space for a special emphasis on urban sovereignty. Sanctuary practices represent one arena in which cities have begun to address substantive problems of social inequality; legal mechanisms utilized for this purpose are reviewed in this context in this article. While sanctuary cities and current urban crises in the United States provide a contextual framework for the discussion, the theoretical framework for sovereignty is examined, as noted, in relationship to the concepts of "city power" and "urban commons". The article argues that current legal literature on "urban commons" and "city power" needs a stronger normative lens and better conceptualization of urban inequality, redistribution, and publicness. Moreover, if cities are to assume greater capacities to govern and to ensure the life, liberty, and the sustainability of their populations, they have to overcome serious constraints in the four domains outlined in the article: (1) surveillance and control of urban space, (2) privatization of public space, (3) the rise of the luxury city, large-scale developments, megaprojects, and (4) homelessness. The linkage between urban constraints and urban sovereignty is further emphasized by suggesting the ways in which cities have attempted to address these problems through, for example, the spaces of commemoration, waterfront access areas and participatory community-based plans ("197-a" plans in New York City), community benefits agreements, affordable housing, and litigation on behalf of the homeless.

2. Capital, Coercion, and City-State Relationships

State-city relationships, in particular, the influence of the processes of urbanization on states, the interactions between the state rulers and urban populations, and the correspondences between urban structures and state types, are not well developed in the literature. Diane Davis has studied conflicts between identity politics and sovereignty in divided cities focusing on specifically urban dimensions of contestation, investigating "how the superimposition of certain sovereignty arrangements on identity-diverse urban locales has affected the built environment of the city or its people in ways that fan the flames of aggression and violent conflict" or "lead to the establishment of a genuinely pluralistic, tolerant, and autonomous form of urban citizenship" [9] (pp. 228–230). Research compiled in Davis' and Libertun de Duren's edited volume finds that conflicts are more likely to arise under "conditions of uncertain or contested sovereignty" and to "emerge in cities where divergent populations are denied access to formal or informal institutions for claim-making, for influencing urban policy, or for advocating for citizenship rights or identity aims" [9] (pp. 247, 251). The research does not sufficiently question identity-based projects and nor does it take into account the ways in which institutions can be captured and populations manipulated by identity-based claims. Nevertheless, the research outlines "the degree to which unity of division among identity groups is facilitated by urban form—whether through symbolic buildings, iconic architecture, or the development of urban projects" [9] (p. 247) and includes, significantly, Lawrence J. Vale's conclusions that "the urban world has been filled with effort to manipulate citizens through provocative acts of narrow subnational nationalism" [10] (p. 207).

Tilly and Blockmans' edited volume *Cities and the Rise of States in Europe, A.D. 1000 to 1800* [11] and Tilly's *Coercion, Capital, and European States, A.D. 990–1992* [12] represent particularly valuable contributions to the study of city-state relationships. First, cities can be defined in relation to the "the formation of dense, differentiated populations having extensive outside connections"; this formation is facilitated by the proximity of "[t]rade, warehousing, banking, and production" [12] (p. 17). Second, cities cannot be simply reduced to "expressions of their dominant classes and surrounding economies" [11] (p. 4). Third, it is important to distinguish between city systems and systems of states. "Europe's systems of cities represented the changing relations among concentrations of capital, its systems of states the changing relations among concentrations of coercion. European cities formed a loose hierarchy of commercial and industrial precedence within which at any point in time a few clusters of cities (usually grouped around a single hegemonic center) clearly dominated the rest" [12] (p. 47).

Citing Machiavelli's notion that "a city used to liberty can be more easily held by means of its citizens than in any other way, if you wish to preserve it" [11] (p. 2), Tilly shows how this notion nevertheless proved inaccurate as states developed into large war machines, although the author can be criticized for an overemphasis on the role of coercion and the war-making powers of the state. The author further offers three conclusions: (1) strikingly different types of states emerge in densely populated urban regions vs. regions that contain few cities; (2) where distinctive forms of urban organization existed during the period of the formation of major states, they survived the growth of state power and continued to play national influence; (3) urban merchants and financiers played considerable influence in the formation of states including its armed forces [11] (p. 6).

Tilly distinguishes between two periods. In the first, between 1000 and 1500 when cities were rare and states numerous, "the rulers of most cities of 10,000 or more exercised something resembling sovereignty within their own walls and their immediate hinterlands" and "[r]elative to territorial lords, urban oligarchies wielded considerable political power" [11] (p. 15). In the second period after 1500, however, "the formation of consolidated states coupled with the proliferation of cities to change the city-state relationship both numerically and politically ... Politically, the odds that the oligarchy of any single city would dominate a state declined drastically. The proliferation of cities facilitated a state-making strategy of divide and conquer, the gradual monopolization of coercive means by consolidated states weakened the defensive positions of cities vis-a-vis national authorities, the expansion of state administrative apparatus (which was itself largely a consequence of war and the preparation for war) gave those authorities increasing ability to monitor and control the urban population" [11] (pp. 15, 16).

In both *Cities and the Rise of States in Europe, A.D. 1000 to 1800* and *Coercion, Capital, and European States, A.D. 990–1992*, Tilly emphasizes a critical point that "[c]ities shape the destinies of states chiefly by serving as containers and distribution points for capital" which "gives the urban political authorities access to capital, credit, and control over hinterlands that, if seized or co-opted, can serve the ends of monarchs as well" and can facilitate the aims of the states (e.g., "containers and deployers of coercive means") to develop their armed forces [11] (p. 8); [12] (pp. 51, 52). While the state represents the chief container of coercion which "maintains a relatively centralized, differentiated, and autonomous structure of its own" [12] (p. 131), Tilly also points to the "development of welfare states, of regulatory states, of states that spend a great deal of their effort intervening in economic affairs [which] mitigated and obscured the centrality of coercion" [12] (p. 52).

Tilly stresses further "the autonomy of [the cities'] ruling classes with respect to would-be and actual state-makers, and the strength of their representative institutions" and shows how "major trading cities and city-states mounted more effective resistance to the penetration of consolidated states than did cities in mainly agrarian regions" [11] (p. 22). Moreover, "[m]ost often consolidated states only gained genuine control over major trading cities when cities had begun to lose their predominant positions in international markets" [11] (p. 22). But the critical factors were, however, the "focus of bargaining over the wherewithal of war" [11] (p. 22) and the fact that "urban institutions themselves seem to have become part of state structure more readily where capitalists predominated" [11] (p. 22).

Two conclusions are particularly relevant for the contemporary context of this research. First, Tilly's emphasis on the ways in which the states are weakened today; for example, "the ability of European states to detect and counteract movements of illegal migrants ... has declined radically even as capital moves ever more freely from opportunity to opportunity, regardless of state interest" [11] (p. 26). "Furthermore, after several centuries in which capital and coercion converged under state command, they now seem to be separating" [11] (p. 26). Thus, increasingly sovereign cities are encountering state sovereigns whose coercion power has been weakened, although the sovereign has in the United States applied threats of defunding and limited redistribution to non-compliant cities.

Second, and of particular relevance to rebel cities, Tilly discusses the conditions under which rebellions have tended to start—namely, when (1) "the state's demands and actions offended citizens' standards of justice or attacked their primary collective identities, (2) the people touched by offensive state actions were already connected by durable social ties, (3) ordinary people had powerful allies inside or outside the state, and (4) the state's recent actions or interactions revealed that it was vulnerable to attack" [12] (p. 101). Current rebel cities show that the sovereign has offended urban standards of justice, that the undocumented, refugees, and asylum seekers and their families have started to develop durable ties with the social community of the U.S., that urban political leadership, namely the mayors of American cities, have a stake in at least symbolically defending this population, and that the United States national leadership is increasingly vulnerable to the mounting opposition including by the legal system. Resistance and protests on the part of sanctuary cities may thus be the current weapons of the very weakest.

3. Rebel Cities

David Harvey has asked whether the city can be "a center of revolution" noting that "[p]olitical and urban social movements have used the city as an agent of social and political innovation in the search to construct an alternative social order and a different sense of the right to the city" [13] (p. 101). This article argues that the city can be theorized as a center of power for the benefit of the excluded if the notions of "urban commons" and "city power" can be expanded and substantiated to address profound inequalities—this possibility is seen in the example of sanctuary cities. And a more inclusive city can indeed be a revolutionary idea, one that depends on increased urban powers and on creating a social and political space to direct resources away from surveillance, privatization, and luxury and towards inclusive and sustainable social planning, thus opening up cities for public participatory processes and for enhanced possibilities of a novel poetics, not only politics, of daily urban life. City sovereignty is after all only significant if it can be claimed by enfranchised citizens as well as a range of denizens, including those who do not have legal rights but certainly have claimed the right of the city.

Referencing the role of migration, Harvey concludes that the right to difference is one of the most precious rights of urban dwellers but warns further that "difference can also result in bigotry and divisions, marginalization and exclusions, sometimes boiling over into violent confrontations" [13] (p. 86). U.S. mayors have most recently offered their response to diversity politics in relationship to the recent restrictive state policies. "To anyone who feels threatened today, or vulnerable, you are safe in Boston", noted Martin J. Walsh, the Mayor of Boston adding at a news conference, "We will do everything lawful in our power to protect you. If necessary, we will use City Hall itself to shelter and protect anyone who's targeted unjustly" [14]. This remark comes in response to the President Trump's executive order which threatens to cut funding to sanctuary cities that refuse to cooperate with federal immigration authorities.

In his Cooper Union speech on 21 November 2016, New York's Mayor De Blasio emphasized, "We don't consent to hatred. And we will fight anything we see as undermining our values. And here is my promise to you as your mayor—we will use all the tools at our disposal to stand up for our people. If all Muslims are required to register, we will take legal action to block it. If the federal government wants our police officers to tear immigrant families apart, we will refuse to do it ... If the Justice Department orders local police to resume stop and frisk, we will not comply. We won't trade in neighborhood policing for racial profiling. If there are threats to federal funding for Planned Parenthood of New York City, we will ensure women receive the healthcare they need. If Jews, or Muslims, or members of the LGBT community, or any community are victimized and attacked, we will find their attackers, we will arrest them, we will prosecute them. This is New York. Nothing about who we are changed on Election Day".

"The right of cities to govern themselves and to come together with other cities, both within a beyond their national borders, increasingly is being grounded in powerful rights arguments" [2] (p. 18). To revitalize democracy today, we must have rebel cities—to borrow David Harvey's notion that is tied to the idea of right to the city, which "primarily rises up from the streets, out from the neighborhoods, as a cry for help and sustenance by oppressed people in desperate times" [7] (p. xiii). Citing Lefebvre, Harvey has in mind "a vigorous anti-capitalist movement that focuses on the transformation of daily urban life as its goal" [7] (p. xvi). But in today's speeches by America's mayors, the right to the city is evoked as the right of resistance to federal authority while recent protests focus on the defense of women's, immigrant, and refugee rights.

A more recent group of protests focuses on the opposition to the President's executive order to ban refugees and immigrants from several Muslim countries, and it is perhaps not an accident that the first protest against the Trump administration, the March on Washington, was organized by the feminist movement. At the time when many think that the feminist agenda has been achieved, women still feel oppressed especially given the sexism, misogyny, and threats to cut funding to reproductive health support organizations arguably ushered with the new administration. Cities are logical locations for feminist struggles as they have, as Elizabeth Wilson has argued [15,16], provided a plank in the gradual emancipation of women.

All of these provide examples of how states can construct a stigmatized other. As Koutrolikou has argued in the case of Athens, the other who is "perceived as a threat faces stigmatisation and exclusions (even criminalisation), while processes of 'othering' may also distinguish the 'rightful' from the 'Others'. It might be the 'terrorist', the 'migrant', the 'rioter' or else, but in any form a group becomes negatively correlated to the emergency while it simultaneously becomes disassociated from the 'deserving', law-abiding citizenry [...]. Legal aspects and ethical/moral representations further intensify such divisions. In this way, we have a differentiation, a de-familiarisation and an enemy-formation tactic, dividing the citizenry between 'us and them' [...], between 'good' citizens and their interests and 'uncivil or threatening others'" [17] (pp. 175, 176).

Sanctuary cities in the U.S. represent a feat against the hostile state and "provide a territorial legal entity at a different scale at which sovereignty is articulated" [18]. Sanctuary cities exemplify what Lippert has termed "sovereignty 'from below'" [19] (p. 547) and are shaped by local legal and political contexts and the solidarity with social movements. Given the most recent federal crackdown on sanctuary jurisdictions, some cities are attempting to assert their sovereignty through legal battles while others are seeking alternatives to formal sanctuary city ordinances; the number of sanctuaries cities is increasing in defiance of the federal authorities. Powell notes that as of 6 February 2017, there were 39 sanctuary cities and five sanctuary states in addition to 633 sanctuary counties [20]; it is thus important to emphasize that sanctuary cities range from small towns and counties to major cities in the United States. Sanctuary cities have been "incorporated into the legal and institutional spaces of local governments" and have attempted to exert moral and legal authority (see [21]; see also, [22] (p. 69)) in cases where in their view the federal government had failed, moving away from their roots in faith-based organizing, however, towards "institutionalized mechanisms of local governance" [23] (pp. 219, 223, 228). San Francisco has already sued the Trump administration over its order to withhold funding ($1.2 billion dollars, in this case of this city) from sanctuary jurisdictions, arguing that the order was unconstitutional [24]. The city has claimed that the order represented "a severe invasion of San Francisco's sovereignty" [25] and has won a legal challenge in anticipation of further legal proceedings and political turmoil [26]. San Francisco has been criticized in the legal community for attempting to impose urban liberal values as a nation-wide policy [27]. While the judge applied the anti-commandeering principle to stop the federal government from coercing San Francisco to undertake the work of the federal entity, an additional hurdle is represented by a section of the federal immigration statute that argues that localities can't withhold information or refuse to cooperate with the federal government [28]. Although this notion should be approached cautiously given the remaining statutory challenges, the argument here is that sanctuary cities show promise in offering an inclusive polity as an alternative to the restrictive state. This argument is applied to the cases in the U.S. in contrast to the U.K. examples [29,30] in which sanctuary cities "reproduce some dominant discourses that sanctuary practices overtly seek to counter" [31] (p. 4). Thus, the argument here supports the claim that "sanctuary's promise lies in its potential to disrupt the state's attempt to monopolize territorial sovereignty and ways of being political" [32] (p. 44). The role of cities, however, ought to be central to this argument, as it is cities that can become sites of crucial networks of solidarity with the undocumented, the asylum seekers, and the refugees. Sanctuary cities in the U.S. are more than just "'pockets' of sovereignty, where citizens assert their visions of justice and contact the state when it drifts too far from social realities" [31] (p. 10). The argument here is that sanctuary cities in the U.S. contest the sovereign power of the nation state and its exclusionary politics towards the asylum seekers, the refugees, and the undocumented and, in the face of recent challenges, especially the federal crackdown, include movement into both increasingly legality (by challenging the federal government in court) and publicness and visibility (by increasing media exposure in seeking an immigration policy reform, for example, the Dream Act, or public reemphasis by Democratic mayors on maintaining sanctuary city policies). This is a critical example of city sovereignty in the contemporary U.S. while sanctuary cities in other states such as in the U.K. seem to be replicating state exclusions. Nevertheless, led by a member of the Global Parliament of Mayors (GPM) steering group, Marvin Rees, the Mayor of the City of Bristol, is proposing a crowd-funding campaign to "support" counterpart U.S. mayors that have sanctuary city status. The GPM campaign would involve crowd-sourcing resources from U.K. cities (Bristol initially), transferring them to an intermediary body nominated by the GPM Secretariat, and providing the funds as a donation to a selected mayor (e.g., Boston/Chicago/Los Angeles/NYC) representing sanctuary cities in the U.S. The campaign would run from February to June 2017 initially [33]. GPM is an example of translocal urban citizenship that provides representation to cities beyond their nation states and proposes even forms of redistribution across sanctuary cities. As Barber argues, what is necessary is "cooperation among networked municipalities and a deployment of collective local power that will establish a democratic and public counterweight to private global capital" [2] (p. 40). "Glocality is proving that local government works more efficiently and productively when mayors cooperate globally, forging networks for common action" [2] (p. 85), as the Global Parliament of Mayors' call for crowd-sourcing resources indicates.

4. Rebel Governance

Studies of rebel governance are similar to the literature on rebel cities as both point to the inadequacy of state-centric approaches to the study of governance [34] (p. 286). Rebel governance obtains particular relevance in the cases of state violence which victimizes the local population or that which has failed to attend to the basic needs of the population [34] (p. 7).

The rebels' activities clash "with the dominant perception of rebel groups, especially those in the developing world, which, since the end of the Cold War, have been caricatured as little more than war lords" [35] (p. 3); they have also been referred to as "bandits, militias, rebels, guerillas, warlords, insurgents, even freedom fighters and terrorists" [35] (p. 8). However, "in order to ensure their visibility insurgent leaders cannot only be concerned with the establishment of a coercive apparatus (domination) but must also gain a degree of consent from the civilian population (hegemony)" [35] (p. 8). Rebels have thus shown a capacity to meet the needs of the local population, to collect taxes, to engage in active public work projects building roads and infrastructure, to provide services to the civilian population, to respond to health care and educational needs of the population, to provide shelter to civilians, to ensure food provision, and to respond to social problems such as theft, drug use, and prostitution [35] (p. 4). Rebels can further encourage civilian participation in popular assemblies, provide administrative services, and organize and regulate commercial production activities [34] (p. 287). Mampilly cites Ernesto "Che" Guevara who influenced rebels around the world and whose Guerrilla Warfare "underlined the importance of demonstrating concern for social welfare of local residents through the provision of public goods" [35] (p. 12). Moreover, "provision of public goods could have an ameliorating effect on the insurgency's ingrained need to use the violence in pursuit of a political agenda" [35] (p. 13). There are, of course, different types of insurgencies; "[c]ommunist insurgencies are more likely to engage in governance involving greater social administration and other interventions than groups espousing conservative social beliefs" [34] (p. 292).

Variations in rebel governance are attributed by Mampilly to "the initial preferences of leadership and their interaction with a wide variety of local and international social and political actors" [35] (p. 3). Rebel governance is also dependent upon the pre-conflict relationship between state and society (see also, [34] (p. 289), the (weak) state capacity before the civil war, in particular state abuse or alienation of civilians (Wickham-Crowley cited in [34] (pp. 7, 290)), and the "ethnic composition and the ultimate strategic objective of the group" [35] (p. 16). Government structures are constantly transformed during the course of warfare and are influenced by military capacity and political economy of warfare (see [34] (p. 291)). Furthermore, rebels' own views, which can be strategically formulated, are "malleable, not fixed" and change in response to the conflict and the demands of insurgency [34] (p. 290).

Rebel governance is also significant for post-conflict peace efforts and insurgent government practices should, according to Mampilly, be seen as a precondition for recognition in the international law arena [35] (pp. 7, 24). Rebels also engage in strategies of internationalization and in active diplomacy which is driven by a political logic and the rebels' need to demonstrate that they can "behave like states" [36] (p. 124). Huang finds that "secessionist groups, for whom international recognition is essential for attaining independent statehood, and groups that organize domestically by investing in social service provision or creating legal political bodies, are more likely to become wartime diplomats" [36] (p. 124).

"Like governments of traditional states, rebel leaders must negotiate with civilians in exchange for their loyalty" [35] (p. 9). Mampilly sees governance as an "interactive process" involving also a "surprising institutional interplay" [35] (pp. 15, 22) between insurgent organizations and the incumbent government and finds that rebel leadership is far more constrained in their actions than is commonly assumed. Finally, one of the important aspects of the manner in which the rebels challenge the state sovereignty is the appropriation of aspects of state sovereignty—Mampilly terms this "counter state sovereignty" [35] (p. 21). Rebel cities are thus similar to rebel governance in that they both seek to obtain legitimacy that the state has failed to provide.

5. Devolution Revolution?

"The city of God, city on a hill, the relationship between city and citizenship—the city as an object of utopian desire, as a distinctive place of belonging within a perpetually shifting socio-temporal order—all give it a political meaning that mobilizes a crucial political imaginary" [7] (p. xvii). Yet the urban political imaginary is, importantly, legally bound. Current legal rules, instituted by the states, limit cities in pursing their independent paths. To the extent that we can even discuss city power, it is important to emphasize that cities "only have power to the extent that they are given it by statues and constitutional provisions adopted by state governments" [1] (p. 231). Thus, in addition to the challenges of basic municipal service provision and of addressing critical urban problems, "bureaucratic inefficiencies, dysfunctional agencies, regional fragmentation, and democratic deficits" [1] (p. 231) are also influenced by legal structures. "[B]oth the national government and the states", as Barber has noted, "insist on denying cities the right of action on issues critical to their citizens, whether or not the cities being preempted are better positioned to take action" [2] (p. 117).

Cities are locations where citizens should be enabled to have a voice in altering their polity. Beyond the public places that are the sites of assembly, there are "multiple practices within the urban that themselves are full to overflowing with alternative possibilities" [7] (p. xvii)—protests can take place at the airports too, as has been seen recently in the U.S., and claim them as public sites. Uncovering these practices is a part of the "political task, Lefebvre suggests, to imagine and reconstitute a totally different kind of city out of the disgusting mess of a globalizing, urbanizing capital run amok" [7] (p. xvi).

This reclaiming is already taking place through a "successful revolution in urban empowerment" [2] (p. 37) which would represent "a powerful rebuke to national political parties wedded to neoliberal strategies of privatization and marketization as political cure-alls" [2] (p. 39) were the cities themselves not the sites of rampant privatization. Katz and Bradley have termed this metropolitan revolution. "The United States is on the verge of a historic re-sorting, in which responsibilities once reserved for higher levels of government are being fully shared with, even shifted to, cities, metropolitan areas, and the networks of leaders who govern them... [T]he federal government and the states will be motivated to do more with less by giving cities and metropolitan areas greater flexibility to design and allocate what are likely to be shrinking levels of resources" [37] (pp. 11, 12). The authors endorse urban pragmatism but uncritically defer to the global economic changes and their impact on the metropolitan regions.

"Local democratic governments, both in the central cities and the suburbs, have been overwhelmed by the impact of the decisions made by other governments over which they have no control" [1] (p. 233). One of the challenges has been to influence the state government to give greater role to the city and its citizens. As Frug and Barron note, cities should develop a clear list of priorities and present them to the state government [1] (p. 232); the arguments for pressuring the states to become more redistributive should not be abandoned. For the legal system to embrace a vision of the city, one has to be clearly articulated by the Mayor, the City Council, city agencies, and, most importantly, an actively engaged local polity—if the aim of devolution is "enhance public goods and strengthen democracy" and thus oppose privatization [2] (p. 39). Comprehensive, participatory, sustainable city-wide and regional plans are one means of engaging cities to articulate a vision of urban space that should then be supported by the institutions and not become a mere guideline to be circumvented by private, development interests. Susan Fainstein argues that the maximization of the values of equity, diversity, and democracy should direct urban planning and policy towards a just city, noting further that this can be done in an incremental manner within the current system by "constantly pushing for a more just distribution", assuming that the "reform [is] backed by political mobilization" [38] (pp. 166, 170, 176).

One of the challenges in realizing a more equitable city is the fragmentation of urban governance "created by assigning specific issues to uncoordinated government institutions" [1] (p. 233). Regional cooperation represents a solution to this problem. Even though regional proposals are being made without regional agencies to implement them, metropolitan solutions represent the key. As Katz and Bradley have argued, cities and metropolitan regions are inextricably linked [37] (p. vii). "Our nation's top 100 metropolitan areas sit on only 12 percent of the nation's land mass but are home to two-thirds of our population and generate 75 percent of our national GDP" [37] (p. 1).

"Mired in partisan division and rancor, the federal government appears incapable of taking bold action to restructure our economy and grapple with changing demography and rising inequality" [37] (p. 3). Current legal structures are not sufficiently responsive to urban conditions and most states have not changed in a substantive way their city structures for decades [1] (p. 6). But even though current legal rules limit cities' exercise of control, they also empower cities to pursue the global city and the tourist city policies, both of which defer to private development interests, have resulted in increases of social inequality, and have diminished the public purpose of planning. Thus, even the legal rules that empower cities can be seen as limiting equitable development. As Richard Briffault has argued, even though cities may possess formal authority, "their economic and political power in practice is shaped by private investment decisions" (cited in [1] (pp. 33, 34)).

Reformers in the late nineteenth century envisioned home rule as a way for cities "to become significant actors in the promotion of whatever underlying substantive vision of government the urban reformers favored" [1] (p. 36). The reformers, promoting the vision of good government, did not simply seek to increase the powers of the cities but included a mixture of decreased and increased powers depending on the city and the state in question [1] (p. 36). Some reformers pursued limited government on the local level, while others sought to create an efficient bureaucratic form of local government [1] (p. 37).

Local control can have a dual role—"[i]n the U.S. local governments' formal fiscal and land-use authority has often exacerbated inequality by permitting wealthier local governments to shut out poorer citizens. But local authority can also be used to ameliorate inequality" [8] (p. 254). Not only are the large cities diverse in terms of income, ethnicity and race, they are important in promoting civic participation. "The geographically confined nature of local institutions also provides an opportunity to build the kind of civic capacity that political scientists increasingly see as necessary to sustain efforts to implement proposed solutions to seemingly intractable public problems" [1] (p. 50). The response is, however, not to abandon the role of the states that can significantly influence urban issues.

As Fainstein notes, "[t]he purpose of inclusion in decision making should be to have interests fairly represented, not to value participation in and of itself" [38] (p. 175). Citing Mansbridge, Fainstein thus favors "better representation rather than broader participation" noting that "[i]n the selection model, the representative's accountability to the constituent will typically take the form of narrative and even deliberative accountability rather than accountability based on monitoring and sanctions" (Mansbridge cited in [38] (p. 178)). Nevertheless, Fainstein states that "without a mobilized constituency and supportive officials, no prescription for justice will be implemented" [38] (p. 181) and emphasizes that "the role of protest movements is crucial to a more equitable policy" [38] (p. 182).

6. The Limits of "City Power"

Richard Schragger's *City Power* reflects precisely the crucial tension between what cities should do and what cities can do—a tension that is not sufficiently elaborated upon in the study mostly concerned with the latter question. The author argues that the city should be liberated to "pursue ends directed towards the health and welfare of its current citizens"—"[t]he limited connection between governance and growth, the possibility of leveraging immobile capital, and the reality of municipal redistribution suggest that cities can pursue a fairer and more equal distribution of public goods" [8] (p. 248). As Benjamin Barber has argued [39], however, Schragger's account of city power lacks a normative, prescriptive, rights-based argument. Given the bordered nation states' inability to deliver, a space for normative power of borderless cities opens up; Barber argues that networks of cities are the key—an account that is neglected in Schragger's study.

Schragger claims that "[t]he city's policy options are both less constrained and less determinative" [8] (p. 247) emphasizing that cities can govern if they are allowed to. The author notes that cities should focus more on social welfare spending, for example. "Cities should do less of what they cannot do—include economic growth through competitive labor industrial policies—and more of what they can do—provide quality basic services to their residents" [8] (p. 248).

But cities may be more constrained than Schragger's thesis suggests. Schragger's argument requires deeper theoretical development regarding what cities should do. Furthermore it is not clear how far cities can go in accomplishing their goals. It is not apparent, moreover, whether there are policies that state and federal authorities cannot enact or be responsible for or whether they should devolve more power to localities.

Schragger does not say anything regarding cases when federal powers have defaulted on their responsibilities yet he notes "the significant cutbacks in federal and state support for urban initiatives" [8] (p. 160). The author notes further that "[s]ince the 1980s and the pullback in federal funds, urban infrastructure has been a thoroughly private-public enterprise; there simply is not sufficient government will or money to fund even traditional municipal infrastructure—like housing, schools, roads, or parks—absent private investment. In this environment, the traditional public routes for influencing local infrastructure development are diminished" [8] (p. 160).

Schragger discusses urban policies that are limited in their impact or that have only heightened inequalities and discriminatory practices such as the rebuilding of downtown areas and attempts to attract the "right kind" of people [8] (p. 249). He further points out that struggling cities such as Detroit, Camden, Buffalo, and Baltimore, will further not receive the economic development aid that they need. These cities face further challenges given the lack of federal policies. Schragger notes the need for "redistribution at the national level" but also adds that "many of these policies have either failed or not made much of a difference" [8] (p. 250). The author, however, acknowledges that "the current extreme degree of income inequality in the United States is not something that cities can combat on their own" [8] (pp. 251, 252). The study does not elaborate on the role of national urban policy, leaving the significance of federal funding of cities not fully specified or, in the author's terms, a "mystery". Inequality is said to be something that the city creates and something that a city can solve [8] (p. 252), but the author does not sufficiently discuss either of the two.

Examples of economic development that Schragger gives are further suggestive of the ways the city has been shaped to suit the interests of global capital. When the author discusses affordable housing, he positions the discussion in the past ("forty-year span in the middle of the twentieth century" [8] (p. 253)) and does not consider present efforts to construct affordable housing. Furthermore, Schragger discusses regionalism [8] (p. 251) but does not elaborate on concepts such as tax sharing. The author also completely ignores the role of planning, especially city-wide and regional plans that contain sustainable development policies. The author does not discuss the case of the regional growth boundary in Portland.

Schragger's redistributive arguments are weak and include, as has been noted, only one example of city power (minimum wage, which is also an example of state power, it could be argued). The author admittedly wanted to focus on the fact that cities have to be business friendly and to implement policies that would keep businesses within the city limits, thus emphasizing only the policies that are related to the economic role of cities. Schragger thus neglects the social and cultural roles of the urban environment.

Furthermore, the author concludes that equality should be a parameter—he falls short of arguing that it should be the chief parameter—in evaluating the power of localities. "If the formal grant of power to local governments results in massive inequality in the provision of basic municipal goods and services, it should be avoided. If the formal grant of power to local governments enhances the provision of quality goods and services to citizens, however, it should be favoured" [8] (p. 254). But it is not clear who would arbitrate and how localities that exacerbate inequalities would be punished.

Schragger further cites "claims on the city" that would "reclaim democracy" (Soja cited in [8] (p. 254) but his account offers surprisingly little on community power and social movements or other forces that would be reclaiming democracy.

While cities have in the author's view "a significant role to play in producing public goods and ameliorating economic inequality" [8] (p. 255), it is not clear where the resources to do so are going to come from, especially in the resource-constrained cities. This proposal runs the risk of creating two tiers of cities—those resource-rich ones that may engage in amelioration of inequalities and those resource-poor ones which will be abandoned by all levels of government and where inequalities will grow.

This leaves Schragger in the domain of case studies of what cities have actually been doing which is an indication of both the city's power (minimum wage ordinances) and powerlessness (community benefits agreements (CBAs) which may be summarized as deferring to developers after they have bought off the opposition to their projects).

The author's account of redistribution raises the question of agency—who represents the city in the account of city power? Is it the mayor, city council, select institutions, or the community that is able to mobilize and protest? Similarly, rather than the city having power, it could be that more select groups in the city that are powerful, with others powerless.

Schragger's account is significant, nevertheless, in that it argues for an "enlarged realm of urban governance" [8] (p. 136), yet it is unclear whether this means that select projects may have a redistributive component rather than an overall redistribution strategy. When the author mentions "justice and efficacy of particular city expenditures and who benefits and loses from them" [8] (p. 138), he needs a more developed theory of the city's ends.

Furthermore, the relationship between the city and the state is undertheorized and is treated in case by case examples by Schragger. Would the city rely on the state to support its own redistributive goals or are we entering the arena of "rebel cities"? Also, how can city-wide activism be transformed into a state-wide campaign? This leaves us again with the question of how the author theorizes power. Is it a factor of mobilization or is he favoring a strong mayor model of urban governance?

The author does not discuss sanctuary cities or recent struggles to provide protection to immigrants, minority groups, and Muslims. Current debate on legislation, litigation, and circumvention as the ways to counter exclusionary federal policies is further relevant, as are the current progressive efforts by both states and cities.

Discussion of city power can, furthermore, be framed by the current protests against the Trump administration taking place in cities across America and internationally. But Schragger does not focus on city based movements and the study is silent on the role of community-based mobilization or progressive engagement in cities. Likewise, the question of the new responsibilities of cities cannot be fully answered by the arguments in the study. This is all the more urgent given the federal retrenchment of resources for housing, policing, and clean air. But to the extent that cities will be impacted by recently proposed renegotiation of contracts on trade and on migration, the study does not offer any pointers.

Implicit in Schragger's argument is the significance of mayors; again, the study leaves the reader to wonder whether the author is advocating for a strong mayor type of governance. Current urban political moment opens up space for mayoral leadership on the national and international level, making Schragger's account even more relevant. Schragger emphasizes that political power is the key and leaves it up to the mayors to negotiate with the state and the federal government. The author makes a further distinction between local power and city power arguing that local power can be discriminating, exclusionary, and NIMBY, noting as well the role for cities in advancing labor rights, environmental rights, minimum wage laws and affordable housing. Neglected in this account are the ways in which cities can also be sites of exclusion, discrimination, and NIMBY-ism. Schragger, as Benjamin Barber has pointed out, lacks a normative rights-based argument for cities.

As Nestor Davidson has argued [39], the key question is that of urban capacity including pragmatic capacity of urban institutions, which are neglected in the author's account that is characterized by an ambiguity regarding institutions and technocracy. Davidson further points out that the current conflict between cities and the federal government is suggestive of the inevitability of clashes and pre-emption; legal scholarship necessitates thus new theories of authority and autonomy.

Alaina Harkness of the Brookings Institution noted [39] the highly variable capacities of cities to implement policy and stressed that Schragger's study leaves vague the critical question of the resources that cities would need to govern.

Schragger does not focus on the role of U.S. states in improving conditions in cities and is even dismissive of their role given that they have not, in the author's view, taken their responsibilities seriously. While the author emphasizes the question of urban justice, in particular in education and the provision of basic municipal services, this notion is not sufficiently elaborated in the study. This is all the more critical given the question of how to leverage the resources in an environment where federal policies are hostile to cities, although Schragger argued that federal policies of the past, such as the urban renewal policy, have been previously as well characterized by hostility towards the city and its minority residents. Schragger leaves it to political contestation to fight for the resources for the city, acknowledging that poorer cities just may not have the resources to implement policy.

Wendell Pritchett emphasized [39] the role of legal structures that determine the scope of urban governance, expanding Schragger's questions: Should cities govern? and Can cities govern? Into—What should cities govern? and How should cities govern? Pritchett proposes the partnering of successful cities and struggling cities to address the inequity between the resource-rich and the resource poor cities. Pritchett argues further that cities should have abilities to tax revenue, create inclusionary housing and institute rent controls, and should pass other laws protecting employees, not just minimum wage laws.

In conclusion, the account of city power is problematic in its undertheorized role of national urban policy, on the one hand, and community-based mobilization, on the other. While the account of the legal powers of municipalities is significant in that it opens "political space" [8] (p. 154), it is less clear whether political power can be used to substantively address inequalities.

7. Limits of the Urban Commons

The recent debate on the commons is essential for cities and has the potential to enhance an understanding of urban sovereignty. "Urbanization is about the perpetual production of an urban commons (or its shadow-form of public spaces and public goods) and its perpetual appropriation and destruction by private interests" [7] (p. 80). The essential qualities of the commons are critical as they show resistance-laden aspects of the commons. "This common is not only the earth that we share but also the languages we create, the social practices we establish, the modes of sociability that define our relationships, and so forth" (Hardt and Negri cited in [7] (p. 72)). Furthermore, "[t]he human qualities of the city emerge out of our practices in the diverse spaces of the city even as those spaces are subject to enclosure, social control, and appropriation by both private and public/state interests" [7] (p. 72).

The commons is produced through a social practice of commoning which captures "an unstable and malleable social relation between a particular self-defined social group and those aspects of its actually existing or yet-to-be-created social and/or physical environment deemed crucial to its life and livelihood" [7] (p. 73). Furthermore, David Harvey emphasizes that commoning in essence includes "the principle that the relation between the social group and that aspect of the environment being treated as a common shall be both collective and non-commodified—off-limits to the logic of market exchange and market valuations" [7] (p. 73).

Rethinking the City by Foster and Iaione [6] is an important contribution to understanding the urban commons. It would be interesting to further develop the concept of urban inequality, which is addressed at the very conclusion of the paper, in relationship to the urban commons. Foster and Iaione could discuss how cities are chief sites of inequality, especially in the policy arenas that they do control such as development. Following Schragger, it could be argued that cities are politically and legally empowered to engage in development, but the resources that cities do command have gone to upscale development projects which have benefited higher income groups and have reduced the amount of public spaces, contributing to the further privatization of public spaces. Cities have also not done enough planning nor have made urban or regional plans that have addressed urban inequalities.

Foster and Iaione emphasize that cities are "inclusive, shared, sustainable, resilient, innovative, democratically open and responsive to citizen needs" [6] (p. 23). Cities are, however, also sites of conflict, social exclusion, and contain ghettoes and slums. If "commons" is a new way to claim resources as the authors argue, what role will redistribution of resources play in the commons as it is understood as an inclusive polity?

Foster's and Iaione's arguments are particularly strong in their emphasis on the role of "experimental policies" which include "a variety of kinds of civic, neighborhood, and infrastructure goods... produced and managed through different forms of 'pooling' and cooperation between five possible actors—social innovators (i.e., active citizens, city makers digital collaboratives, urban regenerators, community gardeners, etc.), public authorities business, civil society organizations, and knowledge institutions (i.e., schools, universities, cultural institutions, museums, academic, etc.)" [6] (p. 23). The authors may want to emphasize further the role of citizen participation. In the section of the paper in which the authors cite Jane Jacobs [6] (p. 12), the analysis would benefit from a further critique of the rational comprehensive model of planning.

The authors' emphasis on complex systems theory [6] (p. 11) is also risky as it neglects to address aspects of social inequality and other cultural and social factors. For example, when the authors note that "the more heterogenous and numerous are the interacting units and agents, and the more complex the problems facing the city, one could argue the more pressure is placed on centralized government authorities to de-centralize decision making", they do not sufficiently discuss the ways in which decentralization of power could further increase inequalities. Although the authors mention exclusionary practices they do not discuss gated communities, racial segregation, exclusionary zoning, and a lack of comprehensive planning, especially in the suburbs. While decentralization facilitates local participatory action, "[d]ecentralization and autonomy are primary vehicles for producing greater inequality through neoliberalization" [7] (p. 83).

In their discussion of community boards, the authors may want to mention the role of "197-a" plans as a possible achievement of several community boards in New York. But the authors might also note the fact that community boards are appointed rather than elected bodies and that they have historically contained entrenched local elites that would block more robust citizen participation, as well as that they were sites of the local patronage of City Council representatives. Community Boards at their best have engaged in reactive participation, stopping or limiting development projects.

The authors further continue with the view of cities as complex systems and suggest "open forms of governance that might involve broad knowledge exchange through creative collaborations with market actors, users, knowledge institutions and communities" but not all of these actors are of equal order and not all of them have the same powers, possibilities or influence or access to decision-making capacities.

In the paragraph in which Foster and Iaione discuss cities as laboratories of policy experimentation [6] (p. 18), implications for democracy are not developed. Perhaps the sharing economy and the new policy experimentation projects are more suitable for business-friendly innovations. To the extent that sharing can refer to a joint use of resources and can be relevant for sustainability, it appears that the examples cited are mostly suggestive of piecemeal efforts at sustainability rather than a comprehensive policy change.

In the discussion of the Sharing City (the example of Seoul), it is also not clear who has access to these new resources and how these resources have broadened access to information. In the concluding sentence to the paragraphs on the Sharing City [6] (p. 19), "sharing in the market activity and the polis" are equated as if they were of equal order. The paper leaves too much space for market forces to exert their influence and does not discuss implications for democracy sufficiently. It further does not explain the extent to which "smart city" devices would be available in low income neighborhoods and how would immigrant, minority, and poor residents have access to them.

The authors offer a good critique of Smart Cities [6] (p. 21), where they discuss "the increasing inequalities by stressing the gaps between haves and haves nots, and deepening social divisions" thus critiquing Smart Cities for their role in deepening inequalities. The authors' response to this problem assumes, however, a strong participatory policy which may not exist, especially in low-income neighborhoods.

The examples that the authors give of economic sustainability fall short of comprehensive sustainable policy initiatives and are more focused on certain exemplary projects. The authors could further highlight the role of cities in climate change (see, for example, [2]). The authors, moreover, cite affordable housing but do not discuss the right to housing or the decline in public investment in housing. The final paragraphs of this section could be further strengthened by discussing resources that the cities need to deal with natural disasters as well as the resources and commitment needed for sustainable development.

Finally, Foster and Iaione turn to the subject of the city as commons. Their discussion of citizen participation is significant but also telling of the fact that the examples given in the paper include mostly efforts that fall short of levels of citizen power and more resemble examples of tokenism. It is also further unclear how the new system of governance that they advocate will address social inequalities.

The examples given by Foster and Iaione of medieval cities [6] (p. 24) highlight a lack of democracy and domination by elites, as well as a division between poor and rich cities. This makes one wonder whether the paper could have rather been framed around challenges in achieving urban commons, or the difficulty of urban commons, or problems with the concept of urban commons – rather than an endorsement based on historical examples that are mostly indicative of deeper inequalities and not bases on which to build a progressive concept.

It is important to situate the current debate on the urban commons in the context of "the recent wave of privatization, enclosures, spatial controls, policing, and surveillance upon the qualities of urban life in general" [7] (p. 67). In the discussion of the commons as a "shared resource" it is unclear how city policies can be altered when cities have engaged in privatization of public resources.

Thus, a major critique of the concept of "urban commons" is related to the fact that is leaves too much space for private actors seeing them as equal as public actors. What is exactly the role of private actors? Could they take over the commons? How does the commons ensure its publicness? When the authors argue that the commons "presumes co-design and co-production with private and public actors" and note that they "envision common resources as neither private not public" stressing that "[t]he commons exists between the market and the state" [6] (p. 26), they defer to the private interests leaving too much room for market actors whose influence has been already too strong in cities. The danger is that the commons thus becomes "regulated, policed, and even privately managed" and denies open access [7] (p. 71).

Why is it that the commons cannot be chiefly public especially given that the mixture of public and private resource has meant skewing towards the market and diminishing the role of public spaces in the city? The authors do not discuss how the market excludes or does little to include, nor do they elaborate upon other factors that contribute to social exclusion.

Perhaps a way to address this question is to tie the idea of the commons to the concept of a right to the city, as the authors have done in an earlier article (and as they have now accomplished in the most recent version of their paper), where they argue that the city possesses "shared resources that belongs to all inhabitants" and is aligned with "the right to be a part of the creation of the city, the right to be a part of the decisionmaking processes shaping the lives of the city inhabitants, and the power of inhabitants to shape decisions about the collective resources in which we all have a stake" [5] (p. 288). The final points of the paper are suggestive of the fact that the commons can become a manner of improving or enhancing collaborative devices [6] (p. 26) in cities but this point could benefit from more development in the paper and the examples included, as noted, are more indicative of tokenism rather than of true participation. The authors further suggest that cities can establish mechanisms to mediate conflict failing to acknowledge that conflicts may be more deeply rooted and that sometimes exposure of conflicts can be beneficial and can promote urban social change.

While Foster and Iaione end their paper with the examples of how the concept of commons may address urban inequalities, their examples could be bolder and include the fight for a minimum wage increase, job training and job creation initiatives, pre-K for all programs, right to housing and affordable housing, stronger fair-share programs, regional tax sharing, city-wide and neighborhood comprehensive plans, sustainable development programs and other programs that stress redistribution of resources and public sector responsibilities.

Harvey's solution to the problems of urban commons is social mobilization. In his view, the commons is not public until it is made so by "political action on the part of citizens and the people to appropriate [the commons]" and make them into public spaces [7] (p. 73). The commons is thus dependent upon democracy. Harvey points out that the struggle for the creation of the commons is constant. "The common is not, therefore, something that existed once upon a time that has since been lost, but something that is, like the urban commons, continuously being produced. The problem is that it is just as continuously being enclosed and appropriated by capital in its commodified and monetized form, even as it is being continuously produced by collective labor" [7] (p. 77). Politics "is the sphere of activity of a common that can only ever be contentious" (Jacques Rancière, cited in [7] (p. 71).

"Much of the corruption that attaches to urban politics relates to how public investments are allocated to produce something that looks like a common but which promotes gains in private asset values for privileged property owners" [7] (p. 79). The key legal task would be to prevent the corruption of the common. Thus, in one example of the commons that is marred by surrounding upscaling, the High Line in Manhattan, would become a site that would also include affordable housing rather than becoming a commons most easily accessible by the rich residents. Another example includes the "organizers of low-income and precarious labor in Baltimore [who]declared the whole Inner Harbor area a 'human rights zone'—a sort of common—where every worker should receive a living wage" [7] (p. 79).

Developing further Elinor Olstom's notion of polycentric governance based on a "rich mix of instrumentalities", Harvey proposes, following Murray Bookchin, confederal assemblies which "will be given over to administration and governance of policies determined in the municipal assemblies, and the delegates will be recallable and answerable at all times to the will of the municipal assemblies" [7] (pp. 85, 87). Harvey's model is limited in that he insists that the politics of the commons can solely be accomplished as long as it is a part of anti-capitalist struggle, although many of his examples suggest that important achievements can be undertaken even within the current system.

8. Urban Constraints

Cities are the key proving grounds for the new arrangements of governance [40] (pp. 1992, 1993); Erik Swyngedouw, following Harvey, accurately identifies "a desire to construct politically the market as the preferred social institution of resource mobilisation and allocation, a critique of the 'excess' of state associated with Keynesian welfarism, and a bio-political engineering of the social in the direction of greater individualised responsibility" [40] (p. 1998). The new innovative governance-beyond-the-state, in all of its new institutional forms (which include private market and civil society) are, as Stoker notes, characterized by permeable boundaries between the private and public sectors [40] pp. 1992, 1994), and "exhibit a series of contradictory tendencies". Swyngedouw argues that governance-beyond-the-state reveals as well an "undemocratic and authoritarian character" which only supposedly "offer[s] the promise of greater democracy and grassroots empowerment" [40] (p. 1992). Swyngedouw presents an excellent critique in terms of legitimacy, representation, and exclusion tied to the limited and problematic concept of stakeholder (or 'holder') and points out that many groups rejected or opted-out of participation and political action; the author errs, however, in foreclosing opportunities for civil society, which he sees merely as "the Trojan Horse that diffuses and consolidates the 'market' as the principal institutional form" [40] (2003). Egalitarian spaces and spaces of political insurgency are limited in what Swyngedow sees as "a post-political and post-democratic city" (cited in [41]) (p. 2648) characterized by the foreclosure of dissent. While the prospects of resistance arising from the poorest urban populations should not be overstated, the above discussed sanctuary city movement has suggested that cities are sites of a crucial political struggle.

Brenner has similarly argued that the pluralized and variegated formation of sovereignties within cities and regional jurisdictions have, following Ong, formed "spaces of exception" [42] (p. 172), emphasizing that the new rescaled configurations of state sovereignty have "generated new forms of socio-spatial inequality and political conflict that limit the choices available to progressive forces throughout Europe" [42] (p. 172). Brenner falls short of arguing, however, that increases of urban sovereignty, assuming that they can include a serious attempt to address urban inequalities, could contest the rise of the far right-mobilization and challenge state exclusions and "neo-liberal geographies of uneven spatial development" [42] (p. 173)—an argument advanced in this article. Cities have the potential to become agents of global change but face tremendous challenges especially as they are increasingly discharging the responsibilities of the sovereigns. While cities can be seen as incubators of democracy, sites of bottom up citizenship, civil society, and voluntary community, there are also simultaneous worrisome trends which are a result of concrete urban policies influenced by the processes of globalization and urban restructuring and increased security concerns. (For comparison, see Benjamin Barber's account of urban inequality [43] (pp. 177–209)).

(1) Surveillance and control of urban space

In his book on war and cities, Ashwort cautioned that the period of 1945–1989 was a "brief, curious and unique interlude in world history" [44] (p. 202), a precarious era of unsteady avoidance of world wide warfare, not forgetting of course post-colonial struggles. Writing in 1991, the author pointed out that the notion that we live in an unsafe world was not evident to generations born after 1945. Ashwort writes defensively regarding the study of cities in the context of military analysis, which for most scholars occasioned discussions of medieval fortifications. It has become evident, however, that defense strategies were among the crucial variables in contemporary urban development and planning [44] (p. 196). Historical examples are still significant, however, not only because of the heritage of fortified cities, but given that close scrutiny offers plentiful evidence of the influence of military technologies and military geo-politics on urban form, the morphologies of cities, and their very locations, even if the term "militarization" of urban space may not be appropriate and should be used with caution.

While new technologies, and political and institutional alliances made urban intervention possible, what is significant here is the capacity to employ the resources of the state and its military and political priorities to render urban contexts of the past irrelevant and a new urban future (one of the controlled, surveilled city) not simply inevitable but necessary. This is one example where the "militarization" of space has broader implications in that it can be used to justify a specific future space of the city. This may have a significant impact on limiting the urban spaces of democracy (see also, [45]). In another example, in the case of Athens, Koutrolikou has documented how a politics of fear as "a spatial manifestation of urban crisis" (constructed as a state of emergency) may evolve into a moral panic which can feature a new construction of the public and "its enemies" and can be used impose a new definition of (il)legality [17] (pp. 174, 175).

Stephen Graham has argued that the provision of "security" in the present political ideology has begun to overwhelm in importance the other functions of national states such as social welfare, education, health, infrastructure development: "security" has become the sole criterion of political legitimization [46]. One of the chief problems in cities is fear and insecurity, facilitating the increased surveillance of city's public spaces. The "militarization" of urban life takes several dimensions and is evident in many spheres such as "the design of buildings, the managements of traffic, the physical planning of cities, migration policies, or the design of social policies for ethnically diverse cities and neighborhoods"—all of these are brought together under the umbrella of "national security" [46] (p. 11). Urban environments are saturated by surveillance systems, checkpoints and defensive urban design. Additional examples of the militarization of space include: "Tanks protect airports. Troops guard rail stations. Surface-to-air missiles sit around office blocks housing meetings of international leaders. Combat air patrols buzz around Manhattan and London. New York street police now carry pocketsize radiation detectors in hope that they might detects any nuclear 'dirty bombs' smuggled into metropolitan areas. US postal sorting depots have automatic anthrax sniffers. New York's Grand

Central Station now has automatic bio-weapons detectors". Some commentators have even argued that central cities should be actively decentralized to protect themselves from terrorism [46] (p. 12). The "militarization" of urban space is adding to the vicious cycle of fear and insecurity in places already affected by crime, social violence, racism, and xenophobia [46].

One of the responses to urban surveillance and control is offered by spaces of commemoration and reflection—memorials (of the Holocaust, the Vietnam War, 9/11, etc.) as public spaces in which reckoning of the victims can take place and which might also allow for the challenge to dominant narratives of victimhood rather than merely serve the interest of the nation-state.

(2) Privatization of public spaces

Sharon Zukin (1995) has argued that culture is a powerful means of controlling cities. Culture can convey images and memories that symbolize "who belongs" in specific places [47] (p. 1). Culture is furthermore a part of the economic development of cities, fueling the city's symbolic economy (one example is tourism which "bolsters the city's image as a center of cultural innovation" [47] (p. 2); another example is Sony Plaza which intertwines cultural symbols and entrepreneurial capital in creating a new symbolic economy in which retail dominates a public plaza). Zukin relates culture to urban fear and contestation over social difference arguing that this has further contributed to the growth of private police forces, gated and barred communities, and a design of public spaces for maximum surveillance. Private interests have stepped into the vacuum created by the government. "Handing such [public]spaces over to corporate executive and private investors means giving them carte blanche to remake public culture. It marks the erosion of public space in terms of two basic principles: public stewardship and open access" [47] (p. 32). One of the characteristics of the new public spaces is thus the "withdrawal of the public sector and its replacement with the private sector" [47] (pp. 24, 25)—private security guards patrol space, public and private sanitation workers clean it up—for example, in the case of Bryant Park which was during the 1970s associated with crime, disrepair, and the presence of low-income and poor minorities. Homelessness increased during the 1970s—the time of deinstitutionalization when many mental health patients were placed on the street without sufficient support of community facilities. The Bryant Park Restoration Corporation has redesigned Bryant Park, which now includes cultural events, features kiosks and food services, and is patrolled by private security guards. The Park features a fashion design show during which a portion of the park is closed. The Park has also adopted the social design principles by William H. Whyte ("movable chairs"). His additional idea is to bring "normal users" to the park so that there would be less space "for vagrants and criminals to maneuver" [47] (p. 28).

"197-a" Plans—an example of participatory community-based planning in New York—can be seen as one of the challenges to the privatization of urban space—many plans originated in opposition to development projects which were stopped by community protests but in their creation of waterfront access, of public open spaces on the neglected, fenced off waterfront areas, they represent an example of proactive, rather than reactive, planning.

(3) The rise of the luxury city, large-scale developments, mega-projects

Peter Marcuse has argued that the city is quartered, divided according to the lines "of race, of class, of occupation, of ethnicity" [48] (p. 94); its quarters are sometimes congruent, sometimes not and they vary by different times of the day, and they reflect the "spatial arrangements of residential life" and "the spatial arrangement of business activities" [48] (p. 94). Marcuse identifies the rise of the luxury areas of the city—the locations of the "power and profit" characterized by high rise condominiums with their own security. "The new architecture of shopping malls, skywalks, and policed pedestrian malls is a striking physical mirror of the social separation" [48] (p. 95). The homeless and the poor are removed from sight in these areas. According to MacLeod, following Peterson and Florida, "[d]eluxe landscapes coupled with a spirited branding of a city's image will purportedly attract globally mobile investors alongside a creative class of professional and revenue-generating tourists [41] (p. 2630); in these sites, MacLeod argues, citing Purcell, the "premium [is placed] on exchange value of space, perhaps ahead of any use value acquired by people inhabiting it" [41] (p. 2646).

Current policies are characterized by a "single-minded focus on encouraging growth through the vehicle of public-private partnerships" [38] (p. 170). "Within the United States, national subsidies for urban programs have shifted decisively toward supporting private initiatives" [38] (p. 176). Even though affordable housing is the most pressing need in the three cities that Fainstein studied—New York, London, and Amsterdam—the three cities "have been instead engaged in promoting megaprojects that provide only limited amounts of low-income housing" [38] (p. 173). These projects are often criticized by neighborhood groups as they typically feature aggressive government intervention in collaboration with private interests—the taking of property commonly in decaying areas (waterfronts, manufacturing zones, transport infrastructures, historic district renovation). These regeneration projects revitalize the center city and clear the inner-city space of the poor, heightening the contrast with many other areas of the cities experiencing severe deprivation. Fainstein suggests that megaprojects be "subject to higher scrutiny, be required to provide direct benefits to low-income people in the form of employment provisions, public amenities, and a living wage, and, if public subsidy is involved, should include public participation in the profits. If at all possible, they should be developed incrementally and with multiple developers" [38] (p. 173).

Urban policies are shaping cities around the world in a similar manner and this goes beyond the discussion of cultural homogenization countered by localism. Increasing standardization is evident in the similarity of central business districts. Sennett noted that such standardization is necessary to enable the purchasing of square footage of office space in New York from Singapore [49] (pp. 44, 45). Mega-projects, especially those that cater to the global markets (sports events, expositions, residential areas for the global economic elite) feature similar characteristics as they include designer buildings and forms of spectacle in the city. While they display awareness of environmental concerns and an appreciation of urbanity [50] they represent in a manner attempts to depoliticize their developments.

Market driven housing and commercial development are among the most critical factors of socio-spatial segregation. Many developments around the world contribute to the centralization of the higher income groups and peripheralization of poverty in cities. This further contributes to the spatial segregation of the upper-income highly educated groups. This is combined with a lack of investment in low-income areas, which experience lack of services, poor infrastructure, crime and vandalism. The poor are unable to benefit from economic growth which does not reach the periphery of cities. While there are new peripheral locations for the middle classes, there is, however, the emergence of gated communities for the upper-classes who live outside of traditional enclaves.

Fainstein suggests that as a challenge to the current policies the example of the Minneapolis Neighborhood Revitalization Program could be examined—the program successfully diverted funds from "downtown development to community betterment" [38] (p. 182). Fainstein further calls for the reversal of national policies that subsidize private interests, citing European examples, in particular those in the Netherlands where government regulation and ownership are significant.

(4) Homelessness

As Matthew Desmond has noted, "most poor renting families are spending more than half of their income on housing, and eviction has become ordinary, especially for single mothers" [51]. "The National Law Center on Homelessness & Poverty currently estimates that each year at least 2.5 to 3.5 million Americans sleep in shelters, transitional housing, and public places not meant for human habitation. At least an additional 7.4 million have lost their own homes and are doubled-up with others due to economic necessity" [52]. In April 2017, 61,277 people slept in homeless shelters in New York City—an increase from 36,960 in June 2010, according to the Coalition for the Homeless [53]. Moreover, "[h]omeless people remain a visible presence in public spaces: on the streets, in the parks, on plazas in front of expensive apartment houses, in office building atrium lobbies, in subway cars and stations, in railroad terminals, under bridge and highway entrances" [47] (p. 27). Given recent increases in homelessness, there is a worrisome trend of relying upon business improvement districts (BIDs) to clear the homeless from public spaces. A new model for "controlling" homelessness are thus BIDs which allow businesses and property owners to tax themselves in exchange for maintenance and control over public areas. According to the NYU Furman Center newsletter of 18 October 2016, "[i]n Denver, CO, Berkeley, CA, and Portland, OR, for example, BIDs have campaigned to prohibit people from sitting or lying in public rights of way, and even sued to reverse policies that encouraged tent cities and homeless camps" [54]. BIDs "nurture a visible social stratification" [47] (p. 36) with large, high income area BIDs ensuring the prosperity of their areas if the city cannot fund improvements which make the prosperous BIDs stand in contrast to the impoverished city. BIDs' "'clean and safe' initiative increasingly render downtowns as 'interdictory spaces', designed to exclude those adjudged to be 'out of place' and whose class and cultural habitus may diverge from developers and their target consumers" (Flusty cited in [41] (p. 2646)). The BIDs reclaim public spaces to make them safe for suburban shoppers and those who would have abandoned the city because of fears regarding the safety in the city. One response to the BIDs has been a legal challenge. The Coalition for the Homeless sued a powerful BID—the Grand Central Partnership (GCP)—for hiring the homeless as workfare workers below minimum wage and failing to give them job training. According to MacLeod, GCP's expulsions of the homeless "eventually leading to revanchist beatings of homeless people" [41] (p. 2646).

As the example of New York City shows, the provision of affordable housing, which represents one response to the homelessness crisis, has been inadequate, insufficient, and certainly not supported by health, social services, educational and job training programs. Proposed policies, such as those sought by Fainstein, that argue for housing construction for "households with the incomes below the median . . . with the goal of providing a decent home and suitable living environment for everyone" would "require a considerable increase in government involvement through regulation and some increase in public ownership. Thus, development of affordable housing could occur via the governmental, for-profit, and non-profit sectors, but would depend on generous public subsidy and intervention" [38] (pp. 172, 175). Fainstein cites the example of Amsterdam and London where "national governments play a much larger role in financing affordable housing development" and where "planning and allocative authorities are much more decentralized than New York's, have considerable power and have the potential to bring nonelite interests to bear on the planning process" [38] (pp. 179, 182).

According to David Harvey, "State powers are invariably obsessed with maintaining order and erasing difference when both disorder and difference are fundamental to the creativity of urban life . . . In many a city, the homeless find that struggle to be at the very core of their everyday lives. To them, the injustice is palpable while, to the rest of society, they are simply categorized as a public nuisance and administered their just deserts accordingly" [13] (p. 95). Through everyday life, acts, and practices the homeless try to assert their right to the city and right to public space in spite of urban surveillance, the privatization of urban spaces, and the rise of the luxury city.

All four constraints outlined are indicative of the decline of social planning and limited redistributive programs for the poor. All are further suggestive of the increase in gentrification and of the reshaping of the city for the safety of the affluent. All four constraints further indicate the rise of the walls and barriers and the increase in the creation of citadels (see [48]), further affirming Sassen's [55] thesis that global cities are divided between the financial elites and the low-paid service sector workers but that they also represent a strategic site for the disempowered and discriminated minorities [22]. It is, nevertheless, important to emphasize that even though cities have recently developed programs to advance racial equity exemplified in job training and the Government Alliance on Race and Equity national network initiatives, they have historically been complicit in producing racial inequalities and still remain sites of institutionalized racism and racial segregation [56,57]. Urban policies that would challenge the four constraints outlined above can further be enhanced by expanding the notion of "right to the city"—which according to Lefebvre is the right to alter the urban environment and which is actualized not only via social mobilization and political struggle but also through daily actions and practices that encompass a greater range of creative urban experiences and allow for the claims on the city and its public places on the part of the excluded, the disenfranchised and in particular for the context of this argument, the undocumented, the asylum seekers, and the refugees.

Barber recommends "reanimating democracy by devolving power to cities" [2] (p. 62) and finding ways to "globalize democracy or to democratize globalization" [2] (p. 65). A similar proposal by Harvey—"[a]lternative democratic vehicles (other than the existing democracy of money power) such as popular assemblies need to be constructed if urban life is to be revitalized and reconstructed outside of dominant class relations" [7] (p. 137). Social movements against mass incarceration and political struggles for immigrant rights in the United States have recently demonstrated possibilities for a new democratized urban polity. But what is further critical is the use of legal resources, capacities, and institutions as cities claim increasing sovereignty, and the development of regional collaboration as cities become more engaged in sustainable policies.

"The sovereigns cannot govern, but they can still ensure a paucity of municipal resources and jurisdictional competence that makes it impossible for cities to act aggressively and collectively" [2] (p. 114). The starting point for cities today is to prepare institutional and legal infrastructures and capacities to govern, especially given the rise of urban inequalities and the decline of funding from a reactionary, parochial national sovereign that has abandoned its responsibilities.

9. Conclusions

Cities must defend their sovereignty "at least when the urban view of rights is in accord with universal rights as reflected by international law and contradicted by parochial state and national notions denying such rights" [2] (p. 117). Furthermore, as Harvey has argued, "the right to the city has to be construed not as a right to that which exists, but as a right to rebuild and recreate the city as a socialist body politic in a completely different image—one that eradicates poverty and social inequality, and one that heals the wounds of disastrous environmental degradation" [7] (p. 138).

This article has argued for an increase in de facto already claimed city sovereignty, especially in the face of a hostile sovereign, as is the case in the United States today where cities such as San Francisco have become rebel cities suing the federal government to prevent defunding due to their sanctuary status. Current legal literature on "urban commons" and "city power" needs a stronger normative lens and better conceptualization of urban inequality, redistribution, and publicness. Legal rules in the United States limit cities' resources and exercise of control and are insufficiently responsive to urban conditions; Democratic cities in Republican states also face threats of defunding and pre-emption. While the cities may not possess sufficient resources and cannot replace the roles and powers of nation states, the article has argued that cities are not utilizing the powers and resources that they increasingly do possess to sufficiently and substantively address urban inequalities and to expand urban citizenship into a fundamentally inclusive category. Rebel cities' sanctuary policies represent one arena in which cities have begun to address substantive problems of social inequality. Sanctuary cities show effective resistance to the hostile state and are suggestive of an inclusionary polity which would expand the scope of urban citizenship to encompass provision of a range of services, issuing of municipal IDs, and, to an extent, expansion of "right to the city" claims on the part of the undocumented, refugees, and asylum seekers. Sanctuary cities represent "sovereignty from below", but this sovereignty is limited by serious constraints that cities face ranging from surveillance and the privatization of public spaces to the rise of the luxury city and an increase in homelessness. Rebel cities are similar to rebel governance in that they both seek to obtain the legitimacy that the state has failed to provide. This article has outlined the current conditions under which the legal, political, and symbolic sovereignty of cities stands a chance of advancing the prospects of some of the poorest and the most disenfranchised populations, suggesting that resistance and protests on the part of sanctuary cities may thus be the current weapons of the very weakest.

Acknowledgments: For helpful comments and encouragement, I would like to thank the late Benjamin Barber, Sheila Foster, Ira Katznelson, Elliott Sclar, Rose Cuison-Villazor, Randy K. Lippert, Annika Hinze, Emilie Saccone, Laura Wolf-Powers, and the peer reviewers and editors of *Urban Sciences*.

Conflicts of Interest: The author declares no conflict of interest.

References and Notes

1. Frug, G.E.; Barron, D.J. *City Bound: How States Stifle Urban Innovation*; Cornell University Press: Ithaca, NY, USA, 2008.
2. Barber, B. *Cool Cities: Urban Sovereignty and the Fix for Global Warming*; Yale University Press: New Haven, CT, USA; London, UK, 2017.
3. De Haldevang, M. America's Liberal Cities Are Readying to Battle Donald Trump on Almost Every Front. *Quartz* **2017**.
4. Howlett, M.; Ramesh, M. On different types of governance, including especially on "legal governance", situated at the intersection of civil society and the government, "Three Orders of Governance Failure: Policy Capacity, Problem Context and Design Mismatches". In Proceedings of the IPSA World Congress, Montréal, QC, Canada, 2014.
5. Foster, S.; Iaione, C. The City as a Commons. *Yale Law Policy Rev.* **2016**, *34*, 281–349. [CrossRef]
6. Foster, S.; Iaione, C. Rethinking the City. Unpublished work. 2017.
7. Harvey, D. *Rebel Cities: From Right to the City to the Urban Revolution*; Verso: London, UK, 2013.
8. Schragger, R. *City Power: Urban Governance in a Global Age*; Oxford University Press: New York, NY, USA, 2016.
9. Davis, E.D. Conclusions: Theoretical and Empirical Reflections on Cities, Sovereignty, Identity, and Conflict. In *Cities & Sovereignty: Identity Politics in Urban Spaces*; Davis, D.E., de Duren, N.L., Eds.; Indiana University Press: Bloomington/Indianapolis, IN, USA, 2011.
10. Vale, J.L. The Temptations of Nationalism in Modern Capital Cities. In *Cities & Sovereignty: Identity Politics in Urban Spaces*; Davis, D.E., de Duren, N.L., Eds.; Indiana University Press: Bloomington/Indianapolis, IN, USA, 2011.
11. Tilly, C.; Blockmans, W.P. (Eds.) *Cities and the Rise of States in Europe, A.D. 1000 to 1800*; Westview Press: Boulder, CO, USA, 1994.
12. Tilly, C. *Coercion, Capital, and European States, AD 990–1992*; Blackwell: Cambridge, MA, USA, 1992.
13. Harvey, D. The Right to the City. In *Divided Cities*; Scholar, R., Ed.; Oxford University Press: Oxford, UK; New York, NY, USA, 2006; pp. 83–103.
14. Robbins, L. 'Sanctuary City' Mayors Vow to Defy Trump's Immigration Order. *The New York Times*, 25 January 2017.
15. Wilson, E. *The Sphinx in the City: Urban Life, the Control of Disorder, and Women*; Virago: London, UK, 1991.
16. Wilson, E. *The Contradictions of Culture: Cities, Culture, Women*; Sage Publications: London, UK, 2001.
17. Clarke and Tilly cited in Koutrolikou, P. Governmentalities of Urban Crisis in Inner-city Athens, Greece. *Antipode* **2015**, *48*, 172–192. [CrossRef]
18. Bauder, H. Sanctuary Cities: Policies and Practices in International Perspective. *Int. Migr.* **2016**. [CrossRef]
19. Lippert, R. Sanctuary Practices, Rationalities and Sovereignties. *Alternatives* **2004**, *29*, 535–555. [CrossRef]
20. Powell, C. The United Divided States: San Francisco Sues Donald Trump for Sanctuary Cities Order. Available online: https://www.justsecurity.org/37589/united-divided-states-san-francisco-sues-donald-trump-sanctuary-cities-order/ (accessed on 13 February 2017).
21. Cunningham, H. *God and Caesar at the Rio Grande: Sanctuary and the Politics of Religion*; University of Minnesota Press: Minneapolis, MN, USA; London, UK, 1995.
22. Sassen, S. When the Centre No Longer Holds: Cities as Frontier Zones. *Cities* **2013**, *34*, 67–70. [CrossRef]
23. Ridgley, J. The City as Sanctuary in the United States. In *Sanctuary Practices in International Perspectives: Migration, Citizenship, and Social Movements*; Lippert, R.K., Rehaag, S., Eds.; Routledge: New York, NY, USA, 2013.
24. Fuller, T. San Francisco Sues Trump Over 'Sanctuary Cities' Order. *The New York Times*, 31 January 2017.
25. King, R. Liberals Matriculate at Calhoun College; in the Trump Era, Progressives Are Now Most Likely to Secede. *The Wall Street Journal*, 15 February 2017. Available online: https://www.wsj.com/articles/liberals-matriculate-at-calhoun-college-1487204348 (accessed on 22 June 2017).
26. Yee, V. Judge Blocks Trump Effort to Withhold Money from Sanctuary Cities. *The New York Times*, 25 April 2017.

27. Discussion with Rose Cuison-Villazor, 5 May 2017.
28. Correspondence by Sheila Foster, 26 April 2017.
29. Bagelman, J. *Sanctuary City: A Suspended State*; Palgrave Macmillan: New York, NY, USA, 2016.
30. Squire, V.; Jonathan, D. The 'Minor' Politics of Rightful Presence: Justice and Relationality in City of Sanctuary. *Int. Political Sociol.* **2013**, *7*, 59–74. [CrossRef]
31. Lippert, R.K.; Rehaag, S. (Eds.) Introduction: Sanctuary across Countries, Institutions, and Disciplines. In *Sanctuary Practices in International Perspectives: Migration, Citizenship, and Social Movements*; Routledge: New York, NY, USA, 2013.
32. Czajka, A. The Potential of Sanctuary: Acts of Sanctuary through the Lens of Camp. In *Sanctuary Practices in International Perspectives: Migration, Citizenship, and Social Movements*; Lippert, R.K., Rehaag, S., Eds.; Routledge: New York, NY, USA, 2013.
33. Global Parliament of Mayors. Internal memo. From: Mayor Marvin Rees (Bristol, UK)/Consultative Committee, To: Steering Committee, Re: Crowd-funding campaign to support US Sanctuary Cities (appendix to the proposal GPM Support Fund), 3 February 2017.
34. Arjona, A.; Kasfir, N.; Mampilly, Z. *Rebel Governance in Civil War*; Arjona, A., Kasfir, N., Mampilly, Z., Eds.; Cambridge University Press: Cambridge, UK; New York, NY, USA, 2015.
35. Mampilly, Z.C. *Rebel Rulers: Insurgent Governance and Civilian Life during War*; Cornell University Press: Ithaca, NY, USA; London, UK, 2011.
36. Huang, R. Rebel Diplomacy in Civil War. *Int. Secur.* **2016**, *40*, 89–126. [CrossRef]
37. Bruce, K.; Bradley, J. *The Metropolitan Revolution: How Cities and Metros Are Fixing Our Broken Politics and Fragile Economy*; Brookings Institution Press: Washington, DC, USA, 2013.
38. Fainstein, S.S. *The Just City*; Cornell University Press: Ithaca, NY, USA, 2010.
39. Comments made at the Fordham Urban Law Journal event at Fordham University, "City Power: Urban Governance in a Global Age". Monday, 23 January 2017.
40. Swyngedouw, E. Governance Innovation and the Citizen: The Janus Face of Goverance-beyond-the-State. *Urban Stud.* **2005**, *42*, 1991–2006. [CrossRef]
41. MacLeod, G. Urban Politics Reconsidered: Growth Machine to Post-democratic City? *Urban Stud.* **2011**, *48*, 2629–2660. [CrossRef]
42. Brenner, N. Urban Locational Policies and the Geographies of Post-Keynesian Statehood in Western Europe. In *Cities & Sovereignty: Identity Politics in Urban Spaces*; Davis, D.E., de Duren, N.L., Eds.; Indiana University Press: Bloomington/Indianapolis, IN, USA, 2011.
43. Barber, B. *If Mayors Ruled the World: Dysfunctional Nations, Rising Cities*; Yale University Press: New Haven, CT, USA; London, UK, 2013.
44. Ashworth, G.J. *War and the City*; John, G., Ed.; Routledge: London, UK; New York, NY, USA, 1991.
45. Sennett, R. *The Spaces of Democracy*; Raoul Wallenberg Lecture; University of Michigan College of Architecture + Urban Planning: Ann Arbor, MI, USA, 1998.
46. Graham, S. *Cities, War, and Terrorism: Towards an Urban Geopolitics*; Studies in Urban and Social Change; Blackwell Publishing: Malden, MA, USA, 2004.
47. Zukin, S. *The Cultures of Cities*; Blackwell: Cambridge, MA, USA, 1995.
48. Marcuse, P. The Layered City. In *The Urban Lifeworld: Formation, Perception and Representation*; Madsen, P., Plunz, R., Eds.; Routledge: London, UK; New York, NY, USA, 2002; pp. 94–114.
49. Sennett, R. Cosmopolitanism and the Social Experience of Cities. In *Conceiving Cosmopolitanism: Theory, Context and Practice*; Vertovec, S., Cohen, R., Eds.; Oxford University Press: Oxford, UK; New York, NY, USA, 2002; pp. 42–47.
50. Orueta, F.D.; Fainstein, S.S. Symposium: "The New Mega-Projects: Genesis and Impacts". *Int. J. Urban Reg. Res.* **2008**, *32*, 759–767. [CrossRef]
51. Desmond, M. *Evicted: Poverty and Profit in the American City*; Crown Publishers: New York, NY, USA, 2016.
52. National Law Center on Homelessness & Poverty. Homelessness in America: Overview of Data and Causes. Available online: https://www.nlchp.org/documents/Homeless_Stats_Fact_Sheet (accessed on 22 June 2017).
53. Coalition for the Homeless, New York. Facts about Homelessness. Available online: http://www.coalitionforthehomeless.org/the-catastrophe-of-homelessness/facts-about-homelessness/ (accessed on 22 June 2017).

54. NYU. Furman Center for Real Estate and Urban Policy. *Newsletter*, 18 October 2016.
55. Sassen, S. *The Global City: New York, London and Tokyo*; Princeton University Press: Princeton, NJ, USA, 2001.
56. Tracey, R.; Treuhaft, S. The Secret Trumpism of Cities. *The New York Times*, 3 June 2017.
57. Douglas, M.; Denton, N. *American Apartheid: Segregation and the Making of the Underclass*; Harvard University Press: Cambridge, MA, USA; London, UK, 1993.

urban science

MDPI

Communication
Urbanization and Inequality/Poverty

Brantley Liddle

Energy Studies Institute, National University of Singapore, Singapore 119620, Singapore;
btliddle@alum.mit.edu; Tel.: +65-6516-7080

Received: 22 September 2017; Accepted: 24 November 2017; Published: 27 November 2017

Abstract: The level of world urbanization has crossed the 50% mark, and nearly all future population growth is projected to occur in cities. Cities are disproportionately wealthy, but are associated with poverty, too. Addressing the dual challenges of urbanization and poverty is key to achieving sustainable development. This paper performs cross-sectional regressions, based on Kuznets, as a starting point for understanding the relationship between urbanization and poverty/inequality indicators. Increases in gross domestic product per capita unambiguously lowered poverty and narrowed rural-urban gaps. By contrast, levels of urbanization were either unrelated to poverty/inequality indicators and measures of rural-urban gaps, or had a nonlinear effect where, initially, increases in urbanization likewise led to improvements in those areas, while at higher levels of urbanization, increases in urbanization exacerbated poverty and rural-urban gaps.

Keywords: economic growth and urbanization; urbanization and inequality/poverty; Kuznets-type relationships

1. Introduction

World urbanization exceeded 50% for the first time in 2009. According to the United Nations, urban areas will absorb all of the projected 2.5 billion global population growth and continue to draw in some rural population over the next 40 years [1]. Additionally, less developed regions will account for most of the population growth expected in urban areas. While the impact of urbanization on the environment has been studied (e.g., see [2] for a review), understanding regarding the poverty-urbanization relationship is lacking [3]. Yet, those two forces—poverty and urbanization—are apparent causes for the lack of achieving sustainable development [3]. In Kuznets' [4] well-known paper, he demonstrated that there is an inverted U-shaped relationship between income inequality and economic growth, i.e., as countries initially get wealthier, inequality increases, but at some sufficiently high level of wealth/development, further increases in wealth correspond to lower levels of inequality. This short communication uses a simple model that is based on Kuznets' seminal work as a starting point to analyze the impact of urbanization on several measures of both poverty and inequality.

2. Background

Liddle [5]—in an analysis that considered city-based data from three datasets [6–8]; a total of 167 cities—calculated the ratio of a city's gross domestic product (GDP) per capita to the associated country GDP per capita. GDP per capita is higher for most cities than for their respective countries as a whole—the ratio of city-to-country GDPs is less than one for only 35 cities, and less than 0.85 for only 14 [5]. Furthermore, the relative economic importance of cities is stronger in countries with lower GDP per capita [5]. That second point (i) illustrates that cities in developing countries exercise an important migratory pull; and (ii) helps explain that urban areas will be the locus of all UN projected future population growth (over the next 40 years). Indeed, rural-urban migration accounts for around half of the total urban population in Africa [9].

Urbanization and economic development do tend to accompany one another; in part, this is because the industrialization process involves the agricultural labor force migrating from rural farms to urban manufacturing plants. However, slow economic growth has spurred rural-urban migration and led to the phenomenon of urbanization without growth, particularly in Africa [10–13]. Similarly, in the case of India, how fast a state urbanizes is negatively correlated with that state's rate of economic growth [14]. Ultimately, urbanization may be more evidence of economic progress than a catalyst for economic growth, and the/any relationship between urbanization and development may be an equilibrium one [13,15].

Table 1 displays data from the World Bank's World Development Indicators database [16] on various measures of urban poverty and rural-urban differences. Data were collected for all countries not classified as high-income by the World Bank (this meant a maximum of 137 countries, but not all countries have data for each variable). For data that are collected annually, the most recent year was used (typically either 2014 or 2012); for data that are less frequently collected, the average over 2010–2014 was used.

Table 1. Descriptive statistics for urban poverty indicators and rural-urban poverty comparisons. Non-high-income countries.

Indicator	Mean	Median	Maximum	Minimum	Std. Dev.	X-Sects.
Urban electricity access	84.1	98.1	100	12.3	22.1	137
Rural-urban electricity ratio	0.62	0.71	1.00	0.02	0.35	137
Urban water access	93.4	96.7	100	58.4	8.3	131
Rural-urban water ratio	0.83	0.89	1.04	0.37	0.17	128
Urban poverty share	23.0	20.3	61.6	0.65	14.5	68
Rural-urban poverty share ratio	2.34	1.95	9.28	0.99	1.51	67
Urban slum share	46.1	46.2	95.6	5.5	23.7	82

Std. Dev. = Standard Deviation, X-Sects. = cross-sections. Note: Observations taken from 2010 to 2014 [16].

The data do suggest that people in cities tend to have more opportunities than people in rural areas (since people in urban areas likely have more access to resources—electricity, quality water, education, health care, transport, capital, culture/arts—than do people in rural areas, and since access to such resources tends to increase opportunities for quality of life). Nearly all urban dwellers have access to electricity and quality water (the median shares of urban dwellers with such access are 98% and 97%, respectively). The ratio of the rural to the urban share of population with access to electricity/water demonstrates that urban dwellers are more likely to have such access than their rural counterparts. The median ratios are 0.71 and 0.89 for electricity and water, respectively, suggesting the urban population is about 10–30% more likely to have such access.

However, there is poverty in urban areas, too; almost half of urban populations live in settlements defined as slums (the World Bank defines a slum as a house that lacks one or more of the following conditions: access to improved water, access to improved sanitation, sufficient living area, and durability of housing). Moreover, over a fifth of the urban population lives below their national poverty lines. Yet, the share of people living below the poverty line in rural areas is double that, since the median ratio of rural-to-urban poverty share is 2.

3. Analysis and Discussion

Initially, we revisit Kuznets' analysis by also considering urbanization levels via cross-sectional regressions. Cross-country data is particularly useful in studying developmental change; such data allow for the greatest degree of generalization, and are in the spirit of Kuznets' original analysis. We perform pure cross-sectional regressions (in Tables 2–4), since the measurements of the dependent variables differ much more across countries than across time. Furthermore, a cross-section is more appropriate when including nonlinear transformations of variables, since using pure cross-sectional data avoids the statistical complications that arise when such operations are performed on time-series data (see e.g., [17,18]).

Specifically, we use the Gini index as the measure of inequality, and estimate it (i) as a nonlinear function of GDP per capita (in constant 2011 international dollars that are adjusted for purchasing power parity); and (ii) as a nonlinear function of urbanization. The Gini index is based on the Lorenz curve, which plots the proportion of total income of a population that is cumulatively earned by the bottom x% of the population. So, a 45 degree line represents perfect equality of incomes, and the Gini index is the ratio of the area that lies between the 45 degree line and the Lorenz curve. Hence, a Gini index of 0 represents perfect equality.

The data are from the World Bank's World Development Indicators [16], and the observations are from 2013 for GDP per capita and urbanization and from the average over 2007–2013 for the Gini index (which is stable over time, and, for many countries, is observed/recorded only occasionally). All variables have been converted to natural logs so that their estimated coefficients can be interpreted as elasticities. The cross-section contains 133 countries (which include high-income countries), and the regression results are displayed in Table 2.

Table 2. Kuznets-style cross-sectional regression. GINI index is dependent variable.

Independent Variables	
GDP per capita	0.60 *** (0.20)
GDP per capita squared	−0.04 *** (0.01)
Urbanization	−0.81 * (0.45)
Urbanization squared	0.13 ** (0.06)
Adjusted R^2	0.20
Observations	133
Turning points	
GDP per capita	US$1711
Urbanization	23%

GDP = gross domestic product. Notes: All variables in natural logs. White-heteroskedasticity-consistent standard errors in parentheses. Statistical significance is indicated by: *** $p < 0.01$, ** $p < 0.05$, and * $p < 0.1$ [16].

For the polynomial model considered here, an inverted-U relationship between the dependent and independent variables is said to exist if the coefficient for the linear term, β_1, is statistically significant and positive, while the coefficient for the squared term, β_2, is statistically significant and negative. Moreover, whenever the estimations suggest a parabolic relationship (i.e., one coefficient is positive and the other negative), the implied turning point, τ—or the level of the independent variable at which the sign of the relationship between dependent and independent variable changes—can be calculated by:

$$\tau = exp(-\beta_1/(2\beta_2)) \tag{1}$$

The regression confirms the expected inverted-U relationship between income inequality and income. The turning point of under US$2000 per capita is well within the sample range—indeed, the mean income is over US$14,500, and the median is over US$9300. Interestingly, urbanization has a U-shaped relationship with inequality, i.e., initially, increases in urbanization are associated with lower levels of inequality, but ultimately, increases in urbanization are associated with higher levels of inequality. Again, the estimated turning point of 23% urbanization is well within the sample range; both the mean and median levels of urbanization are around 55%. This finding that higher urbanization can lead to more inequality in a cross-sectional context echoes the results of a recent, time-series-based, China-only study [19].

Next, we revisit the variables on urban poverty and rural-urban differences introduced in Table 1 to determine whether/how the level of income or urbanization is associated with those indicators via cross-sectional regressions (income and urbanization data are the same as described above). As before, the variables have been converted to natural logs so that their estimated coefficients can be interpreted as elasticities. We believe that income should improve these measures monotonically, so we do not consider a polynomial of GDP per capita. However, we do allow for a possible nonlinear relationship with urbanization level (urbanization squared was usually insignificant, and only significant results for this transformation are shown in the table). The regression results are displayed in Table 3.

Table 3. Cross-sectional regressions of the effects of GDP per capita and urbanization on urban poverty indicators and rural-urban poverty comparisons.

Regression	I	II	III	IV	V	VI
Dependent Variable	Urban Electricity Access	Rural-Urban Electricity Ratio	Urban Poverty Gap	Urban Poverty Share	Rural-Urban Poverty Share Ratio	Urban Slum Share
GDP per capita	0.28 *** (0.05)	0.67 *** (0.10)	−1.19 *** (0.17)	−0.90 *** (0.13)	0.19 ** (0.07)	−0.42 *** (0.09)
Urbanization	−0.08 (0.09)	3.29 * (1.83)	−5.87 ** (2.34)	1.17 *** (0.18)	−0.39 *** (0.13)	−0.19 (0.15)
Urbanization squared		−0.42 * (0.25)	1.08 *** (0.36)			
Adjusted R^2	0.39	0.52	0.43	0.41	0.07	0.47
Observations	128	128	47	67	66	78
Turning point		49%	15%			

GDP = gross domestic product. Notes: All variables in natural logs. Sample excludes all countries World Bank-designated as high-income. White-heteroskedasticity-consistent standard errors in parentheses. Statistical significance is indicated by: *** $p < 0.01$, ** $p < 0.05$, and * $p < 0.1$ [16].

For the share of urban population with electricity access and the share of urban population living in slums (i.e., Regressions I and VI), GDP per capita had the expected, statistically significant impact. For urban electricity access, a one % increase in GDP per capita leads to a 0.3% increase in access; whereas, for urban slum share, a one % increase in GDP per capita leads to a 0.4% fall in the share of people living in slums. For both of those regressions, the level of urbanization was insignificant. For the rural-to-urban share of people living in poverty (i.e., Regression V), both income and urbanization were statistically significant, but the associated R-squared for the regression was very low, i.e., the model had a poor fit.

Urbanization had a more interesting relationship for the other dependent variables. For example, for the rural-to-urban electricity access ratio (i.e., Regression II), urbanization had an inverted-U relationship. A one % increase in GDP per capita raised the ratio by two-thirds of a percent—i.e., the rural-urban electricity access gap narrows at higher income. Initially, higher urbanization levels are associated with a higher access ratio/narrower gap as well, but at urbanization of 49%—approximately the mean and median for the 128-country sample—higher levels of urbanization are associated with a lower access ratio/larger rural-urban gap (i.e., disproportionately less electricity access for rural populations). In other words, at higher levels of urbanization, rural populations are more likely to be "left behind." Perhaps, at high levels of urbanization, there is less interest/incentive for governments to invest in rural infrastructure.

The urban poverty gap regression (Regression III) reveals a similar nonlinear relationship with respect to urbanization. The urban poverty gap is the urban population's mean shortfall from the poverty lines (counting the nonpoor as having zero shortfall) as a percentage of the poverty lines—so the measure reflects the depth of poverty and its incidence. Again, not surprisingly, GDP per capita has a strong negative relationship; indeed, increases in GDP per capita reduce this gap more than proportionally. Urbanization now has a U-shaped relationship with the urban poverty gap; however, because of the definition of the dependent variable, the basic relationship is the same as with the rural-to-urban electricity access ratio, i.e., initially, increases in urbanization are associated with an improvement (i.e., lower urban poverty gap), but ultimately, urbanization is correlated with a worsening in poverty.

What is particularly surprising about Regression III is the relatively low turning point for urbanization; indeed, the turning point is only 15%, whereas, the mean/median is approximately 40%. It is possible that when urbanization increases because of rural to urban migration, those rural migrants settle in marginal urban areas so that urban poverty increases. However, one should be mindful of the relatively small sample size of Regression III (only 47 out of 128 countries had the urban poverty gap data). Moreover, those countries included in Regression III were disproportionately poorer than the "full sample" (of Regressions I and II). For example, the mean and median GDP per capita for Regression III were only US$5200 and US$3600, respectively, compared to US$8000 and US$6500, respectively, for the 128-country sample (Regressions I and II). Moreover still, the maximum GDP per capita for Regression III was approximately US$14,500, which means the 21 richest countries in the 128-country sample were not included. By contrast, the range of urbanization levels is similar for the smaller sample (Regression III) and the larger ones (e.g., Regression I): 12–78% compared to 12–89%, respectively.

The urban poverty share regression (Regression IV) is similar to the urban poverty gap regression (Regression III) in two ways: (i) the smaller sample of countries are poorer than the larger sample—mean and median GDP per capita are US$6600 and US$4700, respectively; and (ii) increases in urbanization seem to offset improvements from increases in GDP per capita. Indeed, increases in GDP per capita lower the share of urban population living in poverty by nearly one-to-one; however, increases in urbanization appear to more than offset that improvement in poverty reduction (urbanization's elasticity is 1.2). Again, the results could be interpreted as suggesting that, when urbanization increases because of rural to urban migration, poverty among the (newly designated) urban population would increase as well. Indeed, there is evidence that rapid urbanization has caused worsening urban poverty (e.g., [20])—a finding that is in concert with both Regressions III and IV.

Lastly, we consider another method for analyzing potential nonlinearities, i.e., the quantile regression (initially proposed by [21]). A quantile regression estimates the linear relationship between regressors and a specified quantile of the dependent variable (in this example we use quartiles). Among the questions quantile regressions can address are: (i) whether the coefficient estimates vary across different quantiles of the dependent variable; and (ii) whether the coefficients for the median are statistically different from those estimated at the upper and lower quantile.

The quantile regressions typically suggest a uniform impact of urbanization (see Table 4). The main exception to that result is for the Gini index, for which urbanization is significant only at the higher quantiles of the index, i.e., urbanization matters in societies that are the most unequal. There was more evidence of differences across quantiles for income—this was the case for nearly half of the dependent variables as displayed in Table 4 (results for the other quantile regressions not shown, but are available upon request).

The impact of GDP per capita declines significantly when the share of urban population with electricity access is sorted by quartiles (consider the reported *p*-value of the slope equality test between the lower and median quartile and between the upper and median quartile)—an unsurprising saturation effect. A similar pattern is observed for both the rural-to-urban electricity access ratio and the urban poverty share; however, the difference between estimations is only statistically significant when comparing the median quartile with the top quartile. For the rural-to-urban electricity access ratio, that relationship is in concert with the same finding for urban electricity access, as would be expected. Whereas, for the urban poverty share, the quantile regression suggests (surprisingly) that the income effect on lowering urban poverty is significantly smaller in societies with the highest share of urban people living in poverty.

Table 4. Cross-sectional quantile regressions of the effects of GDP per capita and urbanization on select urban poverty indicators and rural-urban poverty comparisons.

	Dependent Variable	Gini Index	Urban Electricity Access	Rural-Urban Electricity Ratio	Urban Poverty Share
1	**Quantile/s**				
GDP per capita	0.25	−0.09 ** (0.04)	0.33 *** (0.05)	0.73 *** (0.11)	−0.92 *** (0.13)
	0.50	−0.10 *** (0.03)	0.19 *** (0.04)	0.70 *** (0.09)	−0.73 *** (0.15)
	0.75	−0.14 *** (0.04)	0.10 *** (0.04)	0.29 ** (0.12)	−0.46 ** (0.17)
Slope equality test	0.25, 0.50	0.69	0.00	0.75	0.15
	0.50, 0.75	0.18	0.01	0.00	0.07
Urbanization	0.25	0.09 (0.11)	−0.11 * (0.07)	0.33 (0.22)	1.09 *** (0.23)
	0.50	0.08 (0.08)	−0.05 (0.05)	0.11 (0.21)	1.10 *** (0.27)
	0.75	0.19 *** (0.06)	−0.06 (0.05)	0.02 (0.19)	0.78 ** (0.30)
Slope equality test	0.25, 0.50	0.91	0.24	0.27	0.95
	0.50, 0.75	0.098	0.78	0.60	0.23
Observations		133	128	128	67

GDP = gross domestic product. Notes: All variables in natural logs. Sample excludes all countries World Bank-designated as high-income. White-heteroskedasticity-consistent standard errors in parentheses. Statistical significance is indicated by: *** $p < 0.01$, ** $p < 0.05$, and * $p < 0.1$. For slope equality test, p-value shown [16].

4. Conclusions

Cities are disproportionately wealthy—a key reason why the world is becoming more urban. Yet, cities are associated with poverty, too. Increases in GDP per capita unambiguously lower poverty and narrow rural-urban gaps. By contrast, levels of urbanization were either unrelated to measures of poverty and rural-urban gaps, or had a nonlinear effect where, initially, increases in urbanization likewise led to improvements in those measures, but at higher levels of urbanization, increases in urbanization exacerbated urban poverty and rural-urban gaps. Thus, this paper, using a broad cross-sectional analysis, has confirmed the results of several regional and single-county studies [14,19,20] that rapid/excessive urbanization can lead to greater poverty and inequality.

Given the tenuous causal relationship between urbanization and economic growth/development [13,15], urbanization policies should be motivated by goals like improving equality (i.e., rural-urban gaps) in health and educational access (and not by encouraging economic growth). How cities are formed likely has an impact on urban poverty and whether rural-urban gaps are reduced or exacerbated. Future work could seek to improve the understanding regarding the potential nonlinear relationships among urbanization and some urban poverty measures and rural-urban differences.

Acknowledgments: A version of this paper was presented at the workshop on Urbanization in Asia: Economics and Social Consequences, held at Seoul, 15–16 December 2016. The author appreciates comments from both the workshop's participants and a reviewer/discussant, as well as financial support from ADBI to attend the workshop. Additionally, comments from the participants of the International Population Conference, Cape Town, South Africa, on 2 November 2017, as well as from anonymous reviewers, helped to improve the final version.

Conflicts of Interest: The author declares no conflict of interest.

References

1.	United Nations. *World Urbanization Prospects: The 2014 Revision*; United Nations: New York, NY, USA, 2014.
2.	Liddle, B. Impact of Population, Age Structure, and Urbanization on Greenhouse Gas Emissions/Energy Consumption: Evidence from Macro-level, Cross-country Analyses. *Popul. Environ.* **2014**, *35*, 286–304. [CrossRef]
3.	Cobbinah, P.; Erdiaw-Kwasie, M.; Amoateng, P. Rethinking sustainable development within the framework of poverty and urbanization in developing countries. *Environ. Dev.* **2015**, *13*, 18–32. [CrossRef]
4.	Kuznets, S. Economic Growth and Income Inequality. *Am. Econ. Rev.* **1955**, *45*, 1–28.
5.	Liddle, B. Urban density and climate change: A STIRPAT analysis using city-level data. *J. Transp. Geogr.* **2013**, *28*, 22–29. [CrossRef]

6. Kenworthy, J.; Laube, F.; Newman, P.; Barter, P.; Raad, T.; Poboon, C.; Guia, B., Jr. *An International Sourcebook of Automobile Dependence in Cities, 1960–1990*; University Press of Colorado: Boulder, CO, USA, 1999.

7. Kenworthy, J.; Laube, F. *The Millennium Cities Database for Sustainable Transport*; International Union (Association) for Public Transport (UITP): Brussels, Belgium, 2001.

8. International Union for Public Transport. *Mobility in Cities Database*; International Union (Association) for Public Transport: Brussels, Belgium, 2005.

9. Redman, C.; Jones, N. The environmental, social, and health dimensions of urban expansion. *Popul. Environ.* **2005**, *26*, 505–520. [CrossRef]

10. Fay, M.; Opal, C. *Urbanization without Growth. A Not-So-Uncommon Phenomenon*; World Bank Policy Research Working Paper WPS 2412; World Bank: Washington, DC, USA, 2000.

11. Bloom, D.; Canning, D.; Fink, G. Urbanization and the wealth of nations. *Science* **2008**, *319*, 772–775. [CrossRef] [PubMed]

12. Liddle, B. The energy, economic growth, urbanization nexus across development: Evidence from heterogeneous panel estimates robust to cross-sectional dependence. *Energy J.* **2013**, *34*, 223–224. [CrossRef]

13. Liddle, B.; Messinis, G. Which comes First Urbanization or Economic Growth? Evidence from Heterogeneous Panel Causality Tests. *Appl. Econ. Lett.* **2015**, *22*, 349–355.

14. Calì, M. *Urbanization, Inequality and Economic Growth: Evidence from Indian States*; World Bank: Washington, DC, USA, 2009.

15. Henderson, V. Cities and development. *J. Reg. Sci.* **2010**, *50*, 515–540. [CrossRef] [PubMed]

16. World Bank. World Development Indicators. Available online: http://databank.worldbank.org/data/reports.aspx?source=world-development-indicators (accessed on 22 September 2017).

17. Stern, D. Between estimates of the emissions-income elasticity. *Ecol. Econ.* **2010**, *69*, 2173–2182. [CrossRef]

18. Wagner, M. The carbon Kuznets curve: A cloudy picture emitted by bad econometrics? *Resour. Energy Econ.* **2008**, *30*, 388–408. [CrossRef]

19. Chen, G.; Glasmeier, A.K.; Zhang, M.; Shao, Y. Urbanization and Income Inequality in Post-Reform China: A Causal Analysis Based on Time Series Data. *PLoS ONE* **2016**. [CrossRef] [PubMed]

20. Boadi, K.; Kuitunen, M.; Raheem, K.; Hanninen, K. Urbanisation without development: Environmental and health implications in African cities. *Environ. Dev. Sustain.* **2005**, *7*, 465–500. [CrossRef]

21. Koenker, R.; Bassett, G. Regression Quantiles. *Econometrica* **1978**, *46*, 33–50. [CrossRef]

urban science

MDPI

Review

Pipe Dreams: Urban Wastewater Treatment for Biodiversity Protection

Caitlin Cunningham [1],* and Mohammad Gharipour [2]

[1] Graduate Landscape Architecture Program, Morgan State University, Baltimore, MD 21251, USA
[2] Graduate Architecture Program, Morgan State University, Baltimore, MD 21251, USA;
    mohammad.gharipour@morgan.edu
* Correspondence: cait.cunningham@gmail.com; Tel.: +1-410-967-4659

Received: 21 December 2017; Accepted: 25 January 2018; Published: 30 January 2018

Abstract: Wastewater treatment systems in urban areas of the United States have reached a critical replacement age. From century-old, deteriorating systems raw sewage overflows into basements, streets and surface waters. In economically depressed cities, sewage overflows are frequent and heavily fined, costing municipalities millions of dollars. Pollution by untreated wastewater severely degrades aquatic and wetland ecosystems and exacerbates serious risks to public health. Necessary and extensive clean water infrastructure repairs are imperative to protect the health and habitat of humans and other organisms. As accelerating human development contributes to wide spread losses of naturally occurring wetlands, dwindling patches of habitat native plant and animal species rely on for survival are further threatened. Within this alarming situation is an opportunity to rebuild and retrofit our wastewater treatment systems with infrastructure that enhances long-term ecosystem sustainability.

Keywords: urban wastewater treatment; constructed wetlands; habitat loss

1. Introduction

Below the streets of most major urban areas of the United States water infrastructure, including drinking water and wastewater treatment systems, is in a state of widespread disrepair. In many cities pipe failures and raw sewage overflows are frequent and substantial, the result of deteriorating 19th century conveyance structures. In Baltimore, Maryland water infrastructure conveyance pipes burst approximately one thousand times a year. Nearly twenty percent of the water piped from reservoirs for Baltimore's drinking water is lost from leaky pipes before it can even be consumed [1]. In Houston, Texas forty percent of conveyance pipes are in need of replacement. Excessive heat waves and a long period of drought led to eleven thousand pipe ruptures in 2011, costing Houston one quarter of its existing clean water resources for that year. In Miami, Florida sewage pipes have failed approximately sixty-five times between 2009 and 2011, polluting streets and waterways with over 47 million gallons of raw sewage [2]. In Baltimore, heavy rain events cause frequent sewage overflows into local streets and water bodies from leaky conveyance pipes while wastewater treatment plants discharge raw sewage from relief valves located on streams. Homes adjacent to sewage overflows in Baltimore are at times flooded with raw sewage during major storms while local waterways are contaminated to such an extent that zero human contact is advised. Limited signage or contribution to public awareness by Baltimore city agencies has put citizens and tourists at risk of contracting waterborne diseases [3].

Deleterious effects of water pollution by sewage coming from large urban areas are of increasing concern. Sewage overflows contribute to excessive nutrient pollution that feeds harmful algal blooms. Harmful algal blooms suffocate organisms by blocking light and depleting oxygen sometimes producing hypoxic dead zones where no plant or animal life can survive. Harmful algal blooms can cause illnesses in human and animals by direct contact or by exposure to toxic algal bacteria contamination in drinking water or seafood. In 2014 city officials of Toledo, Ohio warned residents against contact with municipal drinking water due to a three hundred square mile algal bloom in Lake Erie that caused levels of bacterial toxicity surpassing the capacity of the city's treatment plants [4]. Drinking water contaminated by harmful algal blooms can cause severe stomach flu-like symptoms, neurological damage and in some cases death from liver toxicity [5]. The pollution of waterways with wastewater contributes to: decreased life and biodiversity in aquatic ecosystems, proliferation of harmful bacterial diseases and loss of critical carbon storage in our oceans. Ultimately, ecosystems that provide water resources we rely on in order to live on are in danger of collapse as a result of increasing development and anthropogenic pollution of the environment [6].

Approximately half of the terrestrial space left on earth has been altered by human clearing and development, precipitating wide spread loss of species diversity [7]. Efforts to retain native species are critical to maintaining our native ecosystems, ecosystems that support human communities by supplying services like water purification, protection from natural disasters and pollination of crops. Native species are the support systems for the ecosystem services critical to human survival. Urbanization is the fastest growing type of land-use worldwide and one of the most destructive land-use types to local ecosystems, contributing to accelerated extinction of native species [7]. There is a vital need to conserve our native species while appreciating opportunities provided within the novel and diverse ecosystems that comprise our urban environments [8]. What can be done in an urban context to increase resiliency and ecosystem health and to protect our water bodies from collapse? Two ecological concepts provide a theoretical foundation for sustainable improvements to urban wastewater treatment systems. Reconciliation ecology, as articulated by ecologist Michael Rosenzweig, is the concept of consciously planning shared habitats for humans and wildlife in order to mitigate loss of biodiversity [9]. Closely related to reconciliation ecology is the concept of urban ecological mutualism [10]. Coined in 2008 by urban planner and landscape architect Brooke Ray Smith, urban ecological mutualism depends on a critical departure from a linear waste creation and disposal paradigm to a closed-loop resource paradigm. In closed-loop resource systems, waste that is created is repurposed without the creation of additional waste for the lifetime of the material. For the purposes of wastewater treatment, urban ecological mutualism refers to treatment and conveyance methods that have positive impacts on both humans and wildlife [10]. The design of urban clean water infrastructure, defined as the combination of drinking and wastewater infrastructure, has historical precedence dating back to Roman times. The clean water infrastructure of most US cities relies on large quantities of fresh water to produce food and products and to manage human, industrial and agricultural waste. Water clean enough to wash a baby is currently used to flush our toilets and wash our cars. An enormous amount of energy is required to convey and treat wastewater in our current water paradigm of usage and release. Innovations integrating the reuse of water, including wastewater systems that rely on reuse or treatment of used but not contaminated "gray water" on-site can make efficient use of a nominal resource [11]. Most of our current treat and release systems built with ubiquitous hard "grey" infrastructure do little to support ecological health while discharging pollution, increasing sedimentation and replacing habitat to the detriment of human and ecosystem health. An overall reimagining and redesign of current clean water infrastructure is necessary to address a state of disrepair and the increasing impacts of climate change on the hydrologic cycle, including heavier rains and increasing droughts. "Green" infrastructure systems that treat wastewater effectively and remove anthropogenic pollutants are modeled after naturally occurring systems such as wetlands. Constructed wetlands are artificially designed natural filters offering ecologically beneficial treatment to polluted waters released from anthropogenic sources.

The following review of literature in conservation ecology, landscape architecture and environmental management seeks to illuminate inadequacies in existing systems that treat and release wastewater coming from dense urban areas of the United States. Brief historical precedence of the formation of existing systems is given to provide a foundation of understanding wastewater infrastructure development in the majority of urban areas in the U.S. and the state of these systems as they exist today. An examination of literature regarding ecological strategies for the conservation of biodiversity in human dominated regions provides a conceptual framework for the use of green infrastructure to protect vulnerable ecosystems. Further examination of literature concerning current conservation and green infrastructure planning strategies and their relationship to human health was performed in order to assess the overall feasibility of land-based wastewater infrastructure in urban regions. Finally, a case study of existing wastewater treatment infrastructure is presented alongside case studies of constructed wetland wastewater treatment systems in order to illustrate potential outcomes of green, land-based wastewater treatment.

2. A Brief History of Wastewater Infrastructure

The practice of discharging human waste into surrounding water bodies is likely as old as the first human settlements. Historically, wastewater is managed by using gravity to discharge wastewater directly or indirectly into topographical lowlands, to areas where wetlands already existed or exist as a result [12]. Advanced wastewater treatment methods date back to the early pipe filters and sewage canals of Indus Valley settlements in 26-1700 BCE. The complex, extensive sewer networks of ancient Rome separated water resources into aqueducts and included many smaller networks to drain sub-regions of their wastewater. Public baths and latrines were constructed to dissuade people from using the streets for disposal. Simultaneously, wetlands were drained for to erect Roman city foundations [13].

Following the fall of the Roman Empire, a dark age of limited and inadequate sanitation persisted in European countries and the United States for a period of nearly a thousand years. In urban areas of the early nineteenth century United States and much of the developed world, raw sewage from homes was dumped into public cesspools that were left to fester and breed disease before collection by sewage workers [13]. By the mid-19th century an abundance of water could be piped into homes, only to be later flushed out into human waste cesspools, causing frequent overflows and further spreading waste and disease. Sanitary engineers advocated for a solution in flush-based pipe connections from that would move water and waste from public cesspools to local water bodies. Throughout the twentieth century convenient water bodies were explicitly relegated to the role of wastewater dumps, reflecting an implicit idea that the "streams are nature's sewers", [14]. In 1854, the British physician John Snow proved outbreaks of waterborne diseases were the result of contaminated water supplies from leaking sewage pipes. Following Snow's correlation of disease and raw sewage contamination, cities in the United States took on massive sewage conveyance projects to protect potable water sources. Massive engineered sewer networks were built to address enormous excrement increases following the rapid growth of cities and industry in 19th century Britain and the United States. Developing modern sewer systems meant a large-scale transformation of native hydrology, not unlike historical Roman water infrastructure [14]. The replacement of cesspools and stagnant alley ponds carrying bacterial diseases required significantly greater volumes of flushable water. Continuous clean water pouring from taps meant greater demand for fresh water from reservoirs, requiring massive dams and further environmental disruption [15]. In order to install a comprehensive sewage system at that time in the low-lying city of Chicago it was necessary to raise most of the city with thousands of jackscrews to install sewer pipes that could convey wastewater with enough gravity [16]. At the time, common knowledge dictated water had the ability to "purify itself" of sewage and industrial pollution. The solution to the issue of water pollution and the threat of disease was dilution. This philosophy of dilution paved the way for the flush-based mechanisms of our modern waste removal infrastructure [14].

The importance of wastewater management to public health cannot be understated. Mortality rates in the US lowered by 40% from 1900 to 1940, partially as a result of rapid decreases in diseases transmitted via sewage [14]. Elsewhere bacterial diseases continue to cause public health devastation through the contaminated water supplies of countries with inadequate or damaged sanitation systems, such as in Haiti and Ghana. The Clean Water Act of 1972 was passed in the United States as part of a growing effort to reduce the amount of pollution entering waterways. The Clean Water Act necessitated the construction of numerous new wastewater treatment facilities in order to meet more rigorous water quality standards and the added demands of growing populations and. Many of the plants built following the Clean Water Act are long overdue to be updated with "add-on processes" necessary to meet pollution loading regulations [17]. Pollution reductions currently mandated by the Environmental Protection Agency as an effort to meet the goals of the Clean Water Act have led to heavy fines in municipalities that lack adequate resources to repair their crumbling sewage infrastructure. The economic cost of updating failing systems is often prohibitive to the repair of inadequate systems. In the United States, large-scale wastewater infrastructure is now reaching "replacement age", a crisis level state of disrepair in many cities that lack the resources for rebuilding [3]. As our century-old systems in the US fail during a time of limited financial means alternative systems and add-on processes are imperative to protect clean water resources and our ecosystems; and to prevent human contact with disease.

3. Strategies for Ecosystem and Clean Water Protection: Ecological Mutualism and Reconciliation

Mutualism is an ecological term referring to a species interaction wherein both or all species benefit. In the work of ecological urban planner Brook Ray Smith, the term *urban ecological mutualism* is defined as a model of urban ecosystems wherein infrastructure is more self- sustaining and less defined by systems of conveyance and linear disposal. Mutualistic ecosystems ideally operate in closed loop-systems where all wastes produced are repurposed [10]. For example, Phosphorus is one of the most difficult nutrients to remove from wastewater [18]. The industrial byproducts alum sludge (a byproduct of drinking water purification) and oyster shells (a landfill problem in Korea) were captured from the linear waste stream and used to purify industrial discharge in constructed wastewater treatment wetlands in a study performed at the Korean Institute of Water and Environment in 2007. The repurposed media of alum sludge and oyster shells filtered and removed Phosphorus effectively [18]. Alum sludge removed significant phosphorus in another study performed in Ireland in 2009 at the Centre for Water Resources Research [19]. The measurement of an effective design incorporating urban ecological mutualism is the extent to which humans and other species communities benefit from the shared landscape over time. Infrastructure design incorporating this concept requires an emphasis on resource optimizing and energy-usage minimizing, especially in repurposing waste as a resource. In ecologically mutual wastewater treatment systems, waste is repurposed as a resource [10]. Wastewater filtered through constructed wetlands can irrigate crops, parks, gardens, or golf courses [20]. The organization Metropolitan Water Reclamation District of Greater Chicago is now capturing phosphorus from wastewater to sell as a high-quality fertilizer. A large wastewater treatment in suburban Chicago extracts captured phosphorus and sells it to a company to turn it into non-water-soluble fertilizer that fertilizes only when the plant releases acids to signal its need, reducing phosphorus runoff concentrations. Encouragingly, the selling of phosphorus from waste treatment will net the district around two million dollars per year. A retrofit to perform the capture is thirty million dollars, meaning a fifteen-year return on the investment and a significant percentage of phosphorus being converted into a reclaimed fertilizer. According to David St. Pierre the director of the Metropolitan Water Reclamation District of Greater Chicago: "we [should be] moving from a waste paradigm to a resource paradigm", [21].

Urban ecological mutualism is an ideal outcome of systems designed in accordance with the principle of reconciliation ecology. The ecologist Michael L. Rosenzweig articulated the term reconciliation ecology in 2003 as the science and practice of reconciling human use of the earth with that of other species in order conserve species diversity. According to Rosenzweig, setting aside land for habitat reserves is inadequate to mitigate massive conservation losses. Large-scale habitat networks in direct contact with human environments are necessary to prevent further losses of biodiversity. It is important for landscape designers to work in tandem with ecologists to interpret studies gathered in nature reserves that indicate the habitat necessities of specific species. Using green infrastructure in wastewater treatment has the potential to accommodate the needs of various native species [9]. Wildlife corridors, for example, are of vital importance in developing urban habitats that offer benefits to both humans and wildlife. Wildlife corridors are generally located along streams in urban areas and allow the passage of species from isolated patches into neighboring habitats to ensure long-term species reproduction and survival. Greenways are trails connecting humans in urban areas to networks of green spaces and are used both for recreation and commuting. Wildlife corridors along streams often operate as both habitat links and human pathways, they provide a mutually beneficial public health service to citizens along with the connectivity necessary for the survival of species diversity [22]. Because sewage overflows are most often deposited into streams due to their gravity-dependent design, the prevention of such overflows is important to developing these multi-functional corridors in urban areas. Repairs to current gravity-fed centralized wastewater treatment systems are necessary to protect existing wildlife corridors and greenways. There is potential for retrofits to existing low-lying wastewater valves in streams to redirect sewage overflows to adjacent treatment areas and away from sensitive stream ecosystems, reducing the length of conveyance pipes (and conveyance repairs) necessary to redirect overflows to centralized treatment areas.

A paradigm shift to infrastructure with ecologically beneficial design would benefit people by lowering infrastructure costs for municipalities in the United States. In the highly developed (40% urbanized) Capital Region of Minnesota, frequent flooding from storm water and sewage overflows have necessitated new storm and sewage water management infrastructure to control excessive pollution inundation of surface waters. The city decided against a standard sewage pipe collection system costing approximately two and a half million dollars in favor of an approximately two-million-dollar green infrastructure system. The green infrastructure system consists of eight decentralized land-based storm water management designs including underground storage and infiltration facilities, a storm water pond and rain gardens [23]. Installing landscapes as infrastructure is a way to lower energy costs, to retrofit existing infrastructure and to replace the need for more expensive gray infrastructure construction and maintenance. According to the Environmental Protection Agencies 2008 Clean Water Needs Study, the total cost of wastewater and storm water infrastructure need in the US is 298.1 billion dollars, 192 billion of which is needed for wastewater treatment. Though limited funding exists for clean water infrastructure in most cities, reliance on traditional and costly centralized impervious "gray" infrastructure persists despite its limited ability to improve water quality [24].

With the need for replacement there now exists an opportunity for multiple professions to contribute to newer greener types of infrastructure that are inclusive of the ecosystem services that sustain human habitats and protect sensitive species in an ecological mutual paradigm. It is possible to plant the "green" of green infrastructure to support biodiversity and ecosystem resiliency. This new type of infrastructure can contribute to environmentally sensitive remediation and development. A multi-layered approach to infrastructure using land-based strategies could effectively address multiple problems simultaneously while reducing energy needs, pollution stress and infrastructure costs.

4. Strategies for Biodiversity Conservation and Green Wastewater Infrastructure

In the last few decades a new paradigm has emerged in urban storm water management, shifting our storm water infrastructure from large scale centralized capture and release conveyance systems to a smaller-scale, decentralized practices modeled according to principles of low impact design (LID) and best management practices (BMPs) that filter and infiltrate polluted storm water closer to the source. Low impact design practices seek to mimic pre-development conditions based on naturally occurring hydrology while BMPs exist as decentralized green infrastructure treatment facilities at the scale of blocks or singular buildings. If land based systems similar to common LID practices and BMPs are to be used to treat wastewater, the scale of such systems is of particular importance, especially in dense urban environments where public greenspace is at a minimum.

Land sparing is the conservation technique of setting aside land outside of human development for nature reserves [25]. It is considered by a 2015 study to be the best option for preserving habitats necessary for the survival of the largest variety of species on the planet [7]. As the population of the world's cities grows, strategies for development that involve minimal impact on local ecosystems are vitally important. In a typical *land sparing* configuration, extremely compact intensive urban growth is separated from large contiguous conservation lands. Landscapes designed for human activity that simultaneously provides wildlife with habitat is referred to as land sharing. Land sharing in an urban context provides significant public health benefits while cultivating public understanding and sympathy for biodiversity losses and the goals and imperatives of conservation [7]. In the case of wastewater management, centralized systems are compatible with a land sparing approach. Wastewater treatment in urban areas of the US overwhelmingly consists of large-scale, extensively piped conveyance systems with centralized treatment facilities. Alternatively, wastewater treatment performed in decentralized systems of more numerous smaller-scale treatment facilities is more compatible with a land sharing model.

A 2014 study conducted by research ecologists evaluated Rio de Janeiro, Brazil and Portland, Oregon evaluated the ecosystem benefits of land sparing (Rio) and land sharing (Portland) models. The Rio model of a dense urban area surrounded by large tracts of natural land performed a better job of sustaining ecosystem services including cleaning water and air, reducing noise, supporting pollination and storing carbon. The same study found in densely urbanized areas, land sparing resulted in greater population sizes for the majority of species studied. The model of land sparing was also found to do a better job of mitigating the urban heat island effect [26]. The researchers found development occurring at moderate levels such as that in suburbs causes natural lands to lose their ability to provide ecosystem services at a far greater rate than denser developments [27]. It is recommended by the researchers that City planners and policy makers adopt land sparing strategies in areas that will be densely urbanized in the future, by leaving large blocks of greenspace undeveloped [26].

Close to half of the population of the world lives in "highly modified human dominated landscapes", that are growing even more disconnected from nature. Worldwide forty percent of people live in urban regions and that number is expected to increase to sixty percent by 2030. Without access to the natural world, city dwellers suffer from what ecological researcher James Miller calls an "extinction of experience" that comes with severe risks to human health. Beyond public health, a lack of experience of biodiversity can lead people to disaffection and apathy towards nature. Childhood experiences are particularly important to combat the origins of estrangement from the natural world [28]. Land sharing regions such as Portland that offer residents many small public parks gave residents a greater sense of well-being and improved mental health, according to the 2014 study of Rio de Janeiro and Portland. Use of public greenspaces and satisfaction with those greenspaces was found to be higher in land sharing regions [26]. Emphasis on land sparing could decrease human-nature interactions, negatively affect public health outcomes and reduce public interest in biodiversity by limiting access. In the midst of rapid urbanization, development and infrastructure retrofitting designs that preserve biodiversity and minimize negative impacts on local species are an urgent matter [26]. Biodiversity enhancing strategies need to be carefully planned within urban areas to achieve measurable conservation benefits. According to researchers in the Department of Biology of Lund University in Sweden, land sparing could be executed simultaneously at multiple spatial scales to the greatest effect for local biodiversity. With appropriate planning, conserving smaller scale areas for habitat may better facilitate the movement of species between habitat fragments and provide greater resources to nomadic species [29].

The scale and distribution of wastewater treatment systems presents a complicated challenge for local ecologies. Wastewater in most major urban cities in the United States is ideally treated by the piping of flushed effluent to large-scale centralized, energy consumptive wastewater treatment plants that release treated effluent to adjacent water bodies. In the centralized systems of areas with varying topography, energy intensive pumping stations are in necessary for conveyance structures to traverse changing elevations en route to a limited number of treatment plants. Though significant technological advancements have been made in wastewater treatment plants in the United States, economic constraints, remain a barrier to major improvements in financially distressed urban areas such as Baltimore, Maryland [30]. Due to the deterioration of century old pipes that make up conveyance structures, storm water infiltration is a major contributor to sanitary sewage overflows. To control sewage overflows due to heavy storm water inundation, the US cities Chicago and Milwaukee have dug deep tunnels into bedrock over three hundred feet below ground in order to hold and convey sewage overflows in massive temporary holding quarries. These deep tunnel systems allow for better overflow storage in increasing heavy rain events brought about by climate change. However, significant pumping is necessary to move water stored in deep tunnels back to ground surface and the deep tunnel system requires highly dangerous construction and maintenance work [31].

Decentralized wastewater management systems are those that collect, treat and discharge or reuse wastewater at or near the point of origin as opposed to relying on extensive conveyance networks. In rural areas of the US and in some developing countries and towns such as Mobile, Alabama decentralized wastewater treatment strategies have been implemented as economically feasible and environmentally sustainable solutions to local small-scale wastewater management. In sparsely populated areas of developing countries, decentralized treatment can provide cost effective alternatives to extensive sewer pipes and systems [32]. In the United States, twenty-five percent of the population is served by decentralized wastewater treatment systems [18]. Wastewater treatment essentially consists of collection, treatment and disposal. In centralized systems, especially in countries with low and sparse population density, sixty percent of the total wastewater treatment budget goes to collection costs [32]. Onsite or neighborhood scale wastewater treatment systems offer an opportunity to capture and treat waste closer to the source within the built environment, reducing the need for conveyance structures and minimizing related retrofits [33]. While a smaller-footprint centralized treatment plant may seem to require less land than multiple and potentially more land-intensive decentralized green treatment systems, the methods and scale of conveyance are a necessary part of the central structure. Centralized treatment may seem to operate as a land sparing method in terms of land use, however the frequent failures of their extensive subterranean conveyance structures have result in deleterious environmental impacts to vulnerable shared habitats. Appropriate placement and design of green infrastructure wastewater treatment systems is critical to supporting remaining habitat fragments within treatment sites.

Constructed wastewater treatment wetlands typify low impact land-based filtration and green infrastructure design, allowing for multiple beneficial environmental and anthropogenic functions. Unlike their predecessors, storm water ponds, constructed wetlands filter and remediate pollutants instead of just containing overflows. Constructed wetlands treat polluted domestic or industrial wastewater using plants and engineered soils. They mimic natural filtration processes with native vegetation, soils and microbial communities. Design of these systems involves variable criteria including: wastewater constituents, plant species, substrate materials, flow direction and retention times [34]. Constructed wetland systems for wastewater treatment can be land-intensive, according to some estimates: a system for wastewater from 10,000 persons requires twenty acres of land [35]. However, recent advances in wastewater treatment methods such as using "biohedge" matrices to grow decomposing microbes can reduce land-intensiveness of such treatment systems [36]. Biochar, a byproduct of agricultural biomass waste, was found by researchers at Kwandong University in Korea to greatly enhance constructed wetland function due to its highly porous structure and low economic investment. When used as a soil amendment Biochar effectively absorbs heavy metals, remediates contaminants, improves fertilizer retention and increases hydraulic capacity in constructed wetlands [37]. Novel design of constructed wetlands can also make use of adjacent natural wetlands as a final polishing treatment beds for wastewater coming from pretreatment systems. Excessive nutrients in wastewater are remediated by plant communities in the natural wetland, providing nutrients that can have a positive impact on growth rates, resulting in a mutually beneficial relationship [38].

Constructed Wetland treatment systems have the potential to function compatibly with land sharing conservation methods if treatment wetlands are designed to have multiple functions as educational centers, recreational parklands and wildlife habitats. Careful analysis of multiple environmental, economic and social factors is necessary to address the scale and placement of such systems and any proposed land based retrofits to existing water infrastructure.

5. Potential Benefits of Green Wastewater Infrastructure

Purified, potable water clean enough to wash a baby is currently used for flushing our toilets, watering our gardens and washing our vehicles. The energy cost of conveying and treating wastewater is one of the largest consumers of energy in most municipalities and a major contributor to carbon emissions in the United States [11]. Though it may not seem so, raw sewage is composed of 99% pure water. Roughly half of wastewater is from toilets, the remaining half: called "greywater" comes from sinks, bathtubs, showers and washing machines [17]. Treatment processes in systems such as constructed wetlands are far less energy intensive, use fewer chemicals for disinfection, create less toxic sludge as a treatment byproduct and landfill waste and emit less greenhouse gases through construction and operation compared to standard treatment methods [33]. Greywater, water that has not come into contact with human waste, can be recycled for non-potable reuse on building sites or purified in onsite treatment facilities. A combination of composting toilets and greywater treatment through constructed wetlands is ideal for new developments, operating onsite with a low energy footprint. However, constructed wastewater treatment wetlands for small sites could potentially carry a larger footprint and require better soil drainage than is possible for dense urban areas. Installation of such systems would depend on the actions of existing building owners, zoning and developers. A system will be necessary in most urban areas to continue to treat wastewater coming from existing conveyance networks even as newer developments are incentivized to incorporate LEED methods of wastewater management, storage and reuse with the ultimate goal of reducing wastewater production and potable water usage. A move toward green infrastructure that supports natural filtration processes of the hydrologic cycle is essential to the protection of public health and clean water resources. There is a need for green space in human dominated landscapes to influence greater understanding of the necessity of conservation efforts [26]. Exposing communities to the processes and pitfalls of contemporary clean water infrastructure has multiple potential benefits: behavioral changes, stewardship and development of interest in research and participation in clean water complexities. Addressing cultural barriers affecting public acceptance of green infrastructure systems requires education to change our understanding of waste management and to overcome discomfort with unfamiliar treatment systems such as composting toilets [33] and (potentially) greenspaces that support wildlife while treating wastewater.

The ecologist E.O. Wilson described biophilia as the innate human tendency to seek out novel and diverse organisms and to explore and associate with other living things. *Biophilia* is a significant and formative process of our mental development [39]. Biophilic design is a strategy in landscape architecture that seeks to mimic natural systems in order to reconnect humans to nature in urban environments. Land based wastewater treatment systems have the capacity to foster our innate love of nature while promoting environmental stewardship and public understanding of conservation needs and practices through education and direct experiences with diverse ecosystems [27]. Interaction with the natural world through urban greenspaces provides multiple public health benefits to city residents. Public greenspaces are importance for facilitating social capital, the value of collective social interaction in people's lives. Lack of social capital is as major a factor in determining health and mortality as smoking and obesity are. The amount of greenspace accessible in one's environment is a major predictor of mental health status among residents, when factoring in both the benefits of physical activity and of social cohesion. The amount of public green space in communities is positively associated with lower body mass index (BMI) in children along with reduced odds of BMI increases over time. Physical activity early in life is critical to creating sustaining physical activity in adulthood. Parks in urban environments at least two and a half acres in size have significant effects on reducing air temperatures, lowering the risk of heat related illnesses exacerbated by the urban heat island effect. Consistent and accurate reporting on the health co-benefits of green infrastructure would promote its necessity as a fundamental public health practice [40]. Urbanization and lack of green space is associated with increased incidences of depression and mental illness. A longitudinal study from researchers at the European Centre for Environment and Human Health in 2014 reported significant and sustained gains in mental health following relocation to greener areas. Researchers in environmental science, biology, neurology and psychology at Stanford University report walking through a natural area affects the brain in meaningful ways walking for the same duration through an urban environment does not. The Stanford study found walking in a natural setting markedly decreased levels of rumination (commonly referred to as brooding) in participants, suggesting a powerful connection between greenspace and mental well-being [41]. Urban environments cause attention fatigue as a result of required sustained directed attention on a greater variety of sensory input. The ability of natural environments to ameliorate symptoms of mental fatigue has positive effects on symptoms of Attention Deficit Hyperactivity Disorder, both improving concentration and self-discipline. Greater access to natural environments can provide urban residents with an opportunity to recover from attention fatigue and improve cognitive function. By planning urban landscapes to address a lack of available greenspace, green infrastructure has the capacity to function as public greenspace with associated ancillary benefits to public and ecosystem health. People are attracted to both constructed and preserved wetlands for a variety of reasons, often to relax and observe wildlife [17]. Preserved wetlands such as intact marshland provide critical habitat for many species. Coastal Marshes and tidal wetlands provide habitat for native nesting and migratory birds, including great blue herons, snowy egrets and the American oystercatcher. Shoreline and upstream development are the greatest threats to tidal wetlands, adding excess sediment and nutrients to tributaries that blocks photosynthesis and degrades wetland habitat [42]. Increasing the resiliency of shore habitat is critical to providing a natural buffer from storm surges as tidal habitats become further fragmented due to sea level rise. A recent report issued by the evidence-based collaborative research group, Science for Nature and People Partnership (SNAPP) used advanced flood modeling to determine the direct impact of coastal wetlands had on annual property damage from storms. They looked at data from two thousand storms in New Jersey, US to determine the effect shoreline wetlands had on property damages. The study found shoreline wetlands reduce annual property damages by over twenty percent, a significant reduction in vulnerable areas. On the Atlantic coast of the US, wetlands saved an estimated $625 million in damages caused by Hurricane Sandy (2013), the second costliest hurricane in US history [43].

The intention of using constructed wetlands as water treatment facilities is to meet water quality imperatives with minimal disturbance to existing wildlife populations [17]. At this time, a small number of constructed wetlands have been designed with the specific intention of contributing to wildlife conservation. Barriers to design that prioritize wildlife conservation potential are: lack of understanding of ecological and conservation principles and needs, added costs, dearth of design manuals that could outline design techniques and lack of clear and obvious benefits to local communities. Effluent coming from surface flow constructed wetlands already contains a fundamental part of the wetland food chain and has less negative environmental impact on surface waters when discharged [20]. In some cases when treatment wetlands feed nutrient-rich effluent to tertiary wetlands, the treatment wetland acts as a nutritional support system for an already established and bio-diverse wetland habitat [17]. Constructed wetlands can be designed and managed to optimize wildlife and biodiversity potential in urban areas. Projects enacted to enhance biodiversity in the urban environment need to take into account the habitat value possible within the context of a densely built environment. Conservation studies and practices are generally species specific and management that increases populations of one species may not be effective for another [44]. Designers, engineers and land planners need to intentionally collaborate with conservation biologists and ecologists to restore and retrofit existing native habitat for species that are expected to gravitate due to warming temperatures [45]. Areas of treatment wetlands may need to be separated from human contact by design in order to promote wildlife conservation goals and protect public safety.

The use of constructed wetlands to treat urban wastewater has both potential positive benefits along with complicated design challenges of scale, siting, design and systemic cohesion. Careful implementation and design of green infrastructure for wastewater is imperative to protect public and ecosystem health in a manner feasible for large urban populations. Positive effects of replacing gray infrastructure with green infrastructure are evident in enhances to ecosystem services that benefit human populations and support habitat for dwindling native species. In urban regions, greenspace and green infrastructure can mitigate negative effects of human development by mimicking natural hydrologic processes. There is potential for large treatment wetlands to develop into important habitat, even if the system itself becomes obsolete in time. For example in Toronto, Canada, a barrier island called The Leslie Street Split unintentionally evolved, following decades of neglect, from a construction waste fill project in the 1950s into a designated and protected wildlife reserve. The Leslie Street Split now exists as a public educational park, wildlife habitat and barrier island protecting Toronto from shoreline erosion [46].

6. Case Studies of Wetland Wastewater Treatment Facilities

The use of constructed wetlands to treat urban wastewater has both potential positive benefits along with complicated systemic design challenges. Despite these challenges, some municipalities have been able to construct or retrofit wastewater treatment systems with constructed wetlands with successful outcomes. In order to understand the potential of constructed wastewater treatment wetlands to enhance and protect biodiversity, a closer look into diverse existing wastewater treatment systems is necessary. The following case studies contrast existing constructed treatment wetlands systems with an example of a wastewater treatment system typical in urban areas of the United States as a method of better understanding feasibility issues effecting the implementation and long-term sustainability of green wastewater systems.

6.1. Existing Urban Wastewater Treatment Plants: Baltimore and Surrounding Counties, Maryland (1860s–Present)

A sewage commissioner was appointed in 1859 in the city of Baltimore following the discovery by John Snow that correlated sewage contamination of drinking supplies to outbreaks of infectious disease. In nineteenth century urban American cities, citizens dumped their human waste into private cesspools that were later emptied out by "night soil" workers, a major industry at that time. The night soil industry lobbied against the sewage commissioner's plans to construct a new massive centralized underground sewer network like the systems constructed overseas [47]. Since the private sewage cesspools of the regions upper classes were the known cause of sewage contamination in drinking water, the new sewage commissioner's plan included the installation of conveyance structure networks connecting all areas of the city. Wealthy residents feared the pipeline connection to the lower classes and protested against a so-called "two-way pipe" that would cause the gaseous "germs" of the lower classes to backflow into the bathrooms of the upper class [48]. After the destructive force of the Baltimore Fire in 1904 left many areas in dire need of repair, Baltimore city mayor Robert McLane made moves to erect the modern wastewater infrastructure the city depends on for wastewater treatment today [47].

Baltimore's current wastewater treatment system consists of two major treatment plants located on the Chesapeake Bay: Back River and Patapsco. The entire system treats two hundred and ten million gallons of wastewater on an average day. Both treatment plants can treat up to two hundred and fifty million gallons of effluent per day, according to the Baltimore Department of Public Works. Nearly 3100 miles of sanitary sewer conveyance infrastructure collect effluent from Baltimore City and Baltimore County, 1400 miles of which are located in Baltimore City. Eight major and ten minor pumping stations convey wastewater to the two centralized treatment plants located on the shoreline of the Chesapeake Bay [49]. Heavy rains falling in the region frequently contribute to sewage overflows that release into urban streams and storm drains. As described by a journalist at the Baltimore Sun: "Whenever the rain pours-and even when it doesn't-the city's streams and harbor are contaminated by raw human waste spilled from corroding, porous sewer lines [to such an extent] that it's unsafe in most places for people to swim or wade." In the inner harbor, a major site of local tourism where people enjoy small boats and kayaks, safe levels of fecal bacteria are reported only 35 percent of the time. Sewage overflows affect homeowners when systems back up into basements [1]. According to the Baltimore Department of Public Works 7500 homes were flooded with raw sewage just in the last 9 months of 2017. The city does not compensate damages to homes from overflowing sewage, leading to lawsuits that cost the city thousands of dollars. Sinkholes caused by the collapse of massive underground sewage pipes have been opening up on the eastside of the city since the late nineties. When these large pipes collapse, other lines of infrastructure sink down into the sinkhole created. In 1997 a collapse in the sewage infrastructure collapsed gas and electric lines causing an inferno that destroyed the streetlights and a couple of buildings. The seventy to eighty-year-old system is not considered adequate to support the loads demanded on it today, nor the population and climate pressures of the future. The environmental nonprofit The Environmental Integrity Project released a study in 2015 detailing the extent of the environmental issues facing upgrades to the severely deteriorating system. A 2002 consent decree between the city of Baltimore and the United States Environmental Protection Agency (EPA) required the city pay a $600,000 penalty for the recurring and illegal dumping of millions of gallons of raw sewage. An agreement was made to overhaul the system and eliminate all illegal sewage overflows by 1 January 2016. Following the decree, the city tripled water and sewer bills, collecting around two million dollars from city residents since 2002 for infrastructure improvements and standard operational cost. Seven hundred million dollars went into sewage infrastructure improvements between 2002 and 2015 with major projects ongoing over the last thirteen years and the city is only half completed with necessary upgrades as of late 2017. In the year 2015 approximately forty million gallons of raw sewage reportedly overflowed, likely far less than the actual amount due to the underreporting by the city. Overflows of less than 10,000 gallons do not even require public disclosure to the regions citizens, even when they occur in highly populated areas frequently traversed by citizens, such as the Jones Fall (Greenway) Trail. Between 2009 and 2013 the city broke the terms of the consent decree 1258 times, resulting in fines of around $830,000 paid in addition to yearly fines already imposed by the EPA [50].

The Back River treatment plant is located on the west shore of the Back River branch of the Chesapeake Bay in Baltimore County, Maryland. It occupies four hundred and sixty-six acres and allows influent to move entirely via gravity due to a designed thirty-five foot elevation change. Close to 1.3 million regional residents living within one hundred and forty square miles are served by the Back River plant [49]. The Back River Treatment Plant is officially one hundred and four years old and suffering from a major problem with a pipe misalignment, severely limiting the plant's ability to handle large rains. Increasing periods of heavy rainfall have led to the release of millions of gallons of raw sewage into the Jones Falls Stream, a tributary that empties into the Chesapeake Bay. The Jones Falls Stream runs adjacent to the Jones Falls Trail, a local greenway popular with cyclists and runners. Bids to build a 36 million gallon holding tanks to temporarily store waste during heavy storms were currently under way as of October 2015 [1]. A massive four-acre orb-web, created by a diverse habitat of spiders was found in the rafters of Back River treatment plant's sand filtration tanks. Spiders are synanthropic species that thrive in built environments, in this case flies in the water provided energy to the spiders without the presence of a predator or competition for resources. They thrive in some treatment plants that have biofilters that host small invertebrates and structures that provide shelter, where they exist in numbers that far outweigh their populations in their native marshlands. The spider population is considered harmless and will be allowed to remain, however repairs are necessary to counteract the weakening effect their webs have on steel ceiling supports. Their population explosion is indicative of species persistence even in barren, built environments [51]. While novel, the spider population indicates an ecosystem out of balance, supporting the rapid proliferation of a single dominant organism type. This is indicative of an ecosystem that lacks a diverse enough variety of species to control excessive population growth.

Patapsco wastewater treatment plant was built in 1918 when the city of Baltimore acquired an extra sixty square miles, leading to a larger area in South Baltimore that was without sewage treatment facilities. The Patapsco plant services effluent conveyed from the Gwynn Falls watershed and the Patapsco river basin, treating nearly sixty-three million gallons per day and servicing around four hundred and fifty thousand people in one hundred and eighty square miles. The site of the plant is on approximately sixty-nine acres at Wagner's Point [49]. The facility failed to adequate meet the state's pollution limits in 2014, leading to a $5000 fine and a two-year extension for necessary nutrient removal upgrades [30]. After a near-record downpour in April 2014, the Patapsco plant released more than three million gallons of raw sewage into the Patapsco River [1].

Large centralized wastewater systems are arguably valuable as *land-sparing* entities when compared with land intensive wastewater wetlands. However, their reach is extensive when we include the vast underlying infrastructure network of conveyance pipes and pumping stations necessary to transport waste to centralized treatment structures. With further human development and increasingly heavy rains prevalent in a changing climate, storm water infiltration of deteriorating sewage infrastructure will intensify leading to greater and more frequent sewage overflows in many urban areas.

6.2. Arcata Marsh and Wildlife Wetlands: California, United States (1986–Present)

The Arcata constructed wastewater wetland performs wastewater reclamation and treatment in a semi-rural small town-scale constructed wetland wastewater treatment system serving a population of around fifteen thousand people. The treatment wetland is located on a 154-acre site in Northern California, two hundred and eighty miles north of San Francisco. In the 1970s point source pollution coming from the regions existing treatment plants led city officials to a proposal for a new centralized treatment system intended to treat wastewater coming from Arcata and the entire Humboldt Bay region. Projections of the regional plant showed significant cost and operational demands while organizational difficulties with surrounding communities delayed progress. To sway public opinion, city officials along with researchers conducted experiments with novel wastewater and constructed wetland treatment systems. From their experiments, they determined constructed wetlands would be sufficient to treat wastewater while contributing to the biological productivity of the existing wetland ecosystem. Estimates show Arcata's portion of the centralized treatment plant would have cost approximately $10 million as opposed to the $5 million spent to retrofit the existing plant with treatment wetlands, a major factor in swaying Arcata officials. The maintenance costs of the system are $500,000 annually compared to the $1.5 million that a centralized plant would have required. The existing Arcata wastewater wetland has now been functional since 1986. The system has met water quality standards while demonstrating the ability of marsh plants, soils and microorganisms to treat municipal wastewater with nominal negative environmental impacts and reduced energy, maintenance and operational needs. The system proved useful for the rearing of native fish species and provides crucial habitat for native species including migratory birds along the pacific flyway. Support and protection of existing local wetlands helped reverse the trend of wetland habitat loss in the region. The site surrounding the existing Arcata treatment plant included nearly forty acres of abandoned brownfields and former wetlands that blocked shoreline access. The restored site now provides shoreline access to the community and an innovative recreational and educational interpretive center. The transformed marsh is now called the Arcata Marsh and Wildlife Sanctuary (AMWS) due to the diversity of the wildlife habitat it supports, including: aquatic species, shorebirds, waterfowl, migratory birds and raptors. Nearly 200 bird species utilize the marsh as a resting place or home. Nature walks along with school and visitor tours are conducted at AMWS. The park is visited by more than one hundred and fifty thousand people every year for passive recreation, art inspiration, scientific research and bird watching. The City of Arcata was awarded funding from the Ford Foundation to build an interpretive center that focuses on educating visitors on the scientific, biological and technical components of the system [17]. The Arcata treatment wetlands are an example of a successful wastewater treatment that positively impacts residents of the region, providing a multiple economic and social benefits beyond just standard and effective treatment of waste. The marsh functions simultaneously as infrastructure and habitat, further evolving to suit the needs of humans and wildlife. The proven success of a cost saving retrofit to what was previously a poorly functioning system provides a strong argument for the implementation of similar systems in other municipalities.

6.3. EcoSistema Filtro (ESF) of the Parco Naturale Regionale Molentargius-Saline, Sardinia, Italy (2004–Present)

The EcoSistema Filtro (ESF) is a nine hundred and fifteen acre wastewater treatment wetland constructed in 2004 within Molentargius-Saline Nature Reserve of Sardinia, Italy. The Molentargius-Saline reserve was established in 1999, between two fast-growing urban cities in Italy: Quartu Sant'Elena and Cagliari. The ESF was financed by the Environmental Ministry of Italy as a part of the Molentargius protection plan for the reserve. The ESF is a constructed wetland that provides secondary treatment to effluent coming from the Is Arena Depuration Plant in Cagliari. Following treatment, the ESF supplies purified and bio-chemically balanced water to restored freshwater ponds in the nature reserve. The proximity of the reserve to the two cities that surround has provided an ideal opportunity for educational and recreational activities that are easily accessible to the local population. The park dedicates educational walking tours on the topic of constructed wetland purification processes and the importance of wastewater reuse. It offers recreational activities such as rare bird watching. Ecologists use the site to tag and monitor birds. Some of the reserves research activities are open to public attendance and small groups are invited to assist biologists and naturalists. Though publically accessible, the wetland is carefully managed to prevent negative effects of human interaction by limiting volunteer numbers and human contact as needed to protect the habitat. The Sustainability and Environmental Educational Centre of Molentargius (CEAS) introduces visitors to the ESF and provides didactic texts, audio-visuals, educational project space and amenities for events. The ESF has developed in just the last decade into an important habitat for a variety of vulnerable native species of plants and animal including many waterfowl. A study performed by Italian botanical and conservation researcher began recording a floristic survey of plants in the ESF in 2005 one year after the plant was first constructed. Following the years 2006–2007 researchers have recorded a continuous development of species richness with increases in native species, threatened species and alien species. Native species have persisted strongly in the wetland, a positive indication of successful species conservation long-term. The persistence of native flora indicates quality habitat for native non-plant species such as lepidoptera, birds and aquatic species that compose the important trophic foundation of the wetland food chain. The success of the ESF shows great potential for artificial ecosystems to preserve and enhance biodiversity with in a peri-urban context. Ancillary benefits of the Ecosistema Filtro to surrounding human communities include clean water, educational activities and ecotourism [52].

6.4. Wastewater Treatment Facilities: Cannon Beach, Oregon (1980s–Present)

In 1982 the city of Cannon Beach, Oregon received approval for a plan to use constructed lagoons and wetlands to support wastewater treatment in an existing wooded wetland, in order to meet new and stricter regulations enacted by the Clean Water Act of 1972. Though the permanent population of the town of Cannon Beach was only around sixteen hundred, the system was designed to handle population increases during the summer tourism season. The system treats one hundred and eighty million gallons a year, meeting strict effluent standards from the United States Environmental Protection Agency. The treatment system is comprised of thirteen miles of sewage conveyance pipes, nine pumping stations, an analysis laboratory and a series of lagoon and wetland treatment cells. Twelve and a half acres of facultative lagoons and two aerated lagoon cells and sixteen acres of wetlands comprise the multistage system. Wooded wetland cells serve as a polishing system before treated effluent is discharged into Ecola Creek. In the summer months shade from surrounding trees inhibits algae growth. A natural wetland was altered using dykes to contain water control structures, allowing for minimal alteration to the existing ecosystem. The cost of the system in 1985 was 1.5 million dollars, eighty percent of which was funded by a grant from the Environmental Protection Agency. The operating costs of the system represented just twelve percent of the total sewer department's budget from 1992 to 1993. Only one full time staff and two part time staff are needed to operate the wetlands and perform lab work. The system does not produce offensive odors and contributes to a development pattern that is not disruptive to the surrounding environment. The treatment system was maintained to meet greater demands approximately a decade after installation by dredging sludge from lagoons and improving aeration methods. Other system improvements have included an ultraviolet disinfection replacing the need for chlorine disinfection, significant because the chlorine discharged from wastewater treatment plants distress aquatic habitats even in trace amounts. The Cannon Beach treatment wetlands have effectively reduced the volume of city effluent discharges to Ecola Creek, improving overall water quality and habitat in the riparian zone. Civic involvement in the project has heighted awareness of the city's ecological and geographical context and issues related to water infrastructure. The site is used for study by the local school system and nature tours are organized for various citizen groups [17].

The Cannon Beach wastewater wetland system is an example of ecologically sensitive integration of wastewater infrastructure into a surrounding landscape. It has demonstrable economic, recreational and educational benefits to permanent and seasonal residents of Cannon Beach. Ancillary benefits to the local ecosystem include habitat creation and the protection of existing wetlands from destructive development practices. The add-on improvements exemplify the flexibility the system possesses in its ability to incorporate newer treatment technologies while maintaining effective outcomes.

7. Towards a New Wastewater Paradigm

In many urban areas of the United States sewer treatment systems are ticking time bombs, sporadically hemorrhaging evidence of a large-scale infrastructure crisis below our feet. For decades investment in anthropogenic structures that house and convey human beings throughout the landscape have outpaced maintenance of structures conveying less economically productive necessities. The United States American Society of Civil Engineers estimate nine hundred billion gallons of sewage water teeming with destructive nutrient and chemical pollutants spill every year from miles of failing wastewater treatment systems. Multiple sinkholes have appeared in cities like Baltimore as sewage pipes woefully past their usable lifetimes collapse below city streets [53]. Orchestrating the vast repairs necessary to maintain our ecosystems is a complicated imperative, however essential to preventing further casualties of inadequate sanitation.

Wetlands cover 5–8% of land worldwide. Nearly half of the wetlands in the United States have been destroyed as of 2015 and we lose nearly sixty thousand acres yearly [54]. Only in the last fifty years have the public and policy makers begun to recognize the vital ecosystem services wetlands provide. Numerous wetlands were drained and cleared prior to the 1960s, when they were considered disease-harboring garbage "swamps" devoid of value [55]. These bogs and wet seams where land meets water are where the highest concentration and diversity of life resides. A density of crabs, invertebrates, reptiles and fish are found and supported by these fertile habitats. Great blue heron, osprey, bald eagles and numerous species of birds rely on tidal wetland habitat for migrating, feeding and nesting. One third of wetland breeding bird species are considered highly or medium vulnerability to future effects of climate and development stressors [54]. From an anthropocentric perspective, tidal wetlands represent the most desirable tracts of waterfront real estate, as attractive to humans as they are to wildlife. Shoreline property is highly sought for its worth economically and valuable as a source of dilution waters used by shoreline wastewater treatment plants for effluent dilution. Shoreline development provides easy access to cooling waters for power plants and desirable spaces for boats in expanding marinas. Tidal marshes are considered highly vulnerable habitat by the United States Environmental Protection Agency, with significant losses along the Eastern coast of the United States [55]. Degradation of shoreline wetland habitat used by migrating birds since the 1970s has contributed significantly to the extinction of avian species. Conserving existing wetlands and implementing living shorelines that restore tidal ecosystems as an alternative to inflexible shoreline bulkheads is vital to restoring bio-diverse habitat and mitigating species extinction [56].

Our current water infrastructure paradigm exists on a continuum between destructive anthropogenic drainage systems and natural drainage systems wherein our anthropogenic systems are heavily prioritized. With wastewater treatment systems in urban areas of the US now at a crucial replacement age, there is an opportunity to develop new systems and retrofit existing systems to mutually benefit humans and other forms of life. Research and development of green infrastructure treatment systems exists in enough capacity to allow for collaboration between science, engineering and design fields to develop innovation in green wastewater infrastructure. As human populations and developments swell, flexible land-based systems can provide and protect habitat from destructive effects of ongoing urbanization and development. Wetland habitats that purify effluent can provide edge and riparian habitat and nesting sites for a multitude of species, enhancing long-term ecosystem diversity and stability. A new, resilient, ecologically mutual paradigm for wastewater treatment is imperative to benefit the long-term viability of human beings and native species. Increasing population size and progressive densification in urban areas means more pressure on existing systems to meet greater demands. Sea-level rise, climate change and predicted future water scarcities will all further limit the resiliency of our water infrastructure and the ecosystems we rely on to provide clean water. Reducing reliance on current energy intensive systems is crucial to maintaining long-term sustainability of treatment and conveyance systems [11]. Wastewater treatment in the United States currently accounts for 1.5 percent of all annual energy use [57]. Systems that require low-energy input and maintenance and those that contribute to energy production are highly desirable, economically and for long-term resiliency. Novel and ecologically mutual treatment practices can be implemented through green infrastructure with the capability to perform multiple functions in a low-impact, adaptable form [58]. The reuse of gray water along with storm water management practices of rainwater capture, treatment and infiltration can ideally constitute a large part of future water conservation efforts [11]. As a part of a network of sustainable water treatment practices, constructed wetland treatment parks can enhance human experiences of *biophilia*, provide educational experiences in conservation and ecology and improve public health. Wastewater treatment facilities have the potential to handle effluent treatment from urban areas while creating and maintaining habitat supportive of conservation efforts [10]. By embracing a clean water infrastructure paradigm that learns from and mimics naturally occurring land-based filtration processes we have the opportunity to repurpose large flows of wastewater as a valuable resource for enhancing biodiversity.

8. Conclusions

This paper demonstrates that: (1) wastewater treatment systems in urban areas of the US are in a state of disrepair leading to significant negative outcomes affecting human and non-human habitats; and (2) green wastewater infrastructure strategies that support native hydrology with positive environmental impacts are integral to the protection of the clean water humans and other species rely on for survival; and (3) The use of constructed wetlands in green wastewater infrastructure has great potential to ameliorate biodiversity losses in urban ecosystems while supporting and enhancing densely populated anthropogenic environments with multiple benefits to human health. Considering the scholarly gaps, further research is necessary to understand how land-based systems can replace or supplement current treatment infrastructure in practice, including implementation phasing and the remediation of existing brownfields necessary for transformation into healthy wetland ecosystems. Greater understanding of the bureaucratic processes influencing the development and implementation of green wastewater infrastructure as pertains to specific municipalities and any laws governing wastewater treatment practices is also needed to influence future developments in wastewater infrastructure.

Author Contributions: Caitlin Cunningham performed the review of literature and wrote the paper. Mohammad Gharipour provided guidance, feedback, review and editing.

Conflicts of Interest: The authors declare no conflict of interest.

References

1. Wheeler, T.B. No End in Sight for City's $1.1 Billion Overhaul of Leaky, Polluting Sewers. Available online: http://www.baltimoresun.com/news/maryland/bs-md-sewer-overhaul-20150904-story.html (accessed on 13 December 2017).
2. Rabin, C.; Morgan, C. Miami-Dades Leaky Pipes: More than 47 Million Gallons of Waste Spilled in the Last Two Years. Available online: http://www.miamiherald.com/2012/05/14/vfullstory/2799249/miami-dades-leaky-pipes-morethan.html (accessed on 15 December 2017).
3. Tong, S. Baltimore Sewers: Time Bombs Buried under the Streets. Available online: https://www.marketplace.org/2015/02/25/sustainability/water-high-price-cheap/baltimore-sewers-time-bombs-buried-under-streets (accessed on 11 December 2017).
4. Barber, S. Lake Erie's Toxic Algae Bloom Forecast for Summer 2016. Available online: http://www.ecowatch.com/lake-eries-toxic-algae-bloom-forecast-for-summer-2016-1891172391.html (accessed on 20 November 2017).
5. United States Environmental Protection Agency. Harmful Algae Blooms & Drinking Water Treatment. Available online: https://www.epa.gov/water-research/harmful-algal-blooms-drinking-water-treatment (accessed on 3 January 2017).
6. Jorgensen, S.E. Water Quality: The Impact of Eutrophication. *Lakes Reserv.* **2001**, *3*, 1–25.
7. Soga, M.; Yamaura, Y.; Shinsuke, K.; Gaston, K.J. Land sharing vs. land sparing: Does the compact city reconcile urban development and biodiversity conservation? *J. Appl. Ecol.* **2014**, *51*, 1378–1386. [CrossRef]
8. Del Tredici, P. *Wild Urban Plants of the Northeast: A Field Guide*; Cornell University Press: Ithaca, NY, USA, 2010; ISBN 0801474582.
9. Rosenzweig, M.L. *Win Win Ecology: How the Earth's Species Can Survive in the Midst of Human Enterprise*, 1st ed.; Oxford University Press: New York, NY, USA, 2003; ISBN-10: 0195156048.
10. Smith, B.R. Re-Thinking Urban Wastewater Landscapes: Constructed Wetlands for Urban Ecological Mutualism in San Francisco. Master's Thesis, University of California, Berkeley, CA, USA, 2008.
11. Broaddus, L. Radio Interview by Susan Bence. All Things Considered, National Public Radio. Available online: https://www.npr.org/programs/all-things-considered/ (accessed on 29 January 2018).
12. Brix, H. Treatment Wetlands: An overview. In Proceedings of the Conference on Constructed Wetlands for Wastewater Treatment, University of Gdansk, Gdansk, Poland, 11–12 November 1995; Toczylowska, I., Mierzejewski, M., Eds.; Technical University of Gdansk: Gdansk, Poland, 1995; pp. 167–176.
13. Lofrano, G.; Brown, J. Wastewater management through the ages: A history of mankind. *Sci. Total Environ.* **2010**, 5254–5264. [CrossRef] [PubMed]
14. Benidickson, J. *The Culture of Flushing: A Social and Legal History of Sewage*; UBC Press: Vancouver, BC, Canada, 2007; ISBN 0774841389, 9780774841382.
15. Boone, C.G. Obstacles to Infrastructure Provision: The Struggle to Build Comprehensive Sewer Works in Baltimore. *Hist. Geogr.* **2003**, 152–166.
16. Cutler, I. *Chicago: Metropolis of the Mid-Continent*; Southern Illinois University Press: Champagne, IL, USA, 2006.
17. United States Environmental Protection Agency. Constructed Wetlands for Wastewater Treatment and Wildlife Habitat: 17 Case Studies. Available online: https://www.epa.gov/sites/production/files/2015-10/documents/2004_10_25_wetlands_introduction.pdf (accessed on 3 January 2017).
18. Park, W.H. Integrated constructed wetland systems employing alum sludge and oyster as filter media for P removal. *Ecol. Eng.* **2009**, 1275–1282. [CrossRef]
19. Babatunde, A.O.; Zhao, Y.Q.; Zhao, X.H. Alum-sludge based constructed wetland system for enhanced removal of P and OM from wastewater: Concept, design, and performance analysis. *Bioresour. Technol.* **2010**, 6576–6579. [CrossRef] [PubMed]

20. Rousseau, D.P.L.; Lesage, E.; Story, A.; Vanrolleghem, P.A.; De Pauw, N. Constructed wetlands for water reclamation. *Desalination* **2008**, *218*, 181–189. [CrossRef]
21. Klettke, R. Phosphorus for Sale. *Landsc. Archit. Mag.* **2015**, *10*, 46.
22. Groves, C.R.; Game, E.T.; Anderson, M.G.; Cross, M.; Enquist, C.; Ferdaña, Z.; Girvetz, E.; Gondor, A.; Hall, K.R.; Higgins, J.; et al. Incorporating climate change into systematic conservation planning. *Biodivers. Conserv.* **2012**, *21*, 1651–1671. [CrossRef]
23. United States Environmental Protection Agency. *Case Studies Analyzing the Economic Benefits of Low Impact Development and Green Infrastructure Programs*; EPA841-R-13-004; United States Environmental Protection Agency: Washington, DC, USA, 2013; pp. A37–A45.
24. American Rivers; The Water Environment Federation; The American Society of Landscape Architects; ECONorthwest. *Banking on Green: A Look at How Green Infrastructure Can Save Municipalities Money and Provide Economic Benefits Community-Wide*; American Society of Landscape Architects: Washington, DC, USA, 2012.
25. Romnee, A.; Evrard, A.; Trachte, S. Methodology for a stormwater sensitive urban design. *J. Hydrol.* **2015**, *530*, 87–102. [CrossRef]
26. Soga, M.; Yamaura, Y.; Aikoh, T.; Shoji, Y.; Kubo, T.; Gaston, K.J. Reducing the extinction of experience: Association between urban form and recreational use of public greenspace. *Landsc. Urban Plan.* **2015**, *143*, 69–75. [CrossRef]
27. Stott, I.; Soga, M.; Inger, R.; Gaston, K.J. Land sparing is crucial for urban ecosystem services. *Front. Ecol. Environ.* **2015**, *13*, 387–393. [CrossRef]
28. Miller, J.R. Biodiversity conservation and the extinction of experience. *Trends Ecol. Evol.* **2005**, *20*, 430–434. [CrossRef] [PubMed]
29. Ekroos, J.; Odman, A.M.; Andersson, G.K.; Birkhofer, K.; Herbertsson, L.; Klatt, B.K.; Olsson, O.; Olsson, P.A.; Persson, A.S.; Prentice, H.C.; et al. Sparing Land for Biodiversity at Multiple Scales. *Front. Ecol. Evol.* **2016**, 3–11. [CrossRef]
30. Ruetter, M. City Slapped with Small Fine, Given Two More Years to Complete Sewer Plant Improvements. Available online: https://www.baltimorebrew.com/2014/12/24/city-slapped-with-small-fine-given-two-more-years-to-complete-sewer-plant-improvements/ (accessed on 25 October 2017).
31. Moser, W. Deep inside Chicago's Deep Tunnel. Available online: http://www.chicagomag.com/Chicago-Magazine/The-312/December-2011/Deep-Inside-Chicagos-Deep-Tunnel (accessed on 13 December 2017).
32. Massoud, M.A.; Tarhini, A.; Nasr, J.A. Decentralized approaches to wastewater treatment and management in developing countries. *J. Environ. Manag.* **2009**, *90*, 652–659. [CrossRef] [PubMed]
33. District Wastewater Management. Available online: http://ecodistricts.org/wp-content/uploads/2013/05/Water_Manag1.pdf (accessed on 17 November 2017).
34. Upadhyay, A.K.; Bankoti, N.S.; Rai, U.N. Studies on sustainability of simulated constructed wetland system for treatment of urban waste; design and operation. *J. Environ. Manag.* **2016**, *169*, 285–292. [CrossRef] [PubMed]
35. Klockenbrink, M. Small Towns Build Artificial Wetlands to Treat Sewage. *The New York Times*, 29 November 1988.
36. Valipour, A.; Raman, V.A.; Ahn, Y. Effectiveness of Domestic Wastewater Treatment Using a Bio-Hedge Water Hyacinth Wetland System. *Water* **2015**, *7*, 329–347. [CrossRef]
37. Gupta, P.; Tae-woong, A.; Lee, S. Use of biochar to enhance constructed wetland performance in wastewater reclamation. *Environ. Eng. Res.* **2016**, *21*, 36–44. [CrossRef]
38. Doyle, T. Effects of Wastewater on Forested Wetlands. Available online: https://www.nwrc.usgs.gov/factshts/104-02.pdf (accessed on 22 February 2016).
39. Wilson, E.O. *Biophilia*; Harvard University Press: Cambridge, MA, USA, 1984; ISBN 0674074424.
40. Coutts, C.; Hahn, M. Green Infrastructure, Ecosystem Services, and Human Health. *Int. J. Environ. Res. Public Health* **2015**, *12*, 9768–9798. [CrossRef] [PubMed]
41. Bratman, G.N.; Hamilton, J.P.; Hahn, K.S.; Daily, G.C.; Gross, J.J. Nature experience reduces rumination and subgenual prefrontal cortex activation. *Proc. Natl. Acad. Sci. USA* **2015**, *112*, 8567–8572. [CrossRef] [PubMed]
42. Wetlands. Chesapeake Bay Program. Available online: http://www.chesapeakebay.net/issues/issue/wetlands#inline (accessed on 20 December 2016).
43. Narayan, S.; Beck, M.W.; Wilson, P.; Thomas, C.; Guerrero, A.; Shepard, C.; Reguero, B.G.; Franco, G.; Ingram, C.J.; Trespalacios, D. *Coastal Wetlands and Flood Damage Reduction: Using Risk Industry Based Models to Assess Natural Defenses in the Northeastern USA*; Lloyd's Tercentenary Research Foundation: London, UK, 2016.

44. Dearborn, D.C.; Kark, S. Motivations for Conserving Urban Biodiversity. *Conserv. Biol.* **2008**, *24*, 432–440. [CrossRef] [PubMed]

45. Dance, S. Rare Pair of Tropical Birds Take Roost in Locust Point Drawing Birdwatchers. Available online: www.baltimoresun.com/features/green/blog/bs-md-brown-booby-20150921-story.html (accessed on 1 September 2017).

46. Belanger, P. Landscape as Infrastructure. *Landsc. J.* **2009**, *28*, 79–95. [CrossRef]

47. Woods, B. *Sinkhole: What Is Happening Beneath the Ground Downtown?* Baltimore Citypaper: Baltimore, MA, USA, 2016.

48. Puglionesi, A. The Manmade Marvel of the Baltimore Sewers. Atlas Obscura. Available online: http://www.atlasobscura.com/articles/the-manmade-marvel-of-the-baltimore-sewers (accessed on 22 October 2016).

49. Bureau of Water and Wastewater. Baltimore City Department of Public Works. Available online: http://publicworks.baltimorecity.gov/Bureaus/WaterWastewater (accessed on 11 November 2015).

50. Pelton, T.; Bernhardt, C.; Burkhart, K.; Lam, S. Stopping the Flood Beneath Baltimore's Streets. Environmental Integrity Project Report. Available online: http://www.environmentalintegrity.org/wp-content/uploads/2016/11/FINAL-SEWAGE-REPORT.pdf (accessed on 3 January 2016).

51. Greene, A.; Coddington, J.A.; Breisch, N.L.; De Roche, D.M.; Pagnac, B.B., Jr. An immense concentration of orb-weaving spiders with communal webbing in a man-made structural habitat. *Am. Entomol.* **2010**, *56*, 146–156. [CrossRef]

52. De Martis, G.; Mulas, B.; Malavasi, V.; Marignani, M. Can Artificial Ecosystems Enhance Local Biodiversity? The Case of a Constructed Wetland in a Mediterranean Urban Context. *Environ. Manag.* **2016**, *57*, 1088–1097. [CrossRef] [PubMed]

53. American Society of Civil Engineers and The Economic Research and Development Research Group. Failure to Act: Closing the Infrastructure Investment Gap for America's Economic Future, 1-31. Available online: http://www.infrastructurereportcard.org/wp-content/uploads/2016/05/2016-FTA-Report-Close-the-Gap.pdf (accessed on 30 November 2016).

54. North American Bird Conservation Initiative, U.S. Committee. *The State of the Birds 2010 Report on Climate Change*; United States of America; U.S. Department of the Interior: Washington, DC, USA, 2010.

55. United States Environmental Protection Agency. Wetlands Overview. EPA843-F-04-011a. 1-4. 2004. Available online: https://www.epa.gov/sites/production/files/2016-02/documents/wetlandsoverview.pdf (accessed on 1 November 2017).

56. Horton, T. *Turning the Tide: Saving the Chesapeake Bay*; Island Press: Washington, WA, USA, 2003; ISBN 1610911164.

57. Logan, B.E. Research-BioEnergy, Overview of Microbial Fuel Cells, Pennsylvania State University. Available online: https://www.engr.psu.edu/ce/enve/logan/bioenergy/research_mfc.htm (accessed on 21 February 2016).

58. Lovell, S.T.; Taylor, J.R. Supplying urban ecosystem services through multifunctional green infrastructure in the United States. *Landsc. Ecol. Rev.* **2013**, *28*, 1447–1463. [CrossRef]

urban science

Article

Social Resistances and the Creation of Another Way of Thinking in the Peripheral "Self-Constructed Popular Neighborhoods": Examples from Mexico, Argentina, and Bolivia

Chryssanthi (Christy) Petropoulou

Department of Geography, University of the Aegean, University Hill, 81100 Mytilene, Greece; christy.p@aegean.gr; Tel.: +30-22510-44825

Received: 13 February 2018; Accepted: 14 March 2018; Published: 19 March 2018

Abstract: This study refers to urban social movements, creative social resistances, and the collectives that are emerging today in "self-constructed popular neighborhoods" ("barrios de auto-construcción popular" in Latin-American, Spanish bibliography; "quartiers d'auto-construction populaire" in French bibliography and "self-help housing" in Anglophone bibliography), with a special focus on the new characteristics of these movements and the poetics of their daily practices. Firstly, a cartographic approach is explained through the concept of eco-landscapes; a qualitative analysis follows based on interviews and a review of the secondary literature. In particular, this research focuses on cases of movements and collectives in *villas* in South Greater Buenos Aires, *barrios* of Ciudad Nezahualcóyotl in the Metropolitan Area of Mexico City, and *barrios* of El Alto in the Metropolitan Area of La Paz. It shows that the poetics of creative resistances question the symbolic power of territorial stigmatization.

Keywords: urban social movements; other societies in movement; *autoconstrucción popular*; self-help housing; change habitus; urban banishment; Mexico City; La Paz–El Alto; Buenos Aires; creative social resistances

1. Introduction

This study refers to urban social movements, creative social resistances, and the collectives that are emerging today in the peripheral "self-constructed popular neighborhoods" (self-help housing), with a special focus on the new characteristics of these movements and the poetics of their daily practices. It examines whether these struggles, through the creation of another way of thinking in everyday life (beyond the mainstream frames of reference), contribute to reversing:

(a)   the biopolitical [1] state practices [2] in the peripheries of Latin American cities;
(b)   the "fatal triangle of stigmatization of the urban precariat" [3]; and
(c)   the politics of neo-colonial "urban banishment" [4].

It focuses on neighborhoods in El Alto (Metropolitan Area of La Paz), Nezahualcóyotl and (Metropolitan Area of Mexico City), and the South of Greater Buenos Aires. Firstly, it analyses the concept of "neighborhoods or settlements of spontaneous origin" [5] or "neighborhoods of self-help housing," or "barrios de autoconstrucción popular" focusing specifically on Latin American cities. Then, it presents the notions of "urban social movements" [6] and "habitus" [7]. Finally, it poses the question of whether "creative social resistances" and "other societies in movement" [8] actually contribute to transforming the habitus, and whether they therefore constitute "crack capitalism" initiatives [9]. The paper presents a comparative approach of urban social movements in these neighborhoods and a synthesis of the new characteristics [10] of contemporary "creative resistances." In this study, the concept of "creative resistance" refers to all those collectivities that offer not only an anti-systemic logic but, also, that express creative action in everyday life. Specifically, I argue that a transformation in aspects of the habitus is possible, if *creative resistances* acting in these neighborhoods relate to the "tradition of rebellion" and "other worlds in movement" as well as ideas of anti-capitalist, anti-patriarchal, anti-colonial, and ecological global social movements. The term "creative resistances" has been also used in some texts in a different way that attributes to it a more conciliatory approach relative to the dominant ideology of the culture industry. The present text will not enter this debate.

2. The Concept of "Self-Constructed Popular Neighborhoods" Focusing Especially on Latin American Cities

We are not the poorest. We are the ones who, like Maldonado, have chosen not to live subordinate.

—Mario   from   Villa   23,   "Garganta Poderosa" [11]

In the international literature, the term "self-constructed popular neighborhoods" reflects different views of the authors and complex procedures that vary from country to country, from city to city, but also from district to district. The precise meaning of this term varies qualitatively according to what we are referring: the relation with legislation, social characteristics, historical particularities, and colonial or neo-colonial points of view on forms of urbanization and modes of planning. For example, in the Anglo-Saxon, French, and Spanish literature we can find the terms "spontaneous settlements" (mode of space production with poor houses without urban plan), "squatters' settlements" (mode of space production with land squatting), "irregular settlements" (mode of space production without legislation, not only for poor people), "slums" [12] (poor settlements or neighborhoods in the center or the periphery of the city), "colonias populares" (social production of the space) "bidon-villes" (trash-materials of construction in the first period of construction) and the specific terms about neighborhoods (initially land squatting) such as "favelas" (Brazil), or "villas" (Argentina), etc.

Self-constructed popular neighborhoods are variously called:

- In the Metropolitan Area of Mexico City, "colonias populares" (referring to the work position and the type of labor force of the population), "asentamientos irregulares" (referring to the urban planning legislation) and "ciudades perdidas" or "bidon-villes" (referring to the first period of occupation); they are located in what was previously suburban space.
- In the Metropolitan Area of Buenos Aires (Greater Buenos Aires), "villas" and "asentamientos irregulares" and actually, in the first period of squatting, "villas de emergencia"; they are in the South and West periphery of the city.
- In the Metropolitan Area of La Paz–El Alto, "barrios populares" and "asentamientos urbanos irregulares", although, in most cases, the irregularity is related only to construction "outside of the urban plan", without "building license/permission."

In Latin America, the generation of such districts is historically intertwined with the acceleration of forced urbanization, especially during 50's. During this decade, self-constructed popular neighborhoods (self-help housing) were officially considered marginal (a quite erroneous position insofar as most of the inhabitants constituted the main workforce in the city). The predominant idea of "marginality" is supported by Lewis's theory of "culture of misery". Such a perception stigmatizes the social and moral life in these neighborhoods.

The stigmatizing definition of such settlements as "malignant tumors" [13] has served the criminalization and suppression of urban social movements and other radical organizations developed in these areas, especially during periods of dictatorship (1976–1983, in Argentina and 1964–1982 in Bolivia), as well as during the period of squatting repression in Mexico (1976–1985). In contrast to this stigmatizing discourse, Liberation Theology played an important role in supporting self-constructed popular neighborhoods [14].

In the same period, many urban social movements and organizations, with either Maoist, Trotskyist, Guevarist or Anarchist/Libertarian influences, propose and participate in the organization of squatting and the neighborhoods' construction by communities themselves. Liberation Theology supported this new type of autonomy of "social housing" in self-constructed popular neighborhoods.

During 1968–1985, urban movements in these neighborhoods organized a strong Latin American Coordination against mass repression. The influence of ideas of urban movements in the academic works is important:

- Turner (1976) recognizes the freedom of self-help housing and focuses on the element of self-management [15]. Finally, Habitat I, the first United Nations Conference on Human Settlements (1976), accepted self-help housing practices as a possible response to accelerated urbanization.
- From a populist approach, the so called "commodification debate" proposes the regularization of the urban situation of informal settlements and the transformation of their inhabitants to smallholders.
- Neo-Marxist approaches are very critical to understanding self-help construction practices, and the support that this process produced: that is, the manipulation through debt and the illusionary adoption of a middle-class ideology (*embourgeoisement*) by inhabitants. Emilio Pradilla Cobos [16] and Rod Burgess [17] see the limits of this urban process and propose a national housing politics controlled by the working class.
- On the contrary, Turner [18] proposes the idea of self-help social housing (in HABITAT II) and the organized self-management of neighborhoods. "Turner's central thesis argued that housing is best provided and managed by those who are to dwell in it rather than being centrally administered by the state" [19].

In Latin America, the neoliberal policy of the Chicago School (Freedman) officially began with the Chilean and Argentinean dictatorships. After the dictatorships' fall and the crises in the mid-1980s, the policy of commercial and political integration was implemented by the International Monetary Fund (IMF), the World Bank, and other mechanisms of transnational actors. These institutions have implemented the 10 neoliberal guidelines of the so-called "Washington Consensus" (a concept introduced by economist John Williamson in 1989). Harvey's concept of "accumulation by dispossession" constitutes a critical approach to this neoliberal proposition [20]. In 2001, the Argentinean crisis led to the questioning of this model [21]. Revolts and regime change in Bolivia, Ecuador, and Venezuela have contradicted these directions [22], whereas progressive Brazilian governments have not substantially disputed them [23]. In the same period, World Bank policies followed the following directives:

- In the 1980s, World Bank proposed a sort of "laissez faire" urbanization with essential support being provided directly to the inhabitants, through microcredit loans, programs administered by nongovernmental organizations (NGOs), or local government funding, mostly without an urban plan. The populist politics of many Latin American parties regarding cities were both the basis of this proposition and accelerated the process of informal (but not self-managed) settlement construction.
- In 2003, the World Bank and the Inter-American Development Bank proposed the liberalization of land markets that, they claimed, could "reshuffle roles of public and private sectors" [24,25]. This was a newer neoliberal politics that clearly abandoned any state support of "social housing".

In reality, the contemporary global crisis of the capitalist system has led to a new situation of mass deprivation and devaluation through which entire populations are converted into "impoverished masses" [26], which usually reside on the outskirts or interiors of cities, as in urban slums, and in remote rural areas. Attempts to control the masses are not new; yet, modern methods, developed through new technologies, have introduced transformations in the control process. After the destruction of the Twin Towers in New York (September 2001), neoliberal policies have been complemented by totalitarian biopolitical control policies. The so-called preventative control practices and the interventions by special army forces that were initially adopted in United States cities (especially in ghetto and meta-ghetto areas [3]) were then generalized throughout the globe, especially in the self-constructed popular neighborhoods. Thereafter, through mass media propaganda, these same neighborhoods have been criminalized, throughout Latin America, particularly in Colombian, Chilean, and Brazilian cities.

Despite the repression, self-help construction and self-management processes continue ([27], p. 217). Many urban social struggles change the everyday conditions of life in these neighborhoods. During 1990s, and contrary to the "culture of poverty", a "culture of resistance" has been developed, created at the core of social movements and of collective life. This "culture of resistance"—influenced by various radical artistic movements [28]—becomes of particular importance in the era of globalization [29].

> "Understanding the evolution of these neighbourhoods requires a dialectical linking of their internal processes with the historical development of their country and region, as well as with international processes that variously favoured or limited their development. These neighbourhoods keep changing all the time (visually as 'landscapes', economically, socially, and culturally), but also include several elements of a 'tradition of rebellion' or of 'servitude' that marked their emergence. So, they often figure in our minds as an allegory: how we talk about them and what we take them to mean depends on what we are looking for. In fact, their description is basically related to their landscape: small simple houses on small land parcels with unpaved roads made without the necessary infrastructure. It is a landscape that changes at different rates depending on the intervention of social movements, the state, or, in most cases, the solidarity among families" (Petropoulou [5], pp. 816–826).

This process of construction, except for its first stage, is not totally "spontaneous"; today, these settlements constitute an organic part of the city, with two or even three-story houses, retail and basic social services, and social diversity (comprising poor and lower-middle class people of different ethnicities). For all the above-mentioned reasons I define these neighborhoods as "settlements of spontaneous origin" [5], or self-constructed popular neighborhoods.

In this text, the term "auto or self-constructed popular neighborhoods" is chosen (the translation of the term used in the Spanish-language literature, "autoconstrucción popular"), and refers to the construction of neighborhoods in a collaborative way, which are not just single-family residences). I prefer this to the term "self-help housing" (from the Anglophone literature) because the latter is more individualistic (and reflects a colonial perspective; for a critique of colonialist philosophy see: Dussel [30]), referring to the type of housing rather than the resident himself. Moreover, it does not immediately refer to the construction of a neighborhood by a community.

This work focuses on "self-constructed popular neighborhoods" in neighborhoods that have a "tradition of rebellion" (see: Damianakos, definition [31]) and in which the important contributions of urban social movements transformed the significations of the landscape. It is important to understand that the inhabitants of these districts are not only poor; they are mainly those of the poor and the newly impoverished middle classes who refuse to live in blind obedience.

In all cases of organized squatting by urban social movements I prefer to use the definition "communally constructed neighborhoods" or "squatting and neighborhoods' construction by communities themselves". That is the cases of MTST in Sao Paulo, Francisco Villa, UPREZ and Assamblea de Barrios in Mexico City and other urban social movements and organizations in different Latin American cities.

3. From "Urban and Regional Social Movements" to "Urban and Regional Societies in Movement": Contributions in the Transformation of Aspects of the Habitus

According to Manuel Castells, urban *social* movements differ from simple urban movements in that the former can change the signification of urban space. Urban social movements are "vehicles of urban-spatial processing", or social movements which, opposing the "meaning" of a given spatial structure, create experiences of new "urban functions" and new "forms" [6]. These movements differ from the mobilizations of citizens who are organized around particular issues. When urban movements consciously construct "the rethinking of urban signification" they become "urban social movements"; today, they are part of what Wallerstein defines as "new social movements" [32].

Contemporary social (urban and regional) movements have a deeper role than previous simple urban movements, because they reinvent the values of freedom, dignity, solidarity, and social rights, through various local groups and networks [33]. They reinvent the notion of the *common* and gradually build other collective values (Stavrides [34] and Petropoulou [35]). One of these values, "the right to the city" (Lefebvre [36]), includes all those people who have not officially been considered "citizens" in the past: immigrants, many autochthonous nations, women, and children, among others. Particularly in Latin American cities, where a long tradition of indigenous peoples' (first nations') rebellion exists, the right to the city possibly includes the right to the living well (*sumak kawsay*, *buen vivir*) of all living beings. As Harvey ([37], pp. 1–2) has pointed out, it is not the right to the existing city that is demanded, but the right to a future city. Contemporary urban social movements, then, do not only demand the right to the city but they seek to realize it now in everyday life, as in "nowtopias" (see: Carlsson C. and Manning F. definition [38]).

There are quite a few different approaches taken to analyzing the new characteristics of contemporary social movements and initiatives. Claudia Korol [39], Ana Esther Ceceña [40], and Ouviña H. [41] each defines the new social movements using the terms "popular movements" or "emancipators". In *Crack Capitalism*, Holloway [9] considers that these are "new different worlds". Zibechi [8] argues that there are no longer any social movements in the traditional sense of the term (following Tilly's definition of social movements) but rather "other worlds" or "societies in movement". Sitrin [42] broadly defines them as "societies on the move". Some authors refer to the "prefigurative politics" of movements under the influence of a neo-Gramsian approach (Ouviña [41]); others, from post-hegemonic perspectives, refer to their horizontal prefigurative politics (Kioupkiolis [43]; Cornish, Haaken, Moskovitz and Jackson [44]). Maeckelbergh argues that it "is not possible to separate out 'prefiguration' from 'other' forms of political activity" [45].

This research does not only deal with those collectives that, through a prefigurative politics, consider themselves to be the precursors of another society. This approach about new social movements is different of the Eurocentric approach of Donatella Della Porta and Mario Dianni [46]. In this study, the concept of "creative resistance" refers to all those collectivities that offer not only an anti-systemic logic—such as the new movements to which Wallerstein [32] refers that emerge after 1968; but, also, to those that express creative action in everyday life (Lefebvre [47], Vaneigem, [48]). "Here is the essential role of creative social resistance ... A society within society that is capable of overturning the existing models in the collective imagination" (Papi [49] and Varcarolis [50]).

The essence of this concept, is used, by some alternative groups [51], to describe social collectivities, and alternative urban and artistic practices related to "everyday life" [52]. The rhizomatic qualities of these creative resistances—and, in particular, the principles of connectivity, heterogeneity, multiplicity, non-signifying rupture, cartography, and decalcomania of the rhizome (Deleuze, Guattari notions [53])—can show how fluid identities are in "a constant state of flux owing to their permeability, creating new territories of engagement" ([54], p. 2). In this sense, the point of departure is not *rights* but *necessities* there is an everyday need to create places of free experimentation.

Is it possible to change aspects of *habitus* in an urban space? Let us further examine the concept of *habitus*, one of Pierre Bourdieu's fundamental contributions to sociology, and one of the key terms of his theoretical framework. By *habitus* Bourdieu implies the set of generative schemes from which subjects perceive the world and act on it. *Habitus* is the Aquinian and Boethian Latin translation of the Aristotelian concept of Ἕξις (*hexis*).

Habitus is defined as "a system of durable and transferable dispositions, structured structures predisposed to function as structuring structures", that integrates all past experiences and functions at all times as a structuring matrix of perceptions, judgments, and actions of agents facing a conjuncture or event, which they co-produce ([7], p. 178; [55]).

In this paper, I argue that, in the self-constructed popular neighborhoods, it is possible to change aspects of habitus through the construction of another way of thinking. These neighborhoods have a long history of rebellion, but this alone is not enough: it is possible to change aspects of habitus if "creative resistances" enacted in these neighborhoods are connected with "other worlds in movement" and "new global social movements". I suggest that this process can change the both the self-image of the neighborhood and contribute to its decriminalization by its exterior. In many historical instances we encounter "heroic neighborhoods" that were once "stigmatized neighborhoods".

In the following section, I present three examples, drawn from areas of Mexico City, La Paz–El Alto, and Buenos Aires. These regions have been selected because they feature a long tradition of presence in social resistances and movements. That is, these regions have been characterized by the participation of their inhabitants in struggles, whether over local issues, or over political or labor issues, or over issues of feminist rights; hence, they have a "tradition of rebellion" (see Damianakos' definition: [31]). These political traditions are related to oppressed social strata, which have been marginalized due to their various "unruly" cultural practices; from the point of view of the dominant system, they are "dangerous classes" (see Hobsbawm's definition: [56], p. 82). In this text I do not explore the influences of tradition of rebellion in popular culture. This is the theme of another text (forthcoming).

4. Methodology and Selected Areas of Study

This paper results from a larger research project realized in various Latin American cities in 2015–2017, using oral and videotaped open-ended interviews. The participants have been assigned pseudonyms to maintain their anonymity, except in cases where they themselves requested to be eponymous in the research.

4.1. Interviews and Participate Observation

For the purposes of this research, I selected districts with a tradition of rebellion. The interviews focused on collectives that create "commons" in public space. Some of them share a different lifestyle, a decolonial perception of life, and various practices through which they attempt to create new worlds beyond and outside the capitalist system of production, human exploitation, and ecological disaster. Based on the above characteristics, the following city areas were selected:

- The municipality of El Alto in the Metropolitan Area of La Paz and in particular the districts of Ceja and Villa Ingenio.
- The southern district of Buenos Aires (in particular the neighborhoods of Villa 1-11-14, Villa 21-24, Zavaleta, Villa Soldati, Bajo Flores, Nueva Pompeya, Este Baracas), in Greater Buenos Aires.
- The Ciudad Nezahualcóyotl Municipality in the Metropolitan Area of Mexico City, and in particular the Flores neighborhood.

In the Metropolitan Area of La Paz–El Alto, the neighborhoods of Villa Ingenio (in construction), Villa Dolores and Ceja (formerly central mid-urbanized neighborhoods of popular architecture now combined with low-rise buildings), I interviewed members of FEJUVE (Federación de Juntas Vecinales); ALBOR popular theatre; "Confederación Sindical Única de Trabajadores Campesinos de Bolivia"; a researcher at "Centro de Documentación e Información de Bolivia"; as well as three professors and three students of the National University of Bolivia.

In the Metropolitan Area of Buenos Aires, I interviewed members of Chilavert (a historical, recuperated factory with an important relation to the district of Nueva Pompeya); members of

"Pañuelos en Rebeldía" (the historical Cultural Centre Pompeya—"Universidad Popular Madres de Plaza de Mayo" in the same district); and members of some of the major organizations operating in Villas and participating in Carpa Villera: "Frente Popular Darío Santillán", "Movimiento Popular La Dignidad", "La Poderosa". The last two organizations participate in CETEP. Members of these organizations also participate in CVI. More specifically, the interviews were carried out in statistical units C1, C4, C7 and C8 of INDEC, 2010 [57].

In South Grande Buenos Aires in Villa 21-24 and near Dario-Maxi (Avellaneda) train-station, I interviewed two teachers from the self-administrated state-owned Lyceum, which follows Paulo Freire's principles; two workers from the self-managed Polo Textil cooperative; four members of self-managed collective kitchens, recycling centers, and Club Popular El Dari (a youth cultural center); and two representatives from a hip-hop group and a graffiti crew with which they collaborate in various actions.

In Bajo Flores, Villa Soldati and Nueva Pompeya (South City of Buenos Aires), I interviewed members from two recuperated factories and cultural centers; one social clinic to Villa 1-11-14; the CVI [58] fire-fighting team; the waste collection and sewer cleaning team; the education and political discussion group of CVI; the popular theatre and the collective kitchen in the same Villa. In Villa 31 (C1 unity near the port of Buenos Aires), I interviewed a teacher, a nurse, and a solidarity artist. Various publications in the "La Garganta Poderosa" magazine, the website and a video related to the everyday living conditions in Villa were used as well [11].

In the Metropolitan Area of Mexico, I interviewed members of historical urban movements, such as: Unión Popular Revolucionaria Emiliano Zapata (UPREZ), Asamblea de Barrios (2 different groups) and Francisco Villa (3 different groups) and political alternative groups of artists, poets and teachers participating in social movements.

In the neighborhoods of Maravillas, Flores and Benito Juárez of the Ciudad Nezahualcóyotl (a self-constructed district in the Metropolitan Area of Mexico City, where in 2015 according to INEGI, inhabitants numbered 1,040,000) interviews were conducted with 3 members of "poets under construction" as well as with 2 mural artists; 2 members of cultural Nahuatl groups; 2 representatives of cultural centers; one journalist in a local cultural newspaper; and 3 students and teachers of the school and the University of UPREZ. I also used participatory research methods and conducted interviews in the "El Molino de Iztapalapa" neighborhood, and "Santo Domingo de Coyoacán" in Mexico City (In this paper, I use complementary information from interviews and participatory research in Coyoacán and Iztapalapa: in Santo Domingo Coyoacán, I interviewed members of the Zapata School and the "Centro de Artes y Oficios Emiliano Zapata" and in El Molino de Iztapalapa district (a district that has been built to its greatest extent by urban movements organizations through the three-stage process of occupation, legalization, and construction), I interviewed 2 members of UPREZ and 3 of Francisco Villa (three of its subdivisions) as well as 3 members of community cooperative gardens and several residents (see [59]).

4.2. Organization of Interviews

To analyze the image of the Municipality of El Alto, Nezahualcóyotl, South of Buenos Aires, presented through the press and Internet, two newspapers were explored for each local website, as well as hashtags on social networks, and studies presenting the social construction of the image of the above districts or municipalities. Finally, a review of the secondary literature was conducted in 4 languages (Spanish, English, French, and Greek).

Interviewees were selected through social networks to find those who would like to talk about the actions of their collectives in videotaped interviews. Where this was not possible, the research remained at the level of participatory responsive observation [60] with the agreement of the respondents. The key questions raised in open interviews, and which emerged in the narrations of research participants are summarized below:

- Presentation of the history of the land question, self-help neighborhood, urban and social history and of the collectives' or urban movements' main goals and history.
- Location of collective, its relationship with the neighborhood, its relationship with other collectives of the similar or divergent thematic foci, and participation in networks at local, national, and international levels.
- Issues of housing, environment, health, nutrition, social welfare, education, and culture.
- Presentation of the key activities in organizational processes and the way in which decisions are taken (participatory or representative democracy, or otherwise); the role of women in the organization and its actions.
- Presentation of key issues of discrimination against and criminalization of neighborhood residents.
- Presentations of the actions taken to overturn the image of these neighborhoods given by dominant mass media.
- A critical presentation of the major social struggles in which the collectives participated and their outcomes today.
- A few words about the contribution of the arts to "poetic movements" through actions that change their everyday life: theatre, poetry, visual arts, music, cinema, and dance (among others).

Questions raised by the open interviews:

- Presentation of collectives' relationships with worker-occupied "recuperated factories", the alternative education system (inspired by Paulo Freire and other thinkers); indigenous and feminist movements; anti-mining movements; and movements against hydroelectric plants, oil factories, and major infrastructural projects.
- Presentation of their relationship with other major contemporary revolutionary movements (such as the Zapatistas), Latin American social revolutions (in Cuba, Bolivia, and elsewhere), as well as with progressive governments in Latin America.
- Theoretical issues, such as: How do community members construct, and how does the collective perceive the concepts of the "commons" and of "buen vivir"? Do they consider creating prefigurative models for another society? If so, how does this happen?

5. First Comparative Approach

Most of the movements discussed in the present study were created out of necessity to meet basic daily needs and then became politicized. While in the 1960s left (mainly Maoist, Trotskyist, or Anarchist/Libertarian) political organizations created collectives, which they aspired to turn into urban movements, after 1968, new movements seem to emerge in these neighborhoods, and then, leftist collectives attempted to find a role in the emerging new movements. Since 1989, with the beginning of neo-liberalism and the collapse of the so-called socialist bloc, these organizations have been undergoing a crisis. New subjects appear to have emerged mainly from anarchist politics, the indigenous movement, and the anti-patriarchal, anti-capitalist feminist movement. Major movements are born, experimenting with horizontal and vertical hierarchy structures, which, while seeming to overcome traditional left wing and anarchist organizations, nevertheless act within them but without being able to control them. On the contrary, a series of changes in the daily lives of participants in contemporary movements seem to have started to influence the discourse and practices of both political organizations and anarchist collectives.

Neoliberal politics, since

- 1985 in Bolivia (with the intervention of the IMF and the liberalization of the economy that rendered El Alto as a "city in alert" in 1990 [61]);
- 1986 in Mexico (following the admission of Mexico in the General Agreement on Tariffs and Trade, the liberalization of economy, and the intervention of the IMF and World Bank);

- 1989 in Argentina (with the intervention of the IMF and the realization of directives of the *Washington Consensus*).

In combination with the political disorganization of leftist groups (following the decline of the "socialist bloc" 1989); the Zapatista movement starting in 1994; and the mass social movements in Argentina, Bolivia, and Mexico during 2001–2006 produced a new politicization of urban movements that questioned the role of leftist parties and their strict, hierarchical structures. The role of women and indigenous peoples within urban movements gradually became important. The processes through which urban social movements were and continue to be created in the above-mentioned three Latin American cities—and, in particular, in some of their most characteristic self-constructed popular neighborhoods—is presented below.

5.1. Urban Movements and Self-Constructed Popular Neighbourhoods in Mexico City

We can distinguish certain important periods in the development of Mexico City's self-constructed popular neighborhoods, and urban movements, considering the internal structure of and the political situation in the country.

From the beginning of the 20th century until 1914, Mexico City was a "bourgeois city" and then, a modern city, but only for its oligarchic class. After the social revolution of 1910, the 1919 and 1923 assassinations of Zapata and Villa respectively, and the 1928 decision to concentrate local power in the federal state, until 1934, the city was in disorder. The Revolution (1910–1920), and Mexica, Zapotec, Mixtec, and Maya revolts (among others), create an important tradition of rebellion in everyday life.

The period between 1934 (when Lázaro Cárdenas became President of the Mexican state) and 2 October 1968 (when the Tlatelolco massacre occurred in the center of Mexico City [62]) saw a boom in urban development, and the emergence of small and dispersed urban movements. The role of the working class was important in this transformation. In this period, self-constructed popular neighborhoods multiply; but these slums remain invisible both in maps and in social policy and legislation. Mexico City may be "a city for all", but at the same time it remains, to a large extent, socially and spatially segregated [63,64].

In Greater Mexico City, between 1968 and 1988, we observe the creation, prosperity, and decline (1968–1980) of MUP (Urban Popular Movement) and CONAMUP (National Coordination of Urban Popular Movements, 1980–1988), and, similarly, the decline of the independent, radical, and politicized urban popular movement [65]. Although strictly speaking, not living under dictatorship, Mexicans face severe daily repression. After the 1968 revolt, many students, together with older activists started participating in urban movements. The fusion of urban movements with students' movements produced alternative cultural spaces [29] such as "Escuelita Zapata de Santo Domingo Coyoacán" and many more. During the six years of Luis Echeverría's presidency (1970–1976), the Mexican state undertook profound urban reforms [66,67]. During this period, habitants from Mexico City arrived in Nezahualcóyotl. The first political and cultural interventions in popular neighborhoods began to change habitus and produced the first urban cultures of resistance. In 1969, we observe the first urban movement "Movimiento Restaurador de Colonos (MRC)" in Nezahualcóyotl for political reasons related to the interests of the fractionators. The Nezahualcóyotl municipality administratively belongs to the State of Mexico, created in 1945 and officially in 1963 (Secretaría de Gobernación, 1999). The inhabitants of this municipality at the beginning came from the southern regions (Oaxaca, Chiapas, Guerrero, Michoacán) and from other municipalities and from the United States (rejected from the "Bracero program"), and in 1971, the "strike of payments," in which 200,000 residents participated. This movement "represented a new type of movement and responded to the open political opportunity of the 1968 student movement" [68]; it squatted land to construct schools and markets. It created a system of collective transportation, 10 productive cooperatives, and then started "regularizing" the situation of the neighborhood. The movement was weakened by severe repression and internal divisions. In 1975, in Ciudad Nezahualcóyotl, a new stage began in the history of popular urban movements, with the contribution of leftist groups. Liberation Theology has had an important role in the self-help neighborhoods (barrios).

The decade 1975–1985 was the period of squatting repression. The financial crisis of 1982–1985 (with the revalorization of the *peso* and the nationalization of different enterprises), followed by the big earthquake of 1985 in Mexico City have the effect of multiplying collectives and urban movements [69]. The political organizations of the radical left and other independent groups played an important role in the construction of a dignified life in the city (e.g., alternative schools, canteens, local buses, etc.). Urban popular movements such as "Unión Popular Revolucionar Emiliano Zapata", "Asamblea de Barrios, Unión Popular Francisco Villa" and many more, played an important role in newly communally constructed neighborhoods, along with the contributions of students and architects [29,69]. At the same time, the anarcho-punk scene, inspired by the movements of 1968, came to the fore [70].

Starting in 1986, neoliberal politics [66] in combination with the political intervention of leftist groups have the effect of politicizing of urban movements, yet function with strict, hierarchical structures. Although the role of women and first nations or indigenous peoples' role was important, they themselves and their ideas lacked visibility. In 1988, many urban movements in the Greater Mexico City decided to support the Party of the Democratic Revolution (PRD) and the Labor Party (PT); those movements were transformed into interlocutors with local governments.

Between 1994 and 2006, many divisions were created—and, therefore, much frustration—within various urban movements, because of the participation of their members in different political parties. Economic integration initiated by the North American Free Trade Agreement (NAFTA) in 1993, and the financial crisis of 1994 ("efecto tequila") change the situation of many urban movements. Beginning in 1994, the gradual influence of the ideas of the Zapatista movement (EZLN) on these movements has led them to reconsider issues of autonomy from political parties, and to reposition women's, indigenous, and ecological issues, as well as to experiment with participatory democracy. Parts of such movements have become independent through the creation of new structures; but it is only after 2006 that these ideas have become really important within these movements as a whole.

Since 2006, in the periphery of Greater Mexico City, urban fragmentation and self-help housing are still in progress; although the new legislation is very strict in the interior of the Mexico City (CDMX) (called Federal District DF before 2006) it is not so in all of the Metropolitan Area of Mexico City (AMCM) [71]. The role of narcotics traffickers in traditionally working class neighborhoods has become important. Many homeless people have appeared in the center of the city and have tried to organize politically. During the same period, urban and regional movements have become social movements or "societies in movement" such as the Atenco movement (2006) and the Oaxaca Commune (2006). Liberation Theology does not appear to have an important role among young people active within these movements, which was not the case for other movements such as "The Movement for Peace with Justice and Dignity"; however, indigenous cultural traditions do have an important cultural influence. After their continual repression, newer movements such as "Yo Soy 132" and "Ayotzinapa", as well as many new collectives have emerged in traditional self-help housing *barrios*. These have changed the discourse to include issues related to anti-patriarchal ideas, indigenous cultures, the concept of *buen vivir*, etc. Small cultural initiatives (such as "poets in construction", SECOS, muralists, "Neza Arte Aca" and musicians among others) play a very important role in the process of habitus change and therefore could be considered as "creative resistances" within a "tradition of rebellion".

> "In Nezahualcóyotl we live in circumstances of everyday persecution of young women and considered 'different' young people, and of a systematic depreciation of cultural origins, as well." says Maria [72] (muralist, research participant).

> "With public community-level intervention using mural art, we change the identity of the place and we reclaim the space. Art is not for the museum but for the public space. In a deeper sense, all the people are artists." says Martín Cuaya [73] (muralist, research participant).

5.2. Urban Movements and Self-Constructed Popular Neighbourhoods in La Paz–El Alto

We can distinguish various distinctive periods of development of self-constructed popular neighborhoods, and of urban movements in the Metropolitan Area of La Paz.

At the beginning of the 20th century, La Paz was first the colonial city, and afterward, the modern city of conquerors who dominated the mainly indigenous region. However, the Aymara revolution (such as the siege of La Paz by Túpaj Katari, Bartolina Sisa, and Gregoria Apaza in 1781), the revolution of 1952 and the 1953 rural reforms, bequeathed an important tradition of rebellion to everyday life that has affected the city and has left its mark on new urban landscapes.

The years 1953–1964 saw extensive urbanization, with large migratory flows from the provinces to the capital. The legislative framework related to town planning issues in the peri-urban area of the city was more tolerant toward or did not deal with the issues of the out-of-town building design. In this period, the El Alto Municipality was being built, next to La Paz; the Consejo Central de Vecinos (The Central Council of Neighbors) was officially created in El Alto in 1957.

During the dictatorships (1964–1982), a second wave of immigration took place. Faced with the rise in housing prices in La Paz city center, and under intense political pressure, new city residents, as well as former miners (who, having struggled intensely, were persecuted in 1967, at the same time that Che Guevara was assassinated by the CIA) from the surrounding areas settle in El Alto while commuting to work in the city of La Paz. For this reason, some writers refer to El Alto as the "worker's dormitory city" (Paula Diaz, 2016). In 1960–1970, only a few small demonstrations of urban movements occurred, since the authoritarian political regime did not allow any protests. The inhabitants of the working class neighborhoods actively participated in the 1979–1980 uprisings against the dictatorship. The first Assembly of "Federación de Juntas Vecinales de El Alto" named "FEJUVE–El Alto" was formed in 1979. Their mode of organization is based on the Aymara/Quechua concept of "Ayllu", an Aymara/Quechua word that refers to a "collective process" and "territoriality", is a pre-colonial structure that characterizes many pre-Columbian peoples' participatory democracies—to put it in our own terms—underlying the so-called "micro-governments" [74] that played an important role in the water and gas wars in Bolivia, and in many uprisings in Peru and in Ecuador. "Ayllu" was a means of organization rather than a solely spatial unity in the Inca Empire. According to Prada [75], it has ancient roots in the green revolution in the Andes, when the inhabitants began the systematic cultivation of certain plants, changing the very structures of society itself. The rotation of community representatives and of power, which obey the instructions of the community relates to a structural feature of the society: the availability of labor power and the need to rotate it through various tasks [75]. Contemporary Ayllus have created structured structures (as Bourdieu would say) in the broader Bolivian society (not exclusively in Aymara/Quechua communities) on which the tradition of rebellion is based (as Damianakos [31] would say).

Between 1982 and 1985, Bolivia undertook the restoration of democracy. Nationalization of public utilities (water, gas, oil, and certain mines) progressed rapidly. At the same time, the pressure for democratic representation and the creation of a separate municipality in El Alto was extensive; until 1985, its inhabitants had representation in the municipality, while in 1989 El Alto was institutionalized as a separate municipality and "juntas vecinales" acquired more powers. In the years 1985–1989, the situation was changing rapidly within the context of the economic crisis, which laid the ground for the IMF's intervention.

In 1989–2003 neoliberal development models were applied, starting with the IMF's intervention in 1989, and the implementation of the Washington Consensus Guidelines until the crisis in 2001, which ended with the 2003 uprisings. The period was characterized by the generation of the first new forms of self-organized struggles in working class neighborhoods. In the following period, occupations were multiplied, to meet the urgent housing needs of the unemployed, poor social strata.

FEJUVE-El Alto preserved its autonomy from political parties, organizing a large urban social movement in 1987; although it had a limited role in the "Black February" uprising of 2003, it played a very important role in the so-called "Gas War" or "Red October" of 2003 (see [75,76]). Since 2006, the integration of certain members of FEJUVE in different political parties possibly produced the basis for a division in the movement. Part of this Assembly became an interlocutor of local government, while another part kept a critical, radical point of view.

The "Gas War", or "Red October", was characterized by mass barricades, collective kitchens, and celebrations, as well as conflicts in many areas of El Alto city (see [75,76]). This mode of simultaneous action in many different places has been named by Zibechi as a "multiplicidad" of "society in movement" [8]; it is a mode of action leading to the dispersal of state power [77], not to its renewed establishment, or as Gutiérrez Aguilar R. would say, "disorganization" [78].

From 2006 to the present time, the so-called progressive government favored the strengthening of small businesses, the formation of a new middle class, and massive urban development; these processes brought great changes in the structure of urban movements and in the coordination of "juntas vecinales".

The city extends to the archaeological site Tiwanaku (capital of old empire of Tawantinsuyu) and to Lake Titicaca, without urban planning; rather, houses built with columns of "reinforced concrete" and sometimes using special designs inspired by Aymara traditions, challenge the European architectural tradition.

El Alto is currently inhabited by 650,000 habitants (INE, 2012) and is characterized by significant social diversity. Mariela Paula, [61] questions the academic and official hegemonic discourse on the presumed homogeneity of the city of El Alto.

Fourteen years after Red October, the goals of social struggles are interpreted differently: the current representatives of the Movement for Socialism (MAS) consider them to have been fulfilled, insisting that only the nationalization of water and gas constituted the core demand of the October 2003 struggles. On the other hand, those holding a critical leftist perspective believe that the goals of Red October have not been fulfilled. Mirko Orgáz [79] and other authors agree that only part of the nationalization program has been completed. As Fernando, an interviewed representative of FEJUVE–El Alto, says:

"We are struggling to implement the October agreements. We made these deals because we had no confidence in any representative who could then change political position." [80].

Thus, although the big structures have become almost entirely fragmented, many smaller structures involving young people have emerged, especially in the fields of art and culture, feminism, ecology, and indigenous culture, which can be considered as "creative resistances" with a "tradition of rebellion". A typical example of new collective actions that change everyday *habitus* is the "Theatre of the Oppressed" and the "ALBOR Theatre", in operation since 1997.

"We have been living hunted for many years now. Our life was constantly under persecution" . . .
"We had something to do to talk about our values, and our heroes such as Bartolina Sisa and Túpaj Katari" . . . "Faced with such a situation we began an effort through poetry. We went out to the squares, reading poems, playing music, trying to show that it is possible to sing, dream, to publicly expose a new culture of young people through poetry and other arts" says Willy Flores [81] (ALBOR theatre [82]).

5.3. Urban Movements and Self-Constructed Popular Neighbourhoods in Greater Buenos Aires

We can distinguish distinctive periods of development of self-constructed popular neighborhoods and of urban social movements in the Metropolitan Area of Buenos Aires, and, in particular, in South Buenos Aires. The first period is from the beginning of the 20th century until 1946. This period can be divided into two major sub-periods: city-capital (1880–1916) and modern city (1916–1946), in which there is still no discussion of self-constructed popular neighborhoods outside of the urban plan, despite the fact that they exist (e.g., near the port and in *Retiro*). These areas are inhabited by many rural European immigrants, many of whom lived in the so-called *conventillos*, or tenements, while poor people lived in the first villas. In the 1910s and 1920s, a new tradition of rebellion was being developed in the city, directly related to workers' movements and to those of the so-called lumpen-proletariat; it is expressed in many forms of art such as tango [83]. Between 1930 and 1943—the Infamous Decade ("Década Infame") comprising the first dictatorship and fraudulent democracy, industry was growing rapidly, the migratory flows from Europe were multiplying, and the city was expanding and modernizing; yet, at the same time many self-constructed popular neighborhoods ("villas miserias", "barrios precarious") are inhabited by those workers who, through their labor, "build" the bourgeois city. After the great strike of 17 October 1945, with the participation of workers and inhabitants of working class neighborhoods of South Buenos Aires, "a new political stage is opened, with new social actors. Since then, the labor movement will intervene permanently in the process" ([84], p. 30).

Between 1946 and 1955 (during government of Juan Perón, which supported trade unions), the first discussions of opening the city to the poor, and creating social services began, but these remained unfinished.

The period from 1956 to 1976 is one of continual alternation between dictatorial and democratic governments. This period of great urbanization is characterized by large migratory flows from rural areas, but also from Europe to Buenos Aires. In 1956, about 33,900 residents lived in the villas; by 1976 they numbered 218,000 ([85], p. 76). At that time, the socio-spatial segregation of the city was intensified, and the anti-communist organization regularly attacked the slums (such as the 1974 assassination of Carlos Mujica in Villa Luro).

Even though the 1968 uprisings in Europe and America found Argentina in a period of dictatorship (1966–1973), in May of 1969, large labor and student struggles broke out in Cordoba, [86] Rosario, Neuquén and other cities (such as Cordobazo, Rosariazo and Neuquenazo). "The consequences of the Cordobazo would be glimpsed with the more solid development of a combative current, whose aim was not only the confrontation with the employers but with the traditional union leaderships linked to Peronism" ([84], p. 58). These struggles (coupled with the development of Liberation Theology) have decisively influenced the development of urban movements in working class neighborhoods, particularly in the Buenos Aires [87] villas, where many social resistances developed, demanding the legal recognition of neighborhoods and the provision of social benefits. In addition, in the slums, many members of the movement of the Peronists, the Montoneros (PJ) and the Trotskyist—Guevarist "Ejercito Revolucionario del Pueblo" (ERP-Partido Revolucionario de Trabajadores) acted. All these struggles contributed to the overthrow of the dictatorship in 1973, and to the establishment of a culture of rebellion in the city (e.g., sixties rock scene, theatre, cinema, etc.) [88]—particularly in the peripheral neighborhoods. However, according to my interviews, despite the new ideas coming from Cordobazo, the structures remained highly hierarchical; ecological and indigenous issues were not discussed; women's role, although considered important, was not recognized outwardly, and religion continued to have a dominant say.

The period of the dictatorship from 1976–1983, marked by the U.S. Central Intelligence Agency and IMF's support for Operation Condor, is a dark one: 22,000 people were assassinated and 30,000 were disappeared. It was particularly tough for the city's neighborhoods, as many persecuted militants were involved in the anti-dictatorial struggle. The organization of the World Cup in Argentina in 1978 gave the authorities a good opportunity for their first attempts to criminalize the villas—in particular, villa 31, which was the closest to the city center and the port. Nevertheless, the most important politicized occupations of land by homeless people seem to have started in 1981, under very difficult circumstances that led to the murder of militants. At the same time, the labor movement, as well as the movement of mothers and grandmothers of missing children (Madres de la Plaza del Mayo) were developing. All these struggles, in combination with the Falklands (Malvinas) War (1982) helped to overthrow the dictatorship in 1983.

The post-dictatorial period from 1983 to 1989 is characterized by the demarcation and restriction of villas, while at the same time a densification and a vertical development in the interior of already existing villas from two-story to four-story buildings (with or without mechanical design) take place.

At that time, urbanization policies are promised, but not delivered. Many political exiles returned to Buenos Aires. Until 2003, there was still impunity for those who committed crimes against humanity while following orders ("Leyes de impunidad").

Since 1989, with the intervention of the IMF and following the directives of the Washington Consensus, a neoliberal policy has been implemented. Between 1991 and 2001, based on census data, socio-spatial segregation was intensifying; the city was becoming increasingly polarized, with the poorest living in the South of Buenos Aires ([89], p. 21, chart). Unemployment reached 15%, work in the informal economy accounted for almost one half of all salaries, and poverty reached 40%. The villas were increasingly occupied by impoverished social strata, although many of them (the oldest) maintain mixed socio-economic characteristics.

Since 1992, young people have begun attempts of social self-organization based on horizontal structures and have thus started challenging the hierarchical and patriarchal relationships of the family and the church by participating in new struggles [90]. In 1996 the "piqueteros" movement, born in Neuquén, Salta, Cordoba, and Matanzas [91]. This movement was generalized during the 2001–2003 Great Depression by unemployed people, students and residents of the poor neighborhoods of the district of the cities that made more than 4000 pickets: closing roads with self-organized structures, assemblies, food, cultural actions, etc.. The stigmatization-criminalization of this movement by the mass media did not undermine its influence in the popular neighborhoods. These struggles culminated in the 2001 rebellion in Buenos Aires and in other cities, which involved mostly unemployed young people and students from working class neighborhoods.

The traditional left initially had a critical attitude in relation to this movement, since it considered it to be of a "marginal lumpen-proletariat"; later, however, the traditional left became involved in it. As a matter of fact, as the left became more and more involved in the "piqueteros" movement, some of its components have changed radically, such as Movimiento Territorial Liberación (MTL) [92] and, especially, Movimiento de Trabajadores Desocupados (MTD) ([90], pp. 114–121), both of which claim to have adopted horizontal forms of organization. A significant part of the *piqueteros* is still organizing today, in movements that emerged from the 2001–2003 uprisings, and later participated in the cooperative organizations of the popular economy and on other fronts.

The period from 2003 to the present is characterized by an upsurge in the number of unemployed and redundant workers who are looking for housing without any social policy provisions. The new temporary self-housing "nuevos asentamientos" [85], which eventually turned into permanently degraded or impermanent residences. The recuperated factory and enterprises movement, (in which workers recover factories in bankruptcy, or those that have been abandoned or downgraded for various reasons) also characterizes this period. Some factory workers played an important role in neighborhood assemblies. A typical example is the recuperated Bauen Hotel in the city center (which hosted many assemblies and their members from the province), and the recuperated Chilavert printing factory. Recuperated factories multiplied, having reached 367 in May 2016 [93].

The change in government in 2003, and the prolonged dominance of the progressive Kirchner government did not seem to improve the conditions in these neighborhoods; rather, they became much more militarized. After several struggles (including a major hunger strike at Carpa Villera), some jobs were offered. In December 2010, hundreds of families renting small apartments in villas living in absolute poverty (many of them immigrants from Bolivia, Peru, and Paraguay) decided to occupy an area of 130 hectares in the "Parque Indoamericano", south of Buenos Aires. The police force of Mauricio Macri (mayor of Buenos Aires between 2007 and 2015 and the current Argentinian president) responded to this occupation with massive repression (resulting in 3 deaths); the families were incarcerated and maligned in the media. The need for co-ordination led to the decision to organize the coordinating body "Corriente Villera Independiente" (CVI) through a large assembly in May 2012 in the symbolic square of Plaza de Mayo. One of its most important actions to date was the 53-day hunger strike, which started on 21 April 2014 in the city center ([94], pp. 27–29), and in which women played a particularly important role ([95,96]). This movement became known as "Carpa

Villera". Following the hunger strike, the movement influenced the passage of the Social Emergency Law ("Ley de Emergencia Social").

Self-organized cooperatives of the popular economy and recovered factories operate largely in parallel, with the exception of meetings at conferences (for instance, the Economy of Workers International Gathering in 2017 (see VI International Gathering, http://laeconomiadelostrabajadores. wordpress.com/), or joint local actions. This process has been very severely hit by Mauricio Macri government: the non-implementation of commitments in the "Emergency Law"; the reprivatization of public goods; the stigmatization and militarization of villas. At the same time, the number of recovered factories increased, despite the government's efforts to stifle the alternative economy and criminalize their struggles [97]. Faced with this new government, new movements are emerging, and new alliances are being created among the multiple collectives that emerged in previous years.

Some of the major organizations operating in Villas and participating in Carpa Villera that members have been interviewed are "Frente Popular Darío Santillán"; "Movimiento Popular La Dignidad"; "La Poderosa". The last two organizations participate in CETEP, which brings together many organizations working in the popular economy. Their actions include running collective kitchens, local and alternative clinics, and people's cooperatives; constructing and maintaining housing; conducting urban planning consultations; cleaning; fire-fighting; and organizing cultural activities—including Theatre of the Oppressed, political hip hop, capoeira, reggae, anti-FIFA actions, as well as publishing activities and organizing alternative schools (following Paulo Freire's ideas [98]).

Thus, these collectives must certainly be considered as "creative resistances" with "tradition of rebellion". At the same time, many of the participants in these collectives either keep an intellectual search or are at least aware of the actions of major new Latin American movements—the Zapatistas, the MST and MTST movements, the ecological and indigenous movements, the "Guevaristas"-ALBA movement, the alter-globalization forums, the anarchist, ecological, and feminist movements, etc. There is, therefore, an osmosis of values occurring in everyday life, that slowly changes habits and habitus. Art contributes decisively to this process. However, this is an issue to be explored in a distinct article.

As Maria and Juan (hip-hop and graffiti creators, research participants) say:

> *"the politics of repression and violence (gatillo facil situation) produces an everyday fear for all the young inhabitants in 'popular neighborhoods' ... the solution is to organize ourselves on the path to understand our culture and our body. Art does not change the world, but art is a great companion in the struggle for this change ... Popular education is a way to self-educate as working class, young, free people where we all learn from all. Hip-hop has it as a tool for social change"* [99].

Radical hip-hop plays this role today as it is addressed to everyone, but especially to young people, who embrace it with their lifestyle and appearance.

6. Conclusions and Reflections

The self-constructed popular neighborhoods are districts that were initially ignored (up to 1950) and then integrated (during 1950–1960). Since the 1960s, they have been politically exploited to control people by means of customer relations and microcredit, thus attempting to prevent the emergence of radical movements and collectives within them. Nevertheless, so-called "dangerous" collectives have been created.

It is significant that, in almost all the cases I have examined, the areas under study are socially diverse and not socially homogeneous. They gather people from different regions, Indigenous Americans, mine workers, and young women, introducing to the communities the attitude of everyday autonomous or self-organized life.

Residents in many of these neighborhoods have found ways to meet their everyday needs through shared activities and a collective processes of commons creation (*commoning*); especially those who have been refugees are recreating their lives in the middle of ruins. Many of them have chosen these neighborhoods to have a chance to a dignified life and to enjoy greater freedom, compared to their prior social status.

When walking around these neighborhoods, there are few visible signs that show their history (such as some eco-landscape features); this history can be found only in the narratives of members of creatively insurgent collectives.

If, during the 20th century, there was a great debate about the so-called "communist threat"—because of the first social revolutions that ended with the oligarchical order (e.g., Mexico, 1910; Bolivia, 1952), socialist revolutions (e.g., Russia, 1917; China, 1949; Cuba, 1959; Nicaragua, 1979) and many other failed revolutions—nowadays governments implementing neoliberal policies are afraid of the so-called "self-organized threat": forms of social organization that do not have a command center, which could be manipulated directly or by biopolitical methods. Thus, they prepare their political audience for the repression of social movements by enhancing a vague fear of "difference" and try to prevent inhabitants' self-organization.

In all three Latin American cities in this study, many "creative resistances with a tradition of rebellion" exist, which relate to new movements (societies in movement); they make an important contribution to crack capitalism in everyday life and to slowly transforming the habitus. The rhizomatic way through which their ideas and actions are been propagated is fed by the aforementioned rebellious cultural-poetic actions that favor community and solidarity rather than deep hierarchical structures. Therefore, we could characterize them as "creative resistances" with a "tradition of rebellion" and a rhizomatic way of spreading. Their actions are based on the principles of direct democracy while taking advantage of complex activist practices to guard against malicious infiltration.

Therefore, my reflection, on the issue of what kind of elements could characterize the existence and actions of a network of creative resistances that could change the habitus, concludes with the following basic principles that question the existing dominant codes:

- Independence from political parties and private economic interests;
- Systematic presence through media;
- Openness and free interaction with other social movements and collectivities;
- Participatory Democracy and combination of "horizontality" with other forms of governance through the most immediate possible ways in the internal (anti-hierarchical) dynamics of these movements;
- Trade unionism from below, recuperation of the means of production;
- Cultivation of a different relation with the land and all life (eco-balanced living), ecological gardens, "pacha mama", "buen vivir";
- Contestation of mega-projects and the privatization of commons (mines, oil tankers, water, gas, etc.);
- Recognition of different gender relations, and a critical stance to patriarchy, (feminism, LGBTQ movement);
- Collective processes of commons creation (*commoning*);
- Use of a poetic language as a signifying practice;
- Practice of artistic actions that come from the heart of city's inhabitants and are not just ornamental;
- Interaction between local and global inspiration of creative actions (creative glocality);
- Understanding of "the other" difference. Respect for the different cultures and specifically for Indigenous and Afro-Indian culture;
- Acceptance of sensitivity as a drive not for condemnation but as a creative force of the social movement;
- Understanding of personal time as a special key to coexistence with the other;
- Encompassing rage—whether organized or not—but, if possible, in a poetic and creative way;
- Genuine relationship bonds in daily life and self-sufficiency to meet basic survival needs;
- Recognition that small everyday things play an important role.

All the above elements could be considered as implementing the general principles or basic drives of a "poetic social movement" [33,100].

The structures created in these neighborhoods are neither solely horizontal nor solely vertical. In most cases, these structures alternate. In emergency cases, they become highly hierarchical (military structures), while during peaceful periods, when there is requisite time, they implement horizontal decision-making.

As Sitrin argues drawing on Bourdieu, cultivating horizontalism is not just a matter of changing consciousness, but of undoing ingrained *habitus* through practice [42]. That people can do this is certainly inspiring. However, it also means that horizontalism cannot just spread like an infectious idea. It must become a practical context, as Sitrin points out, within some kind of autonomous territory, whether a factory, a communal kitchen, or behind a barricade.

From a decolonial point of view, through a study of ethno-territorial struggles in Latin America, Arturo Escobar [101] argues that the ontology of another way of thinking constitutes a defense strategy of relational worlds, and the knowledge developed in them, by communities and activists, embodies a far-sighted strategy for the perseverance and fostering of the *pluriverso*.

Finally, the most creative future-change seems to be the embodiment of the attitude "let us all be poets in the present" ([35], p. 570). A reflection on the potential of creating a poetic urban social movement within the space of self-constructed popular neighborhoods, and urban movements is presented in previews texts [33]. These places gave birth to many social movements and to a "culture of resistance" [28]. This reflection can be enriched by the study of actions and practices of various groups such as "Poets in construction" and "CECOS" in Nezahualcóyotl City (Mexico), Theatre ALBOR of El Alto and the Theatre of the Oppressed to the South of Buenos Aires, and their relationship with the neighborhood residents. These groups insist on the importance of constructing a neighborhood "cultural identity" (e.g., cultura Neza, cultura El Alto, etc.)—thereby questioning the mass media's image of the "barrio". This "cultural identity" is opposed to the official representation of "barrios" where the iconic stereotypical representations of 'barrio life' are produced for a white middle and high social class consumer public.

Can "creative resistances" build another way of thinking?

Based on Raúl Prado's approach, I argue that the answer to the above question depends on the "structure of the events" and on the degree of connectivity between "societies in movement" (see: Zibechi [77] and Sitrin [42]) and "creative resistances" in a very large process of "social movements in the everyday life" (see: Psimitis [102]). The poetic, as an important element of "societies in movement" and "creative resistances" as well, will play a crucial role in the making of such connectivity, as it can, over the years, change aspects of habitus. Due to the capitalist system, colonialism, and neo-colonialism, many poor people living in a perpetual banishment from rural or urban spaces (see: Roy [4]), internalize the condition of exclusion; they face difficulties in escaping this *habitus* of marginalization. Contemporary movements create new ways of life [42], and new politics in "new worlds" [77], out of this vicious condition of exclusion.

Holloway [9] notes the limits of Marxist theory on the comprehension of contemporary collectivities and proposes a new approach to understanding them: the process of *crack capitalism* coming to the fore through multiplication of anti-capitalist actions in everyday life. In this paper, I propose that this process of anti-capitalist actions in the everyday life can crack the biopolitical systemic sphere and perhaps change aspects of habitus—if this process relates to the tradition of rebellion and, at the same time, with "societies in movement", ideas of global anti-capitalist, anti-patriarchal, anti-colonial, and ecological movements.

In Mexico, the emergence of this process is visible in "societies in movement" such as the Zapatista movement in Chiapas (1994–present); also evident is their connectivity with a multiplicity of creative resistances and urban-regional and feminist movements such as Oaxaca [103], Atenco [104], Cheran (from 2006 and after). The influence of creative resistances and their contribution to questioning the stigmatization of popular peripheral *barrios* is very important.

In Argentina, the influence of *piqueteros* movement, of the factory recuperation movement and of many other urban and feminist movements contribute to a process through which dignity can emerge in the daily life of peripheral popular neighborhoods and villas; they also contribute to the creation of a multiplicity of creative resistances and "societies in movement" that profoundly question biopolitical state practices.

In Bolivia, the Cochabamba Water War and the Gas War in La Paz–El Alto changed the stigma of the "dangerous neighborhood" and proposed an alternative way of urbanization based on the Aymara/Quechua concept of *Ayllu* (as we have seen, an indigenous mode of organization based on autonomous local assemblies)—therefore becoming actually dangerous for the elite state authorities. During the periods of uprisings, the United States Agency for International Development (USAID) stated it considers the Assembly of "Juntas de Vecinos de Bolivia en El Alto" ("FEJUVE–El Alto") a terrorist organization due to the organizing practice of *Ayllu*. This, combined with other actions, led to USAID's withdrawal from the region in 2009 at the request of the Morales government. It proposed state intervention, along with the institutionalization of local assemblies and strict control of social structures, combined with some improvement in living conditions for at least some social strata [105].

Hence, the important role of *Ayllu* to cracking capitalism in everyday life, and to gradually changing the habitus is clearly revealed. Raúl Prada Alcoreza highlights this process: "The place we are talking about is then the social organization. Not the social structure of Émile Durkheim, but the organization, that is to say, the disposition, the order, the articulation of the social form With Gilles Deleuze and Felix Guattari, we would say, the abstract machine" ([75], p. 22) in a assemblage—agencement). *The definition of the French word agencement does not simply entail heterogenous composition, but entails a constructive process that lays out a specific kind of arrangement.... (wuth) their conditions, their elements, and their agents, or what Deleuze and Guattari call their "abstract machine", their "concrete assemblage", and their "personae".* Thomas Nail [106].

The struggle over authenticity, legitimacy, representativeness, territory, and self-determination continues and the role of social construction of *Ayllu* continues to be important [107]. In all these cases, and the heritage of each of these movements is important in a multiplicity of creative resistances such as poetry, theatre, mural, dance, ecology, new squats, social centers, etc. The connectivity and interaction of all these social actors with other global social movements is underway. Vanden, Funke, Prevost ([108], p. 5) highlights new dynamics of new movements: "powered democratic participation (the new politics) as they unfold in varied ... ways across the world".

This research reveals that the poetics of creative resistances question the symbolic power of territorial stigmatization. A "subversive habitus" ([109], p. 47) and a process of commoning ([110], p. 125) are underway. Perhaps the so-called "dangerous" [111] and "reflexive" [55] social sciences can explore in depth this process.

Acknowledgments: This text would not have been realized without the enthusiastic participation of interviewees in the relative research and the willingness and contribution of Anna Carastathis and Aris Mermigkas in copyediting work, and support and encouragement of Andes Ruggeri, Raúl Zibechi, Hernan Ouviña, Mirko Orgáz, Raúl Prada, Cesar Cisneros, to all of whom I express my gratitude for their time and help. The text is dedicated to the anonymous protagonists of urban social movements, creative resistances, and societies in movement all over the world.

Conflicts of Interest: The author declares no conflict of interest.

References and Notes

1. Foucault, M. *Naissance de la Biopolitique. Cours au College de France 1978–1979*; EHESS with Gallimard and Seuil: Paris, France, 2004.
2. Agamben, G. *State of Exception*; University of Chicago Press: Chicago, IL, USA, 2008.
3. Wacquant, L. Marginality, ethnicity and penality in the neo-liberal city: An analytic cartography. *J. Ethn. Racial Stud.* **2014**, *37*, 1687–1711. [CrossRef]
4. Roy, A. Dis/possessive collectivism: Property and personhood at city's end. *Geoforum* **2017**, *80*, A1–A11. [CrossRef]

5. Petropoulou, C. *Développement Urbain et Éco-Paysages Urbains. Une Étude sur les Quartiers de Mexico et d'Athènes*; L'Harmattan: Paris, France, 2011.
6. Castells, M. *The City and the Grassroots. A Cross Cultural Theory of Urban Social Movement*; Edward Arnold Pub Ltd.: London, UK, 1986.
7. Bourdieu, P. *Outline of a Theory of Practice*; Cambridge University Press: Cambridge, UK, 1972.
8. Zibechi, R. *Autonomías y Emancipaciones. América Latina en Movimiento*; (In Greek: Αυτονομίες και χειραφετήσεις. Η Λατινική Αμερική σε κίνηση); ALANA: Athens, Greece, 2010.
9. Holloway, J. *Crack Capitalism*; Pluto Press: London, UK, 2010.
10. Stahler-Sholk, R.; Vanden, H.; Becker, M. *Rethinking Latin American Social Movements: Radical Action from Below*; Rowman and Littlefield: Lanham, MD, USA, 2014.
11. La Garganta Poderosa. La Garganta Poderosa. Revista mensual Argentina de Cultura Villera. Available online: https://www.facebook.com/La-Garganta-Poderosa-213440425391495/ (accessed on 30 October 2017).
12. Davis, M. *Planet of Slums*; Verso: London, UK; Brooklyn, NY, USA, 2007.
13. Wagner, F. Urban malformation that had to be prevented from spreading through the urban fabric. For a critical view of this see. In *Los Mil Barrios (in)Formales. Aportes Para la Construcción de un Observatorio del Hábitat Popular del Área Metropolitana de Buenos Aires*; Lanham, M., Ed.; Instituto del Conurbano, The National University of General Sarmiento (UNGS): Buenos Aires, Argentina, 2010; Available online: https://periferiaactiva.files.wordpress.com/2015/06/los-mil-barrios-cravino-final.pdf (accessed on 19 March 2018).
14. Schuurman, F.; Van Naerssen, T. *Urban Social Movements in the Third World*; Routledge: London, UK, 1989.
15. Turner, J.F.C. *Housing by People. Towards Autonomy in Building Environments*; Marion Boyards: London, UK, 1976.
16. Pradilla Cobos, E. (Ed.) Autoconstrucción, explotación de la fuerza de trabajo y políticas de Estado en América Latina. In *Ensayos Sobre el Problema de la Vivienda en América Latina*; Universidad Autónoma Metropolitana: Mexico City, Mexico, 1982.
17. Burgess, R. Self-help housing: A new imperialist strategy? A critique of the Turner school. *Antipode* **1977**, *9*, 50–59. [CrossRef]
18. Turner, J.F.C. Issues in Self-help and Self-managed Housing. In *Self-Help Housing: A Critique*; Ward, P., Ed.; Mansell: London, UK, 1982.
19. Spatial Agency. Turner's Text. Available online: http://www.spatialagency.net/database/john.turner (accessed on 10 November 2017).
20. Harvey, D. *Space of Global Capitalism. Towards a Theory of Uneven Geographical Development*; Verso: London, UK; Brooklyn, NY, USA, 2006.
21. Ramos, L. *El Fracaso del Consenso de Washington, la Caída de su Mejor Alumno: Argentina*; Icaria Editorial: Barcelona, Spain, 2003.
22. Escobar, A. Latin America at a crossroads: Alternative modernizations, post-liberalism, or post-development? *Cult. Stud.* **2010**, *24*, 1–65. [CrossRef]
23. Biegon, R. The United States and Latin America in the Trans-Pacific Partnership: Renewing Hegemony in a Post—Washington Consensus Hemisphere? *Lat. Am. Perspect.* **2017**, *44*, 81–98. [CrossRef]
24. Jacobs, M. *Reforming Housing Policies in Latin America Learning from Experience. How Can Housing Finance Policies in Latin America Be Improved?* Inter-American Development Bank: Washington, DC, USA, 2003.
25. Ferguson, B.; Navarrete, J. *New Approaches to Progressive Housing in Latin America: A Key to Habitat Programs and Policy*; Habitat International: Santiago, Chile, 2003; pp. 309–323.
26. Bauman, Z. *Globalization. The Human Consequences*; Polity Press and Blackwell Publishers Ltd.: Oxford, UK, 1998.
27. UN-Habitat. *The Challenge of Slums: Global Report on Human Settlements 2003*; United Nations Human Settlement Program (Un-Habitat); Earthscan Publications Ltd.: Nairobi, Kenya; London, UK, 2003.
28. Berenstein, J.P. Un Dispositif Architectural Vernaculaire. Les favelas à Rio Janeïro. Ph.D. Thesis, Sorbone Paris, Paris, France, 1998, submitted.
29. Nuñez, O. *Innovaciones Democratico-Culturales del Movimiento Urbano-Popular*; Universidad Autónoma Metropolitana: Mexico City, Mexico, 1990.
30. Dussel, E. *Filosofías del Sur, Descolonización y Transmodernidad*; Akal/Inter Pares: Mexico City, Mexico, 2015.
31. Damianakos, S. *La Grèce Dissidente Moderne: Cultures Rebelles*; L'Harmattan: Paris, France, 2003.
32. Wallerstein, M. *Historia y Dilemmas de Los Movimientos Antisistemicos*; Ediciones Desde Abajo: La otra Mirada de Clio, Mexico, 2008.

33. Petropoulou, C. Derecho a la ciudad y movimientos sociales contemporáneos—Por un movimiento social urbano-regional … ¿poético? Desde Nezahualcoyotl al mundo. In *Urban and Regional Social Movements*; Petropoulou, C., Vitopoulou, A., Tsavdaroglou, C., Eds.; Invisible Cities Research Group: Thessaloniki, Greece, 2016.
34. Stavrides, S. *Common Space: The City as Commons*; Zed Books Ltd.: London, UK, 2016; Available online: http://press.uchicago.edu/ucp/books/book/distributed/C/bo23360613.html (accessed on 19 March 2018).
35. Petropoulou, C. Crisis, Right to the City movements and the question of spontaneity: Athens and Mexico City. *City* **2014**, *18*, 563–572. [CrossRef]
36. Lefebvre, H. *Le Droit à la Ville*; Collection Points; Seuil: Paris, France, 1968.
37. Harvey, D. *Rebel Cities*; Verso: London, UK, 2012.
38. Carlsson, C.; Manning, F. Nowtopia: Strategic Exodus? *Antipode* **2010**, *42*, 924–953. [CrossRef]
39. Korol, C. La formación política de los movimientos populares latinoamericanos. *OSAL* **2007**, *8*, 227–240.
40. Ceceña, A.E. *Derivas Delmundo en el Que Caben Todos los Mundos*; Siglo XXI and CLACSO: Mexico City, Mexico, 2008.
41. Ouviña, H. La política prefigurativa de los movimientos populares en América Latina. Hacia una nueva matriz de intelección para las ciencias sociales. *Acta Sociol.* **2013**, *62*, 77–104. [CrossRef]
42. Sitrin, M. Rethinking Social Movements with Societies in Movement. In *Social Sciences for an Other Politics*; Palgrave Macmillan: Cham, Switzerland, 2016; pp. 135–149.
43. Kioupkiolis, A.; Katsanbekis, G. *Radical Democracy and Collective Movements Today. The Biopolitics of the Multitude versus the Hegemony of the People*; Routledge: London, UK, 2016.
44. Cornish, F.; Haaken, J.; Moskovitz, L.; Jackson, S. Rethinking prefigurative politics: Introduction to the special thematic section. *J. Soc. Political Psychol.* **2016**, *4*, 114–127. [CrossRef]
45. Maeckelbergh, M. The Prefigurative Turn: The Time and Place of Social Movement Practice. In *Social Sciences for an Other Politics*; Palgrave Macmillan: Cham, Switzerland, 2016; pp. 121–134.
46. Della Porta, D.; Dianni, M. *Social Movements. An introduction*; Blackwell Publishing Ltd.: Oxford, UK, 2010.
47. Lefebvre, H. *La vie Quotidienne dans le Monde Moderne*; Gallimard: Paris, France, 1968.
48. Vaneigem, R. *Traité de Savoir-Vivre à L'usage des Jeunes Générations*; Gallimard: Paris, France, 1972.
49. Papi, A. Antiviolenti sì Nonviolenti No. *Rivista Anarchica* 2004, *34*, 2. Available online: http://www.arivista.org/?nr=296&pag=19.htm (accessed on 15 March 2018).
50. Varcarolis, O. *Creative Resistance and Anti-Power. Projects and Reflections of the Radical Movement in the 21st Century*; Pagkaki: Athens, Greece, 2012; (In Greek). Available online: https://issuu.com/platform-aii/docs/varkarolis-orestis_dhmiourgikes-ant (accessed on 19 March 2018).
51. Vail, J.; Hollands, R. Creative Democracy and the Arts: The Participatory Democracy of the Amber Collective. *Cult. Sociol.* **2013**, *7*, 352–367. [CrossRef]
52. Yates, L. Everyday politics, social practices and movement networks: Daily life in Barcelona's social centres. *Br. J. Sociol.* **2015**, *66*, 236–258. [CrossRef] [PubMed]
53. Deleuze, G.; Guattari, F. *Mille Plateaux. Capitalisme et Schizophrénie II*; Éditions de Minuit: Paris, France, 1980.
54. Daskalaki, M.; Mould, O. Beyond Urban Subcultures: Urban Subversions as Rhizomatic Social Formations. *Int. J. Urban Reg. Res.* **2013**, *37*, 1–18. [CrossRef]
55. Bourdieu, P.; Wasquant, L. *Una Invitación a la Sociología Reflexiva*; Siglo XXI: Buenos Aires, Argentina, 2005.
56. Hobsbawm, E. *The Age of Capital, 1848–1875*; Mentor Book; Hachette UK: London, UK, 1979.
57. Argentina's National Institute of Statistics and Censuses (INDEC). *Censo Nacional de Población, Hogares y Viviendas 2010*; Argentina's National Institute of Statistics and Censuses: Buenos Aires, Argentina, 2012.
58. Corriente Villera Corriente Villera Independiente 2017. Available online: https://www.facebook.com/corrientevillera/videos/vb.581282611939175/1202104656523631/?type=2&theater (accessed on 15 March 2018).
59. Petropoulou, C. The role of solidarity economy in Latin America "barrios": Cases in Metropolitan Area of Mexico City. In Proceedings of the International Conference on "Changing Cities": Spatial, Morphological, Formal & Socio-Economic Dimensions, University of Thessaly, Skiathos Island, Greece, 18–21 June 2013; Available online: https://www.academia.edu/29677392/The_role_of_solidarity_economy_in_Latin_America_barrios_Cases_in_Metropolitan_Area_of_Mexico_City (accessed on 19 March 2018).
60. Varcarolis, O.; King, D. Voicing researched activists with responsive action research. *Qual. Res. Organ. Manag. Int. J.* **2017**, *12*, 315–334. [CrossRef]

61. Díaz, M.P. Hábitat popular y mercado laboral: El desarrollo urbano desigual de la ciudad de El Alto (Bolivia). *Rev. INVI* **2015**, *30*, 111–146. [CrossRef]
62. Semo, I.; Loaeza, S.; Bellingeri, M. *La Transicion Interumpida. Mexico 1968–1988*; Universidad Iberoamericana: Mexico City, Mexico, 1993.
63. Ward, P. *México. Una Megaciudad. Producción y Reproducción de un Medio Ambiente Urbano*; Consejo Nacional de Cultura y Artes: Madrid, Spain, 1991.
64. Schteingart, M. *Espacio y Vivienda en la Ciudad de Mexico*; El Colegio de Mexico: Mexico City, Mexico, 1991.
65. Ramírez Sáiz, J.M. *El Movimiento Urbano Popular en Mexico*; Siglo XXI: Mexico City, Mexico, 1986.
66. Hiernaux, D.; Tomas, F. (Eds.) *Cambios Económicos y Periferia de Las Grandes Ciudades. El Caso de la Ciudad de México*; UAM and IFAL: Mexico City, Mexico, 1994.
67. Schteingart, M. *Los Productores del Espacio Habitable. Estado, Empresa y Sociedad en la Ciudad de México*; El Colegio de Mexico: Mexico City, Mexico, 2001.
68. Ocotitla Saucedo, P. *Movimientos de Colonos en Ciudad Nezahualcóyotl: Acción Colectiva y Política Popular 1945–1975*; División de Ciencias Sociales, Universidad Autónoma Metropolitana: Iztapalapa, Mexico, 2000.
69. Coulomb, R.; Sanchez Mejorada, C. *Pobreza Urbana, Autogestión y Política*; Centro de la Vivienda y Estudios Urbanos (CENVI): Mexico City, Mexico, 1992.
70. Agustin, J. *La Contracultura en Mexico. La Historia y el Significado de los Rebeldes Sin Causa, los Jipitecas, los Punks y las Bandas*; Grijalbo: Barcelona, Spain, 1996.
71. Legoretta, J. *Efectos Ambientales de la Expanción de la Ciudad de México 1970–1993*; Centro de Ecologia y Desarrollo: Mexico City, Mexico, 1994; Available online: https://books.google.gr/books/about/Efectos_ambientales_de_la_expansión_de.html?id=zJSzAAAAIAAJ&redir_esc=y (accessed on 19 March 2018).
72. Maria (Pseudonym). Interview Given to Christy Petropoulou (personal archive) Related to Muralisme and Woman Actions in Nezahualcoyotl. 1 June 2016.
73. Cuaya, M. Interview given to Christy Petropoulou (personal archive) related to Muralisme in Nezahualcoyotl. 1 June 2016.
74. Mamani, P. *El Rugir de Las Multitudes. Microgobiernos Barriales*; La Mirada Salvaje: El Alto, Bolivia, 2010.
75. Prada Alcoreza, R. Largo Octubre. Genealogía de los Movimientos Sociales. Available online: https://dinamicas-moleculares.webnode.es/news/el-ayllu-en-el-desierto-capitalista-/ (accessed on 15 March 2018).
76. Quispe Huanca, F. *La Caída de Goni. Diario de la Huelga de Hambre*; Ediciones Pachakuti: Qullasuyu, Bolivia, 2013.
77. Zibechi, R. *Dispersar el Poder*; Editorial Abya Yala: Quito, Equador, 2007.
78. Gutiérrez Aguilar, R. *¡A Desordenar! Por una Historia Abierta de la Lucha Social*; Tinta Limon: Buenos Aires, Argentina, 2006.
79. Orgáz Garcia, M. *El Poder de la Nacionalización. La Falsa Nacionalización de Evo Morales y la Venta de Gas a Chile*; Ed. Independiente: Orgáz Garcia La Paz, Bolivia, 2008; Available online: https://books.google.gr/books/about/El_poder_de_la_nacionalización.html?id=umooAQAAIAAJ&redir_esc=y (accessed on 19 March 2018).
80. Fernando (Pseudonym). Interview Given to Christy Petropoulou (Personal archive) Related with FEJUVE—El Alto Movement. 14 April 2017.
81. Flores, W. Interview given to Christy Petropoulou (Personal archive) related to ALBOR theater actions in El Alto, Bolivia. 14 April 2017.
82. Albor, Quienes Somos 2017. Available online: http://albor-arte.blogspot.gr/2009/01/quienes-somos.html (accessed on 18 March 2018).
83. Benedetti, H. *Nueva Historia del Tango. De los Origínas al Siglo XXI*; Siglo XXI: Buenos Aires, Argentina, 2017.
84. Lobato, M.; Suriano, J. *Atlas Histórico de la Argentina*; Editorial Sudamericana: Buenos Aires, Argentina, 2000.
85. Rodríguez, F. Entre la omisión y la expulsión. Un análisis sobre las modalidades de intervención estatal en los Nuevos Asentamientos Urbanos (NAU). In *Barrios al Sur*; Herzer, H., Ed.; Café de Las Ciudades: Buenos Aires, Argentina, 2012; pp. 73–95.
86. Tcach, C. *De la Revolución Libertadora al Cordobazo. Córdoba, el Rostro Anticipado del País*; Siglo XXI: Buenos Aires, Argentina, 2012.
87. De Privitellio, L.; Romero, L.A. Organizaciones de la sociedad civil, tradiciones cívicas y cultura política democrática: El caso de Buenos Aires, 1912–1976. *Rev. Hist.* **2005**, *1*, 1–34.
88. Saborido, J.; de-Privitellio, L. *Breve Historia de la Argentina*; Alianza Editorial: Madrid, Spain, 2006.

89. Rodríguez, G. Segregación residencial socioeconómica en la Ciudad Autónoma de Buenos Aires. Dimensiones y cambios entre 1991–2001. *Población Buenos Aires* **2008**, *5*, 7–30.

90. Zibechi, R. *Genealogía de la Revuelta. Argentina: La Sociedad en Movimiento*; Ediciones FZLN: Mexico City, Mexico, 2004.

91. Retamozo, M. Movimientos Sociales. Subjetividad y Acción de los Trabajadores Desocupados en Argentina. Ph.D. Thesis, Flasco Mexico, Ciudad de México, Mexico, 2012.

92. Poli, C. *Movimiento Territorial Liberación Su Historia. Piquetes, Organización, Poder Popular*; Departamento de Historia, Centro Cultural de la Cooperación Floreal Gorini: Buenos Aires, Argentina, 2007.

93. Centro de Documentación de Empresas Recuperadas. *Worker-Recovered Entreprises at the Beginning of the Government of Mauricio Macri. State of the Situation as of May 2016*; Workers Economy Dossier: Buenos Aires, Argentina, 2016.

94. Ouviña, H. Tomar el Obelisco por asalto para conquistar el derecho a la ciudad. In *Las Voces de los Huelguistas. 53 Días de Acampe y Huelga de Hambre. Carpa Villera*; América Libre: Buenos Aires, Argentina, 2015.

95. Korol, C.; Mosquera, A. *Las Voces de los Huelguistas. 53 Días de Acampe y Huelga de Hambre. Carpa Villera*; América Libre: Buenos Aires, Argentina, 2015.

96. Chaher, S. La Lucha de las Mujeres en la Carpa Villera 2014. *Sandra Chaher*, 19 June 2014. Available online: http://www.comunicarigualdad.com.ar/la-lucha-de-las-mujeres-en-la-carpa-villera/ (accessed on 10 March 2018).

97. Ruggeri, A. INFORME Las Empresas Recuperadas por los Trabajadores en los Comienzos del Gobierno de Mauricio Macri. Estado de Situación a Mayo de 2016. Available online: http://www.recuperadasdoc.com.ar/informe-mayo-2016.pdf (accessed on 10 March 2018).

98. Freire, P. *Pedagogía de la Esperanza: Un Reencuentro con la Pedagogía del Oprimido*; Paz e Terra: Río de Janeiro, Brazil, 1992.

99. Maria and Juan (Pseudonyms). Interview Given to Christy Petropoulou (personal archive) Related to Hip Hop and Graffity Actions in Buenos Aires. 21 March 2017.

100. Petropoulou, C. *Vers un Mouvement Urbain Poétique? Une étude à Mexico*; L'Harmattan: Paris, France, 2010; Available online: https://books.google.gr/books/about/Vers_un_mouvement_social_urbain_poétiqu.html?hl=fr&id=IYMl3FwH42oC&output=html_text&redir_esc=y (accessed on 19 March 2018).

101. Escobar, A. Territorios de diferencia: La ontología política de los derechos al territorio. *Cuad. Antropol. Soc.* **2015**, *41*, 25–38. [CrossRef]

102. Psimitis, M. *Social Movements in the Everyday Life*; Tziola: Thessaloniki, Greece, 2017; (In Greek). Available online: https://www.tziola.gr/book/koinonika-kinimata/ (accessed on 19 March 2018).

103. Esteva, G. The Oaxaca Commune and Mexico's Coming Insurrection. *Antipode* **2010**, *42*, 978–993. [CrossRef]

104. Soto Villagran, P.; Helena Guzman, K. Mujeres, territorio y movimientos sociales. Un análisis del caso de Atenco. In *Urban and Regional Social Movements*; Petropoulou, C., Vitopoulou, A., Tsavdaroglou, C., Eds.; Invisible Cities Press: Thessalonica, Greece, 2016; pp. 255–274.

105. Indaburu Quintana, R. *Evaluación de El Alto*; The United States Agency for International Development (USAID): Washington, DC, USA, 2004.

106. Nail, T. What is an Assemblage? *SubStance* **2017**, *46*, 21–37. [CrossRef]

107. Burman, A. El ayllu y el indianismo. Autenticidad, representatividad y territorio en el quehacer político del Conamaq, Bolivia. In *Los Nuevos Caminos de los Movimientos Sociales en Latinoamérica*; Ejdesgaard Jeppsen, A.M., Balslev Clausen, H., Velázquez García, M.A., Eds.; Tilde Editores: Monterrey, Mexico, 2015; pp. 100–122.

108. Vanden, H.; Funke, P.; Prevost, G. (Eds.) *The New Global Politics: Global Social Movements in the Twenty-First Century*; Routledge: New York, NY, USA; London, UK, 2017.

109. Bourdieu, P. Habitus. In *Habitus: A Sense of Place*; Hillier, J., Rooksby, E., Eds.; Ashgate: Aldershot, UK, 2005; pp. 43–52.

110. Gutiérrez Aguilar, R. *Horizontes Comunitario-Populares Producción de lo Común más Allá de las Políticas Estado-Céntricas*; Traficantes de Sueños, Mapas: Madrid, Spain, 2017; Available online: https://www.traficantes. net/sites/default/files/pdfs/Horizontes%20comunitario-populares_Traficantes%20de%20Sue~nos.pdf (accessed on 19 March 2018).
111. Cisneros Puebla, C. Manifesto for a "Dangerous Sociology". *Athenea Digit.* **2008**, *13*, 171–184. [CrossRef]

urban science

MDPI

Article

Urban Vulnerability in Spanish Medium-Sized Cities during the Post-Crisis Period (2009–2016). The Cases of A Coruña and Vigo (Spain)

María José Piñeira-Mantiñán [1,*, Francisco R. Durán-Villa [1] and José Taboada-Failde [2]**

[1]   Department of Geography, University of Santiago de Compostela, 15782 Santiago de Compostela, Galicia, Spain; francisco.duran@usc.es
[2]   Tysgal Consulting, 15706 Santiago de Compostela, La Coruña, Spain; jtaboada@tysgal.com
*   Correspondence: mariajose.pineira@usc.es; Tel.: +34-881812632

Received: 15 February 2018; Accepted: 6 April 2018; Published: 19 April 2018

Abstract: The economic crisis and post-crisis austerity policies have had harmful effects on urban spaces, mainly in those neighborhoods that have historically been characterized by their vulnerability (social problems, long-term unemployment, low incomes, immigration, etc.). This vulnerability has become more evident in cities that are greater in size (Madrid, Barcelona, Valencia, Seville). However, such casuistry is also observed in medium-sized cities (250,000–500,000 inhabitants) that are prominent urban and economic hubs in their regions. In this article we will analyze to what extent the crisis has impacted the different urban sectors through the analysis of degree of vulnerability. For this, the cities of A Coruña and Vigo—the two main urban poles of the Autonomous Region of Galicia—will be taken as case studies. In addition, we will analyze the proposals to combat vulnerability presented by the ruling parties in their programs for the 2015 municipal elections. Elections that in Spain marked a turning point in the form of governance and priorities to attend (attention to those most affected by the crisis, stop eviction processes, reduction of intra-urban inequality). We will analyze to what extent they have implemented.

Keywords: vulnerability; post-crisis policies; medium-sized cities; Galicia; Spain

---

1. Introduction

Over the last 10 years, Spanish cities have been hit with greater or lesser intensity by a financial, economic and real-estate crisis [1], whose effects include great debt in the public sector. This debt led to fiscal restructuring and a greater privatization of public goods and services. All this occurred at a time when the population demanded more employment, access to public education and health, homes, and access to social benefits in order to reach the end of the month.

Perhaps one of the biggest issues leading to this situation was the repeated denial of the crisis by the government. In 2007, it claimed that the gradual deceleration across the Spanish economy was responding to a correction measure and a restructuring of the economy that would relieve pressure on the construction sector, which until then was inflated. Moreover, it was affirmed that the country could face such economic deceleration thanks to the boom of public accounts, which showed a surplus of around 1.8% of the GDP, and that there were no problems with employment, as there were three million more employed individuals than four years prior. In this context, local governments continued with a neoliberal urban growth model that, far from responding to planning, followed the rules of the market and promoted the construction of public infrastructures and facilities, as well as large residential projects. The population continued to invest in the purchase of homes thanks to their financing being facilitated.

However, in 2011, the European Commission [2] had already warned that the European model of sustainable urban development was under threat because it cannot provide jobs for all. Weakening links between economic growth, employment, and social progress have pushed a larger share of the population out of the labor market or toward low-skilled and low-wage service-sector jobs. An increase in income disparities and a "poor getting poorer" situation is also being observed. In some neighborhoods, local populations suffer from a concentration of inequality in terms of poor housing, low-quality education, unemployment, and difficulty or inability to access certain services (health, transport, ICT). An increase in social polarization and segregation are also being observed. Consequently, spatial segregation processes—as an effect of social polarization—are becoming more frequent, making it increasingly difficult for low-income or marginalized groups to find decent housing at affordable prices, while an increasing number of "society dropouts" may lead to the development of closed sub-cultures with fundamentally hostile attitudes toward mainstream society in many cities.

Ten years after the start of the crisis, some reports, such as that of CaixaBank Research [3], are beginning to show signs of economic recovery (in 2017 the GDP recorded a growth of 3.1% compared to 2016, and the number of unemployed individuals decreased by 471,100 in 2017, representing a decrease of 11.1%). However, Europe warns that even though the economy seems to be growing on a macro scale there are still many cities that seem stuck in a "middle-income trap": the GDP per capita growth from 2001 to 2015 was significantly below the EU average. Although the employment rate has recovered, the unemployment rate is still above its pre-crisis level, and there is a large amount of temporary work with low wage, the manufacturing sector is too small and weak to be competitive, the regional innovation systems are not strong enough, and investments in innovation, skills, and infrastructure are insufficient [4].

That is why the European Commission insists that in order to move beyond the crisis, local governments should generate growth and employment, strengthen their innovation and education centers and put initiatives into action that make their city a safe, inclusive, resilient and sustainable space. In this sense, Ranci, Brandsen, and Satabilenlli [5] affirm that there is a strong connection between the degree of economic competitiveness of cities and the degree of social cohesion. According to these authors, a guarantee of this relationship depends on the following three factors: (i) to what extent the welfare state is able to forge a network of social and economic organizations, (ii) the importance given by citizens to social solidarity and equality, and (iii) the strength of local governments' political investment in supporting local solidarity initiatives aimed at helping the population in situations of vulnerability.

When the crisis began, it became clear that the development model in place until then had not created the necessary mechanisms to face a situation of lasting crisis. This can be explained by the existence of a Welfare State in Spain not guaranteeing a decrease in poverty and inequality. Just as in other southern European countries, social welfare is based on funds stemming from worker contributions. A very different conjuncture to those countries with a social democratic welfare state, characterized by a very strong emphasis on collective bargaining, or those with a Liberal welfare state, also characterized by a strong emphasis on employment for all but in a context of high income inequality and strict work requirements for the recipients of social benefits [6].

In order to face the state of vulnerability in which the Spanish population has been subjected, the welfare state would have to improve its family protection policies, housing policies and a minimum income programme so it could fulfil three analytical functions [7]:

- The "Robin Hood" function that implies a redistribution from better-off members of society to those faced with material or other types of deprivation or those subject to higher social risks. These mechanisms are designed to protect against these risks by delivering poverty relief, providing social housing, redistributing income, and reducing social exclusion. Labor market regulations protect against unfair dismissal and ensure rights for temporary workers. Social risks have evolved over time and now include concepts such as one-parent families and the isolation of old-age pensioners from their families.

- The "piggy bank" function through which the welfare state enables citizens to insure themselves against social hardship and to spread out their income more securely over their lifetime, with pensions being the main element.
- The social investment function that enables the state to invest in social capital. This includes early childcare, state education from primary level through university, out-of-work training, and various types of work-related tax benefits.

In the medium term, it is clear that it will be necessary to rethink the role of the State in relation to the economy. However, for the moment, we must find a solution to the crisis and the state of vulnerability that citizens find themselves in. Local governments should promote urban resilience actions in order to avoid inequality, exclusion and social polarization [8,9].

Throughout this article we will first analyze the factors that determined the crisis in Spain and how alarming levels of vulnerability were reached in the main cities. Second, the degree of vulnerability existing in medium-sized cities will be measured and mapped out using the cases of A Coruña and Vigo as an example. This cartography will allow us to establish a classification of the different urban areas based on their degree of vulnerability. Subsequently we will approach the initiatives that the winning parties in the 2015 municipal elections carried in their electoral programs to reduce vulnerability and improve the quality of life of its citizens. We will check to what extent the proposals have been carried out.

2. Crisis and Vulnerability in Spanish Cities

2.1. Triggering Factors of the Crisis

The 2008 crisis in Spain questioned the current welfare state model, sinking the three main pillars that according to the political economy theory sustain the daily life of the population: the labor market, family structure, and welfare institutions. Understanding how Spain got to this situation requires us to go back to the 1980s, when, on the one hand, the democratic city councils were established and there was a notable institutionalization of local political life; and on the other hand, an economic reactivation began, based on the construction sector, a neoliberal development model characterized by treating territory as a business [10] and deregulation in planning, from which the urban expansion process was designed by a lobby group which saw the participation of owners, developers, banks, savings banks and companies in the sector [11–14].

From then on, cities registered overflowing growth along their immediate peripheries, of such intensity and speed that some authors described it as an "urbanization tsunami" [15]. The traditional city was losing meaning in the face of the protagonism gained by new metropolitan realities. As a result of the centrifugal movements of the medium- or high-income population of the consolidated city toward metropolitan centers in search of better housing conditions, services, schools, higher environmental quality, and security, there was a decline and impoverishment of consolidated urban areas, increasing their degree of isolation and social segregation. Moreover, the creation of new biased urban nuclei by the metropolitan territory generated situations of territorial conflict and tensions between the native population, who saw how their landscape was transformed and their ways of life changed, and the new residents, who wanted to find the comforts that the city offered them in the new residential areas. Processes of residential segregation, which were more evident in the housing developments whose residents remained isolated from their immediate surroundings, turning them into true ghettos of the wealthy population, who preferred to go to the city center to do their shopping or for leisure. In this context, local governments had to face new challenges, such as the creation and improvement of infrastructure (electricity grid, water) and basic services (health, education, refuse collection, urban transport) to satisfy a growing population. The task was not simple due to the fact that urban growth exceeded the municipal administrative limits and required supra-municipal planning that was not carried out due to either a lack of interest, a fear of losing competences, or the lack of an institutionalized figure capable of planning these spaces (like in the metropolitan areas).

However, the local administrations were holding up since the profits of new housing construction and capital gains prevailed over the problems derived from a lack of planning and inefficient management. In fact, despite the crisis beginning in 2008, the reaction by local administrations was delayed, and they even denied that it existed in their localities. It was not until two or three years later that they had a reality check when they could not afford to pay their public debt and had serious cash flow problems in paying for the most basic services, such as electricity and telephony or, in some cases, the payrolls of public employees [16]. By then, unemployment already affected 20.3% of the active population and would continue to increase until reaching 26% in 2012. Social and family-based fragility was evident, as more and more people could not reach the end of the month and could not afford their mortgage payments, leading to the eviction of thousands of families. Many of them found support in family or friends, but others, especially in the case of immigrants, did not have any support network. Social assistance services, dependent on local governments, were overwhelmed by the demand for benefits at a time when their budget items were being cut dramatically to meet public debt payment. The result was a worrying increase in the number of people in situations of vulnerability and a widespread pessimism and fear among the population who, in previous years, saw poverty and social exclusion as a very distant problem, and who now, with the country's new economic and employment situation, found themselves on a tightrope that could break at any moment, endangering their social welfare.

At first, it was thought that the crisis would be temporary. However, its continuation caused the number of people and families who had not paid their mortgages to multiply and part of the financial sector (most Savings Banks took unreasonable risks in their involvement in the construction business) and the public sector to be dragged into bankruptcy. The population began to wonder if the economic growth of the previous years had been an illusion and realized that social cohesion as a crucial ingredient of urban development [17] had been replaced by a new, more radical approach in line with the economic market. Up until then, business owners, bankers, and politicians had focused their interests on growing, building, and obtaining large, fast profits, leaving any social aspects in the background. This, coupled with the emergence of numerous cases of corruption in the government and an interest in rescuing the banks instead of strengthening basic services for the population (health, education, social assistance) led to a resurgence of social and political movements. There were different kinds, ranging from more defensive movements focused on a particular place (against the closure of a company or an eviction order issued to a mortgage victim) to more general movements demanding direct democracy and an end to corruption. These movements fueled the indignados protest with its camps on the streets of all major cities [18].

The municipal elections of 2015 installed representatives of these movements in the local governments of large cities, such as Madrid, Barcelona, and Valencia, and in other medium-sized cities, such as Cádiz, Santiago de Compostela, and A Coruña, where the population demanded a change in the governance model. Aspects such as participation, transparency, shared responsibility among administrations, effectiveness, and coherence took on greater prominence in the new way of running cities [19].

After many decades in which neoliberal governance had intensified polarization of cities' social and urban structure, these new administrations began to devote a substantial part of their public budgets to alleviating the vulnerability found in some neighborhoods, which were forgotten by the administration for decades. The administration began to see the city as a whole, realizing that it was made up of neighborhoods that needed to be considered, rather than just city centers (understood to essentially be historic centers and 19th-century bourgeois housing developments) and certain outlying developments, where state-of-the-art architecture reached its peak of expression in a post-modern city that gave preference to self-investment and urban development over strategic planning.

2.2. The Consequences of a Protracted Crisis over Time

Numerous authors have analyzed in depth the effects of the crisis from an economic, social, political and territorial standpoint [11,12,19,20]. All of them agree that there were three main aspects that had the greatest impact: the housing crisis, the destabilization of the labor market, and social inequality. Based on these, we can classify urban vulnerability into the following three categories (Figure 1):

- Economic vulnerability: considering the fact that many companies have closed, the loss of employment and the prolongation of unemployment situations have led to severe poverty. Unemployment benefits have a maximum duration of two years, so many families now have all members unemployed. The groups most affected by situations of long-term unemployment are those over the age of 45, immigrants, women, and young people.
- Social vulnerability: a decrease in family income has limited the population's access to goods and services, some of which are of prime necessity, such as healthcare (when having to pay for certain medicines) and education (the purchase of books and school supplies).
- Residential vulnerability: being unable to afford the rent and mortgage payments; this situation has caused the number of foreclosures and evictions to multiply.

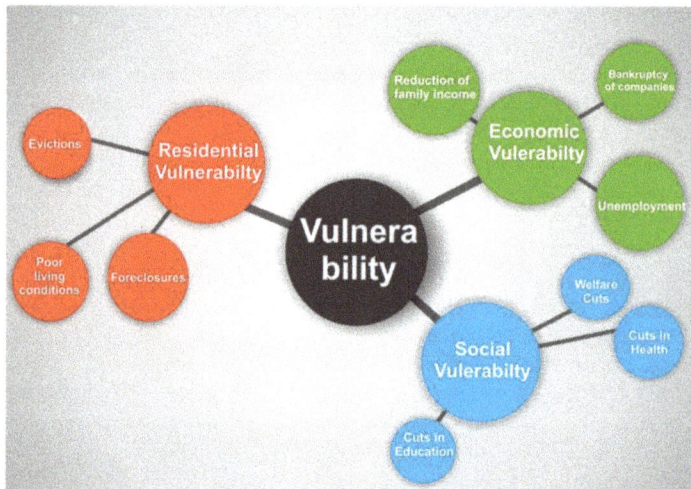

Figure 1. Classification of urban vulnerability.

With regard to the economic vulnerability, two aspects must be highlight: the collapse of the construction sector and the destabilization of the labor market housing crisis. During times of great economic growth, the construction sector came to represent close to 18% of real GDP growth and more than 12% in direct employment. Since the crisis began, it has reduced its contribution to the GDP by 8 points, mainly as a result of the collapse of activity in national public civil works [21], the interruption of large urban projects, and a decrease in new housing purchases. This is confirmed by the data related to visas, licenses, transactions and the volume of new homes started. The latter experienced the greatest decrease of around 95.6%, until 2013 when it began to recover, while licenses and visas decreased by around 83.5% and 92.4%, respectively (Figure 2). Regarding transactions or home sales, the crisis also caused them to be reduced by 68.5%, despite the fact that the price per square meter also experienced a decrease during that period.

On the other hand, regarding to the destabilization of the labor market, it should be noted that the crisis led to the closure of numerous companies and, consequently, an increase in unemployment. The statistics of the College of Registrars indicate that in the period of the crisis (2008–2013), a total of 214,958 companies closed in Spain, at a rate of 23,884 annually. Likewise, during the same period, a total of 1,149,899 dismissal requests were submitted to the Labor Court, which went from 66,249 in

2007 to 146,796 in 2013. The cities with a greater incidence were those of the Canary Islands, with the dismissals of Las Palmas de Gran Canaria representing 1.27% of the working population, and those of the Mediterranean Axis, where real estate development was associated with the tourism product of sun and beach, highlighting the cases of Malaga, Huelva, Almeria, Barcelona, Castellon, and Valencia, where this percentage falls around 0.7% (Figure 3).

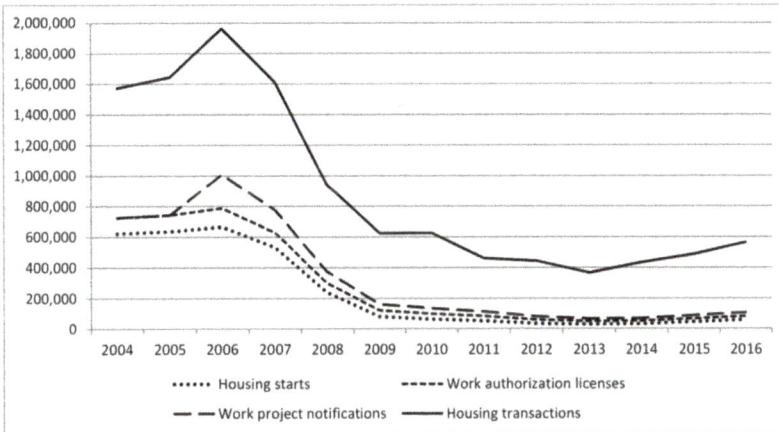

Figure 2. Evolution of Housing starts, work licenses, work project notifications, and housing transactions in Spain. Ministry of Development.

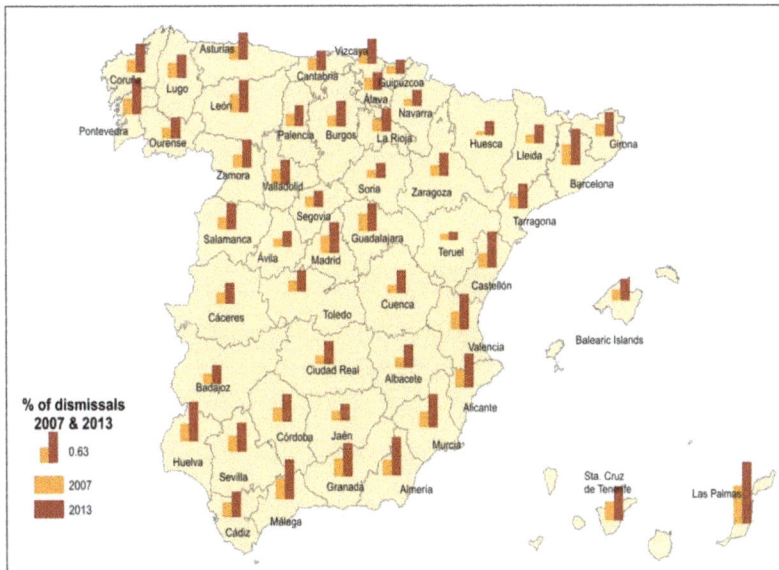

Figure 3. Percentage of dismissals over the entire working population in 2007 and 2013. Judicial Power Statistics.

As a result, the unemployment rate went from 8.5% in 2007 to 25.5% in 2013 [22], with a total of 5,896,300 unemployed individuals. The groups most affected by unemployment were men, immigrant workers, and those who had been unemployed for more than a year. The crisis and its continuation caused thousands of families to see their family income and spending capacity decrease and more and more households to register all their working-age members as unemployed, leading to the social vulnerability increase. Regarding residential vulnerability, Judicial Power Statistics shows that in 2007 foreclosures (the situation prior to eviction) increased by 297% over the previous year, although it was in 2009 when they reached their maximum with a total of 183,676 cases. From then on, the numbers began to fall, but in 2014 a total of 132,863 were still recorded. Of this total, 20.2% corresponded to loans granted in 2007, 17.3% to mortgages signed in 2006 and 12.1% to loans from 2005. This meant that the period 2005–2008, which coincided with the most bullish phase of the bubble, saw a concentration of 61.6% of foreclosures initiated in that year. In absolute values, the cities that saw the highest rate in the period 2008 to 2013 were those located in the provinces of Madrid (with over 70,000), Barcelona and Valencia (which exceeded 40,000), and Alicante, the Balearic Islands and Malaga (all exceeding 20,000). These six provinces accounted for 61% of the total evictions reported in that period. As noted, they are large urban agglomerations and these provinces correspond to established tourist destinations, where the bubble had a greater impact (Figure 4).

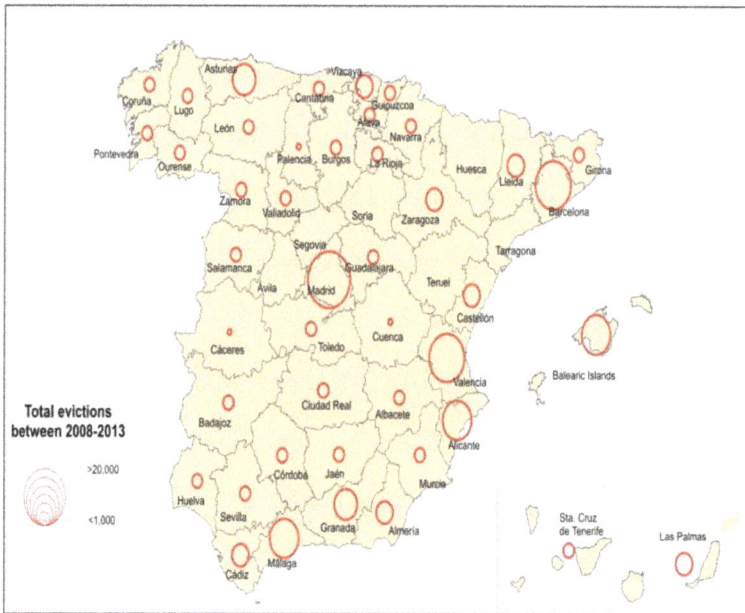

Figure 4. Number of evictions during the period 2008–2013. Judicial Power Statistics.

These figures allow us to assess the degree of tension, anger, impotence, and vulnerability to which Spanish families were subjected since 2008. In a short period of time, many of them lost their employment and housing, and they had to see how the State instead of helping them by offering them official protection housing focused on paying the debt contracted by the banks. It was then that it became clear that housing and urban policies carried out so far developed the creation of a housing park unable to meet the needs of society. According to the Housing Emergency Report in 2013 there was no public rental housing park available to accommodate low-income groups—the percentage of social rental housing did not reach 2% of the total, when the EU-15 average was between 20% and 30%.

The aid to the payment of the rent was scarce and was linked to the budgetary availability, and the private rental market was insufficient (15% of the total) and highly speculative (there were no limits to indiscriminate increases in income). Likewise, the introduction of measures aimed at combating unjustified unemployment and underutilization of real estate had been renounced, as is the case in other countries such as France, where houses that remain empty for 18 months can be requisitioned. That is why Spain had the highest percentage of empty homes in Europe (13.7% compared to 8% in Germany and 6.3% in France) [23,24].

2.3. Map of the Crisis

Since 2014, statistics have shown an incipient recovery in the employment rate—in 2016. it was around 18.63%, and in that same year, the number of foreclosures was reduced by 41,129, 10.62% less than 2015. However, this improvement in quantitative indicators does not seem to be reflected in greater citizen welfare or in a decrease in inequality. As many as 18,083,692 households can currently be counted in Spain, of which 1,610,900 see all their working-age members unemployed [25]. According to a survey of living conditions, 16.6% of people say they have great difficulty reaching the end of the month, 19.0% have difficulty, and 27.0% have some difficulty. As a result, the poverty rate has reached 29.2%, reaching over 40% in some cities of Andalusia, the Canary Islands, Extremadura, and Murcia. To this, we can add the fact that social protection rates are decreasing and the distribution of wealth is changing in such a way that inequality is increasing between individuals with a higher income and those with a lower income. Regarding social protection, the coverage rate of unemployment benefits has gone from 76.5% of the unemployed in 2008 to 56.6% in 2016. The average number of people with unemployment benefits in 2015 was 2.2 million, with a decrease of 27% compared to 2010. The average monthly expenditure per beneficiary has decreased from 2012, going from €920.30 on average per beneficiary to €798.70 in 2016, down 13.2% [26]. The evolution of the labor market continues to show the absence of change in the productive model. Job creation continues to be concentrated in unproductive, low-value-added services (sales, hospitality, ancillary services) with a low impact on the industry and from sectors with medium and high technological intensity. In addition, in January 2017, 91% of signed contracts were temporary and almost a third where part-time, proving the great precariousness of the labor market.

The European Commission shows concern because Spain continues to maintain a high degree of inequality. It maintains that the adjustment measures that have been implemented in Spain have favored the concentration of wealth and the proliferation of poverty in a growing part of the population [27]. This socialization of poverty has made Spain the country in which social inequality has deepened the most, standing at the level of Bulgaria, Greece, and Lithuania [28]. A fact that is confirmed, on the one hand, by the Gini index, which during the crisis period increased by 2.3 points and stands at 34.7 points, while for Europe within the Eurozone it has increased by 0.5 points and stands at 31 points (Figure 5). And on the other hand, due to the fact that if we analyze the distribution of wealth according to the income strata, we can observe that the percentage of the population located in the middle strata has been reduced by six points, the lowest strata has increased by seven points, and the upper strata has remained in the same position [29]. These figures are what caused Europe to issue the Spanish government a warning, berating the scant impact of its social policies when it comes to reducing poverty.

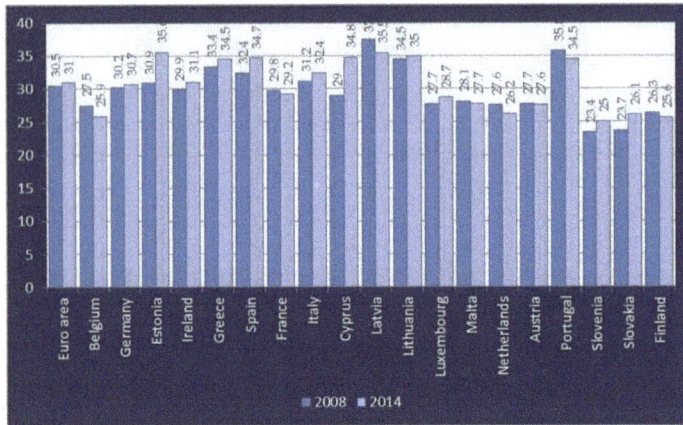

Figure 5. Gini index. Eurostat.

Focusing on the local and mainly urban perspective, it should be noted that the impact of the crisis has not had the same effect on all Spanish cities, making the degree of vulnerability very different. According to the Crisis Atlas [20], a differentiation can be established between those cities that have better withstood the onslaught of the crisis, and those that have been deeply scarred, showing high levels of vulnerability. Regarding the latter, it can be observed that they are concentrated in the following three focal points (Figure 6):

- The Mediterranean coast (especially in the Regions of Valencia and Andalusia), the Balearic Islands, and the Canary Islands, where tourist-based development, particularly in the dense construction on a massive scale of second homes for the middle-income population, generated a deep artificialization of the land, which caused serious environmental and socioeconomic impact and negatively affected the age-old agri-food specialization due to competition for soil or water.
- The metropolitan areas of the urban agglomerations of Madrid and Barcelona, throughout which immigrant and working-class neighborhoods spread, and where the impact of the bubble has left a landscape of architectural skeletons and unfinished spaces, eventually becoming ghost spaces.
- Areas of development, throughout which medium-sized cities are located and where the population and economic activity are concentrated. Worth noting are the Atlantic Axis in the northwest, the Huelva-Seville-Córdoba corridor in the south and the Ebro corridor in the northeast.

What is understood by urban vulnerability? According to the Urban Analysis of Vulnerable Neighborhoods published by the Ministry of Development [30], it refers to any unease or discomfort present in cities brought on by the combination of multiple aspects of disadvantage, in which all hope for upward social mobility and overcoming one's social status of exclusion (or close to it) is considered extremely difficult to achieve. To the contrary, it also entails the perception of insecurity and fear of the possibility of downward social mobility or a worsening of one's current living conditions. In general, the degree of vulnerability is greater in large cities, not only because a larger volume of the population is concentrated, but because individualism and an anomic social climate prevail within them, leading the individual to believe that they cannot count on other people, and that their family relationships are weaker. Moreover, they are the main destination of the immigrant population, which see them as having the greatest potential for finding a job. However, it has sometimes been interpreted that large cities are more prone to receiving a more intense initial impact than medium-sized cities due to their greater openness to the outside and their link to global markets. Furthermore, housing prices are more expensive, costs (such as transportation) are increased, and working conditions may be worse, as there is an ample workforce for a scarce labor supply.

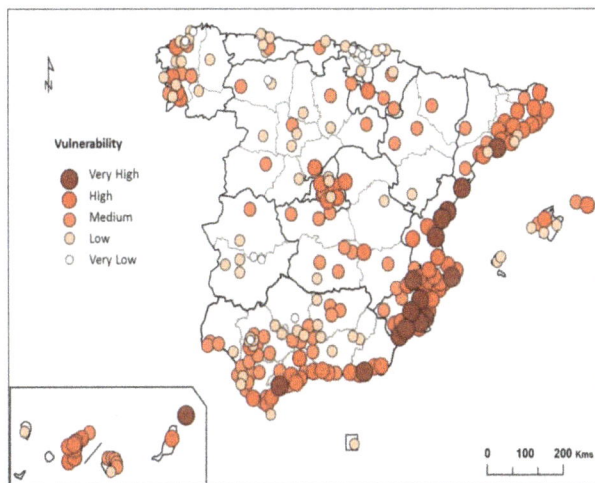

Figure 6. Vulnerability degree in the main Spanish cities [20].

This is not to say that medium-sized cities do not have problems of vulnerability. Their main weaknesses include limited economic diversification, which translates into a high percentage of SMEs, a shortage of innovative clusters, a lack of R&D+I institutions, limited social and cultural diversity—which is perceived in the shortage of local initiatives—little citizen mobilization, local governments with scarce resources and bureaucratic inertia, and low participation in city networks [20]. What happens is that these problems do not often come to light, either due to ignorance or because they do not interest their local governments. However, there is no doubt that these cities have also been affected by unemployment—we can see how their qualified human resources have had to emigrate to find work, and that the local administration has still not offered any plan for social improvement and economic dynamism for the most vulnerable neighborhoods.

Improving the quality of life of its citizens implies an in-depth knowledge of their problems. That is why, in order to measure the degree of vulnerability in medium-sized cities, see to what extent their governments are conscious of the situation and review the measures being taken to overcome this situation, two case studies have been selected: A Coruña and Vigo. These two cities are in north-western Spain, which make up the two main developed areas of the Atlantic Axis, with a similar population (243,978 and 292,817 inhabitants, respectively), but with very different trajectories. What they have in common is that they are both coastal cities, with important fishing ports on a national and international scale. However, while A Coruña is a city mainly offering services, in Vigo, automobile and shipyard industrial activity prevails. As regards local administration, in the first, the Marea Atlántica party has governed since the municipal elections of 2015, a left-leaning party born out of the people's movement and that demands a new model of urban governance based on transparency, real democracy, and social cohesion; in Vigo, the Socialist Party governs, whose representative has been in power for 11 years.

On an urban level, while A Coruña is a compact city, densely populated, and where urban growth has been conditioned by the scarce surface area of the municipality and its location on a peninsula, the urban space of Vigo is fragmented and disorganized. However, in both, we can make out a Historic Center, corresponding to the walled pre-industrial city, in which two areas can be differentiated: the old town, which after a period of serious physical, social, and economic deterioration is recovering thanks to European funds under the URBAN and regional initiatives, the well-known Integral Rehabilitation Areas (ARIs), and a second area, more dynamic and cared for at an urban level, identified as an urban center where commercial and business activity is concentrated and land and housing prices are higher. In this urban space, the value of the land determines residential and economic segregation, since only people with a high purchasing power can afford to purchase real estate and only those establishments or specialized entities with high profits can pay the rent of commercial establishments or offices. From the urban center a set of residential neighborhoods unfolds, in which the working population resides. It is possible to differentiate the following items between them (Figure 7):

- Those developed in the years 1960–1970 by the private initiative, which wanted to build on a massive scale to offer housing to the population coming to the city to work in industry (Florida, Teis, Cabral, O Calvario, Castrelos, and Balaídos in the case of Vigo; or Agra del Orzán, Os Mallos, Monte Alto, A Gaiteira, Castrillón, and Os Castros in A Coruña);
- Those that were built as a result of plans developed by the public initiative, aimed at people with a medium to medium-low purchasing power and/or who were expelled from other urban areas through expropriation processes. In general, they are characterized by having an open urban framework, with buildings in blocks (Coia in Vigo; Polígono de Elviña, Barrio de las Flores, Labañou, Sagrada Familia in A Coruña);
- New residential areas, built after 1990, where there was a concern for design, the quality of housing, green areas, and sports-leisure facilities (Navia in Vigo, Los Rosales and Paseo Puentes in A Coruña).

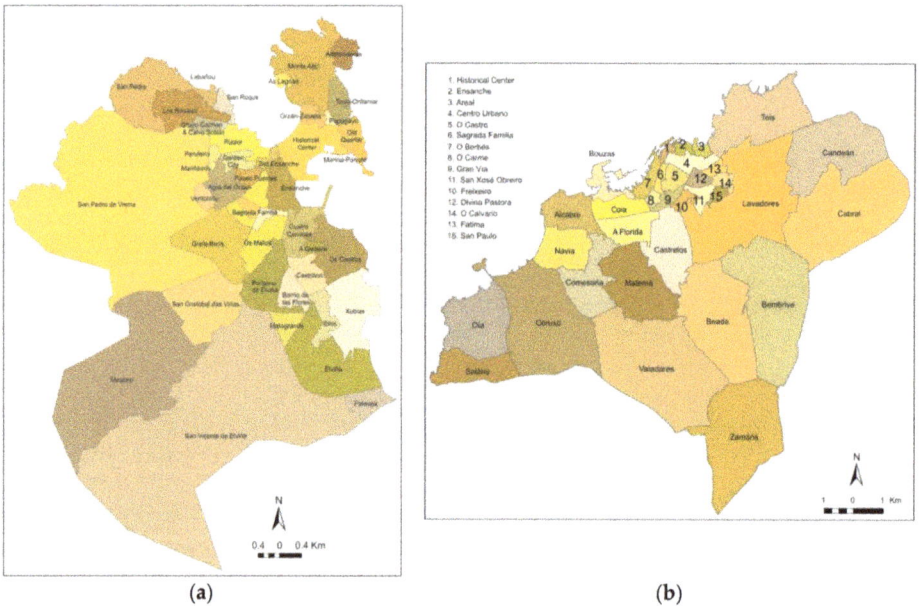

Figure 7. (a) Neighborhoods in A Coruña; (b) Neighborhoods in Vigo.

3. Method

Methodologically, from a geographical standpoint, both the consolidated urban space and the immediate periphery have been considered, although, with respect to the latter, there are notable differences between the cities being studied. In the case of A Coruña, the peripheral settlements are smaller, are very localized, and respond to two well-differentiated typologies: older settlements in which, despite conserving a rural landscape, the ways of life of their inhabitants are completely urban, and recently built housing developments for the well-off middle class. In the case of Vigo, what draws attention is its scattered peripheral growth, the result of urban development based on partial plans, and whose rustic land has not been accommodating, absorbing a large part of the housing deficit required by economically disadvantaged social groups, reaching densities higher than 100 hab/ha [31]. For statistical collection on an intra-urban scale, we have used urban cadastral sections, with these units being the smallest units of analysis. According to the National Institute of Statistics, in 2011 there were a total of 187 census tracts in A Coruña and 243 in Vigo in 2011.

For the calculation of the vulnerability index, we have supervised the research developed by Méndez, Albertos and Sánchez, Subirats and Martí-Costa, as well as Méndez [20,32,33]. However, when collecting the variables of analysis, we perceived that many of the indicators managed to have their origin in surveys, and that there was a significant statistical gap at the census tract scale with respect to important indicators such as the level of income, the number of basic facilities (educational, health) or the population with social benefits; and that in many occasions the sample volume used does not allow a sufficient level of confidence to be reached.

Taking these limitations into account, we combined the variables that put the economic, social and residential stability of the individual at risk into a single measurement. The variables we selected are the only ones offered by the Population and Housing Census published in 2011 by the National Institute of Statistics (INE) and the Galician Institute of Statistics (IGE). It is the last statistical publication to offer detailed and analyzed information on a scale of urban areas.

Each of the indicators has been classified according to the three main vulnerability groups identified in Table 1.

Table 1. Indicators for urban vulnerability.

Socio-Demographic	Socio-Economic	Residential
Ageing	Unemployed	Empty homes
Immigration	Working population replacement	Year of construction
Educational level	Workers with a temporary contract	State of the building

The first group refers to socio-demographic vulnerability, broken down into three aspects. The first focuses on ageing measured by the ageing index. The ageing process gradually transforms an adult subject with good health and full autonomy into an increasingly fragile individual who will gradually become more vulnerable and will have more difficulties developing their own model of life [34]. As a result, the more older population is registered, the more demand there will be for home care services and residences for the elderly. In this sense, it should be noted that A Coruña and Vigo are located in one of the Spanish regions with the highest ageing rate. The second aspect refers to immigration which, although it is understood that in times of prosperity it can be a fundamental contribution to alleviate the effects of an ageing population, in times of crisis it can become an area gravely affected by vulnerability due to the shortage of employment and precarious employment situations; that is, when they are not part of the unemployed population. The third aspect deals with educational level, because we can understand that one of the groups most affected by the crisis and vulnerability are young people with failed schooling and a poor education. The European Commission insists that good education and the acquisition of skills better qualifies an individual to find a job and amass higher purchasing power [28].

With regard to the socio-economic vulnerability aspect, a key factor to take into account is the volume of unemployed workers measured by the unemployment rate. This indicator relates, in an obvious way, to the ability to deal with basic-needs costs, especially in cases of long-term unemployment and with no unemployment benefits. If we relate this indicator to the ageing population, it is of interest to analyze the working population replacement rate, which measures the relationship between individuals 60–64 years of age that are ending their working lives, with people who are in the

15–19 years of age range, who are just starting it. This indicator shows that in the case of an ageing population the number of workers entering the labor market is lower, but essential to maintaining the welfare state. Finally, we have taken into account the volume of workers with a temporary contract, understanding that this type of contract does not guarantee peace of mind and continues to limit their ability to acquire a home or request a mortgage.

The third group of factors relates to residential vulnerability. A lot of research has featured the speculative process which resulted in a housing bubble and a high number of empty houses [11,12,18]. It is possible that developers never got to sell those homes, and if sold, they perhaps remained empty as they had been purchased as investments and not out of necessity. In any case, we can argue two reasons that may account for the number of empty homes: (a) they are unoccupied because the elderly owners pass away or move their residence to live with relatives; (b) are abandoned because they do not meet the appropriate habitability conditions. In any case, we think that the existence of a large number of empty homes denotes a lack of economic dynamism and a prominent demographic gap. Likewise, urban areas with an abundance of empty homes are being affected by squatting. The year of construction was also taken into account, specifically prior to 1970. This decade meant the construction of residential neighborhoods on a massive scale with poor construction quality, which currently suffer certain deficiencies (deterioration of façades, lack of elevators) so these buildings need more improvements. In relation to building state, because those in a deteriorate state determine poor living conditions and lead to degraded urban landscapes.

Once the indicators were selected, they were adjusted through normalization based on the unit, in a way so that values stayed within the range [0–1] where 1 indicates a greater degree of vulnerability. The formula used was $X_{normalized} = (X − X_{min})/(X_{max} − X_{min})$ where X_{max} and X_{min} are the maximum and minimum value of X. Subsequently, the normalized value was multiplied y the weighting value indicated in Table 2. As demonstrated, each of the variables was assigned a weighting value (in percentage terms) so that the sum was 100. The distribution of the weighting responds to the subjective criterion of the authors and to the knowledge acquired through different research financed by Europe and the Ministry of Economy and Competitiveness on the causes of the crisis, its effects and possible alternatives for remedying it. In all of them, it was found that unemployment and temporality are the most important factors when determining situations of poverty, social exclusion and vulnerability, for that reason, a 15% weight was assigned to these variables, while the rest remained at 10%.

Table 2. Weight for each variable.

Type of Urban Vulnerability	Indicator	Weight
Socio-demographic	Ageing	10%
	Immigration	10%
	Educational level	10%
Socio-economic	Unemployed	15%
	Workers with a temporary contract	15%
	Working population replacement	10%
Residential	State of the building	10%
	Empty homes	10%
	Year of construction	10%
Total		100%

With the weights determined, the results were mapped on a choropleth map for which a Geometric Interval was defined, and through which a balance was created between the changes highlighted in the central values and in the extreme values, thus producing a cartographically more comprehensible result.

4. Urban Vulnerability in A Coruña and Vigo

The urban vulnerability index obtained for A Coruña and Vigo tells us that the first has seen a greater impact from the economic crisis, as there are more urban areas in situations of high or very high vulnerability, specifically 39.5% of the cadastral sections, compared to 20.2% registered in Vigo (Figure 8). On the other hand, while in Vigo, 38.7% of the sections are affected by a low vulnerability, this rate does not even reach 23% in A Coruña.

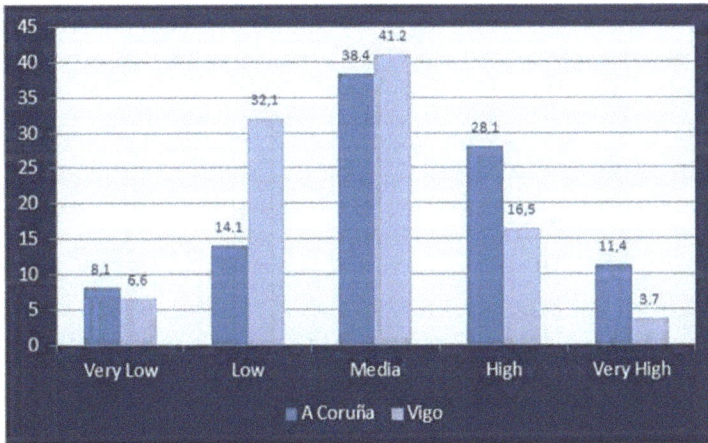

Figure 8. Distribution of vulnerability along urban sectors in A Coruña and Vigo. National Statistics Institute.

Among the factors explaining this situation, we must emphasize that Vigo is characterized by having a consolidated industrial fabric, with the automobile manufacturer Citröen, the canning factories (Albo, Molíns, Alfageme), the fishing industry (Pescanova) and the frozen foods industry standing out. Also in its vicinity is the O Porriño industrial estate, which houses industries committed to R&D+I, and are linked to the energy sector, such as Gamesa, or the chemical-pharmacological sector, such as PharmaMar (antitumor drugs of marine origin), Sylentis (drugs based on gene silencing—RNAi), Zelnova (insecticides, air fresheners), Xylazel (wood protection products), and Genomics (molecular analysis). In A Coruña, however, the business fabric is weaker, with the Petroleum Refinery and the Inditex group, linked to the fashion industry. Secondly, despite A Coruña having a somewhat lower unemployment rate than Vigo (16.28% versus 18.63%), its economy is built on smaller businesses and a service sector based on commerce and tourism—branches of activity in which work contracts are more unstable and have worse working conditions and wages. In this sense, the fact cannot be ignored that its Atlantic climate determines the concentration of tourist activity in the summer months; and that A Coruña has 12 malls, becoming one of the cities with the most land surface area allocated for shopping centers, only to be surpassed by Barcelona and Madrid. This phenomenon has led to the closure of small businesses both in the urban center and in other areas that had traditionally stood out for their commercial dynamism, such as the neighborhood of Agra del Orzán [35]. Finally, the fact that in Vigo there is an urban dispersion of 37% of the population gives a greater capacity for resilience with vulnerability having a lower impact. Although most of its inhabitants work in the industrial or service sector, having a house with a small vegetable garden allows them to have basic food products and reduce family spending. This situation is not registered in A Coruña, where its location on a peninsula and a more irregular topography in the periphery has caused urban development to be concentrated in one part of the municipality and 87% of the population to reside in flats in the consolidated urban nucleus.

If we analyze the degree of vulnerability in the urban center of both cities (Figure 9), the conclusions we can draw are that the areas with a higher vulnerability index respond to both areas in the Historic Center that have been left out of rehabilitation processes and with serious social problems (prostitution and drugs) as well as residential neighborhoods. In relation to the latter, on the one hand, we can differentiate those built in the developmental period (1960–1970), in which private and public housing were combined, where an adult-older population currently resides and where some social conflict has resurfaced due to an increase in criminal action. This refers to the neighborhoods of Monte Alto, Sagrada Familia, Mallos, and Barrio de las Flores in A Coruña. On the other hand, the outlying urban sectors, in which for years there was spontaneous growth, with shanty towns and accessibility problems such as Torre-Orillamar and Adormideras in A Coruña and others that are not yet fully consolidated and in which the landscape is based on housing blocks coexisting with garden spaces and traditional settlements such as Alcabre, Freixeiro, Salgueira, Divina Pastora-Urzaiz and San Xosé Obreiro in Vigo and Elviña, Eirís ,and Mesoiro in the city of A Coruña (Figure 10). In recent years, official housing has been built on these spaces to house the low-income population and shanty town dwellers from areas that were expropriated due to the construction of new infrastructure in the periphery, and the local government wanting them to integrate socially.

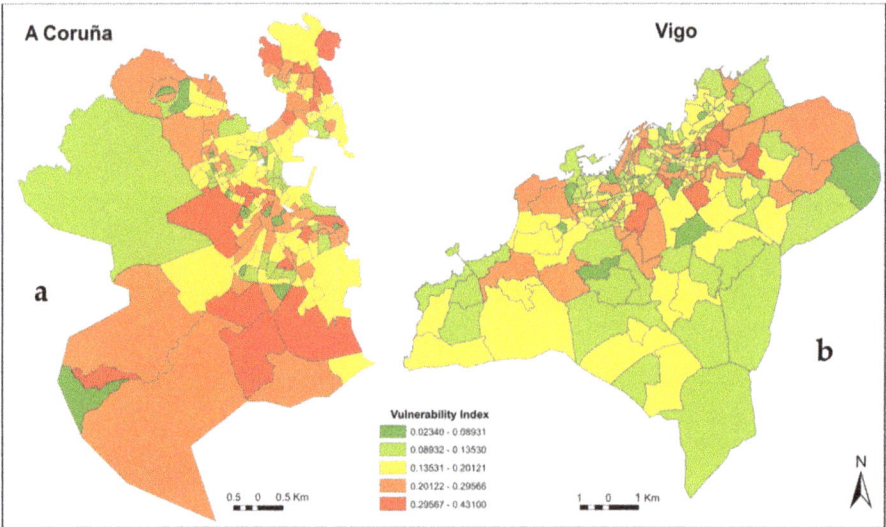

Figure 9. (**a**) Vulnerability Index in A Coruña; (**b**) Vulnerability Index in Vigo. National Statistics Institute.

Figure 10. Neighborhoods of Coia, Barrio de las Flores and Mesoiro. Source: Google images.

Areas with medium-level vulnerability have the greatest presence in both cities. In both cities, they are registered in most of the urban sections that make up the historic and urban center, where some processes of urban renewal have mitigated the deteriorating situation suffered over decades of neglect and where there is interest on the part of local governments to reactivate commercial activity and improve the quality of life of the inhabitants thanks to pedestrianization and urban improvement (lighting, urban furniture, vegetation) initiatives. We can also find them in those residential areas where a process of demographic regeneration is taking place or those built in recent decades, when there was greater concern for better building quality and green areas, and there was a proliferation of townhouses in the immediate periphery. In A Coruña, these would be Los Rosales, Matrogrande, San Critóbal das Viñas, As Xubias, and Palavea. As for Vigo, these vulnerability indexes are recorded in areas such as Navia and Comesaña, Coruxo, Candeán, and Bembrive, where housing developments have proliferated and single-family homes that were once for use on weekends have been converted into main residences (Figure 11).

Figure 11. Neighborhoods Los Rosales, Matogrande and Navia. Source: Google images.

Finally, areas with low vulnerability rates fall under four types of spaces: urban centers and peripheral areas, where the population with the highest purchasing power resides and where land prices are a factor in commercial and residential segregation; waterfronts, where traditional buildings alternate with new ones, all of them of high value—these areas are currently part of the development image of both cities and where intense gentrification processes have taken place (Parrote and the Marina in A Coruña, and Areal in Vigo); some sectors of neighborhoods that, although during the eighties stood out for their social conflict and were a focus of drugs such as Coia in Vigo and the Barrio de las Flores in A Coruña, nowadays have become quieter and of a higher quality thanks to their morphology into an open layout, the abundance of green spaces, and a turnover of residents. Previously an adult population predominated—even though it was part of the middle class, it showed strong differences in terms of its purchasing power—and a large group of young people, submerged in the world of drugs; currently, they are neighborhoods where there is an adult-young, middle-class population occupying the homes that have been left empty as a result of the death of their owners, and who walk safely through the streets since drugs devastated that whole generation of troubled youths. Peripheral urban sectors are those among which can be distinguished those near the beaches where secondary housing has proliferated to spend the weekend or the summer months (Palavea in Coruña, Oia in Vigo) and those in which there still persists a typology of traditional settlement of small houses with orchards, but in which the inhabitants have a totally urban lifestyle (San Pedro de Visma in Coruña, Cabral, Bembrive, Zamáns in Vigo) (Figure 12).

Figure 12. Urban sectors of Parrote, Areal and Oia. Source: Google images.

5. Initiatives to Combat Vulnerability

The 2015 municipal elections marked a turning point in municipal policies in order to tackle the serious consequences of the crisis. All parties in their electoral programs advocated for a change in the way the city is governed and stressed the demand to serve the neediest population and encourage economic growth.

However, once in power, the strategies promoted by local governments to deal with situations of vulnerability were very inconsistent. While some have chosen to accept their fate and react defensively to external pressures, others have decided to consider more proactive responses, arising from decisions and efforts of different people and institutions [36]. Some, such as Madrid or Barcelona, have focused their efforts on the following four key aspects: (a) give more attention to those most affected by the crisis, (b) stop eviction processes and seek alternatives in order to offer decent housing, (c) increase the participation of citizens in the city government and give more power to the urban districts, and (d) reduce intra-urban and territorial cohesion inequality in neighborhoods thanks to a budget distribution that would benefit the most disadvantaged individuals [19]. To do this, the local administration has transferred powers to the neighborhood councils in order to bring the administration closer to citizens and encourage participatory actions. In addition, they have conducted studies on the vulnerability of neighborhoods on the basis of which they have already designed various urgent action projects, mainly focused on offering government-owned homes or housing with social rents, as well as reducing social unrest through the promotion of culture and sport among children.

In the case of medium-sized cities, there are no large-scale measures or an interest in finding out to what extent the crisis has affected its neighborhoods and the population that lives there. It is true that there has been interest on the part of local governments to achieve more cohesive and less vulnerable cities. However, it is a fact that they still do not have in-depth studies of their cities. The statistical data available is scarce and does not cover the complexity of a vulnerability analysis. No field work has been done to obtain qualitative and quantitative information that alleviates the lack of official data (e.g., homeless and socially excluded individuals, families who need help to buy school books, child poverty, etc.), and there has not been a concern to develop intra-urban scale ratios of educational centers or health personnel in relation to the number of inhabitants.

In the case of A Coruña, the A Marea party focused its 2015 electoral program on the following five areas of intervention in order to change the urban governance model and serve the most vulnerable population:

- Strengthen democratic values and citizen participation. To achieve this, it proposed complete transparency in spending, the creation of a digital platform for citizen participation, the creation of participatory budgets and citizen participation in controlling spending; citizen referendums for transcendence issues and the limitation of eight-year mandates.

- Achieve a new territorial and urban model. To do this, it proposed creating a plan to promote the right to property and give a boost to public housing; provide a solution to the city's precarious settlements with a comprehensive integration plan (housing, employment, education, healthcare), create a support program for self-managed urban vegetable gardens and create parking rules to dissuade private cars from entering the city, and educate the population on environmental issues
- Promote justice and social cohesion through the creation of a Municipal Social Income to supplement the income of the neediest individuals; eradication of children's food poverty using the city's school network, eradication of energy poverty, care of dependent individuals through the creation of a Comprehensive Care Plan, creation of a Local Social Inclusion Plan, implementation of educational reinforcement programs to reduce school failure, and implementation of a Local Labor Inclusion Strategy for those Collectives at risk of exclusion.
- Promote a new economic and energy model by diversifying economic activity, encouraging local commerce, developing a Municipal Plan for the promotion of R&D+I, expanding family reconciliation services, carrying out research studies to update the real niches of the labor situation; recognizing the situations of energy poverty, prioritizing ethical banking, and pay off funds in banking institutions that carry out evictions.
- Promote culture, memory, and identity through the creation of a research center facilitating the implementation of cultural projects in the city, the promotion of basic sports and the installation of equipment on the street, the use of cultural and sports facilities by people with some type of disability, meet the demand for municipal nursery schools, and connect cultural infrastructures with the population of the neighborhoods in which they are located.

In Vigo, the city's ruling Socialist Party (in power since 2007) did not publish its electoral program but defined the priorities for its mandate to the media. It is mainly focused on humanizing the streets, creating playgrounds, fostering employment through work promoted by the municipal government (work in play centers and citizen support services like neighborhood caretakers), tax reduction for motorcycles and the promotion of electric bicycles, recovering fluvial spaces through the creation of walking trails, promoting culture and urban art, and increasing the number of flights on offer at the airport. As can be seen, it is still an urban government model that prioritizes work and in which initiatives for the promotion of social cohesion are completely absent.

After three years of governing, there are few initiatives to combat vulnerability that have been launched. The only changes that have been observed are the creation of a transparency portal through which the municipal budget is made public, and the creation of participatory budgets (three million euros) that are available to inhabitants to develop those projects that they consider of interest to improve their neighborhood and the city. However, despite the fact that weekly the mayor attends to the citizens through a radio program to know their problems and needs, it has not yet gone into depth on the state of the issue. Consequently, the only objective data available to the city council are the number of grants offered to individuals applying for RISGA, public assistance to guarantee financial subsistence support to those lacking. In the case of Vigo, only the transparency portal for municipal budgets has been created. A fact that corroborates the total lack of interest on the part of the local government for the situation of vulnerability in which the inhabitants are. It can be said that the mayor is still betting on a "showcase" city model, with attractive and pleasant streets for the walk, but that it hides serious social and economic problems in its neighborhoods.

As a result, the vulnerable population must seek their own resilience mechanisms. Among these are assistance centers such as shelters where they can sleep, and inexpensive kitchens that offer breakfast and lunch to people with problems in their dining rooms, even serving families or individuals who cannot access the dining room by bringing the food to their homes. There are also existing food banks in some neighborhoods, whose staff is voluntary, and other assistance entities such as the Red Cross or Cáritas that distribute food, kits to help children (hygiene and food), family support kits (school material, personal hygiene) and financial aid to help cover basic needs (rental payment, electricity bill), and that travel through the city with their mobile social emergency units, helping the homeless so that people can eat something hot, get warm clothes and receive health care. Lastly, we cannot forget the networks of friends and family members that, in the case of A Coruña and Vigo, continue to be of great importance. The money and food that they contribute is used for survival and causes the recorded degree of vulnerability to be lower than that actually derived from the economic and social situation of families.

6. Conclusions

Although the biggest cities in Spain, such as Madrid, Barcelona, Valencia, and Seville, have suffered most from the impact of the crisis, it has also left its mark on medium-sized cities (250,000–500,000 inhabitants). Here, the closing of companies, unemployment, the reduction of family income, and foreclosures have driven the population into a state of vulnerability. Despite the 2015 municipal elections bringing about greater interest by local governments to improve the quality of life of their citizens, there are still few initiatives that have been implemented to achieve it. In this sense, we believe that as long as local administrations do not stop to find out firsthand the reality of their neighborhoods and what the needs of their inhabitants are, they will not achieve the expected success in reducing levels of poverty and vulnerability. It is true that there is a statistical vacuum limiting the information necessary to carry out in-depth studies and that, since the start of the crisis, local administrations have been affected by excessive control of their local finances and by severe budget cuts applied by the State. For this reason, we find it necessary to promote qualitative studies through fieldwork, population surveys, and participatory actions in order to have a complete vision closer to reality.

Taking what has been noted into account, this article has made a first methodological approach regarding the study of vulnerability on an intra-urban scale, which, although based on the case studies of A Coruña and Vigo, we understand can be applied to other cities with similar characteristics (250,000–500,000 inhabitants). The results obtained signal to us that it is urgent to intervene in historical centers, where the loss of centrality and the predominance of an aging population has led to degradation, and in working-class neighborhoods and the outskirts, where social unrest is increasing. Finally, we believe that vulnerability maps are a key tool from which to visualize the most vulnerable urban areas and to define priorities for intervention.

Acknowledgments: This article was supported by the research project of the National R&D+I I Plan of the Ministry of Economy and Competitiveness: New Models of Government of Cities, and intervention in urban spaces in the post-crisis period (CSO 2016-75236-c2-1-r).

Author Contributions: María José Piñeira-Mantiñán conceived the research; Francisco R. Durán-Villa and María José Piñeira-Mantiñán analyzed the data; José Taboada-Failde contributed to the design of database and cartographic development; María José Piñeira-Mantiñán and Francisco R. Durán-Villa wrote the paper.

Conflicts of Interest: The authors declare no conflict of interest.

References

1. Peck, J.; Theodore, N.; Brenner, N. Neoliberalism resurgent? Market rule after the great recession. *South Atl. Q.* **2012**, *111*, 265–288. [CrossRef]
2. European Commission. *Cities of Tomorrow*; European Commission: Brussels, Belgium, 2011.
3. Fernández, E.; Jefe, E. *Caixabank Research. Informe Mensual*; Caixabank: Barcelona, Spain, 2018.
4. European Commission. *My Region, My Europe, Our Future. Seventh Report on Economic, Social and Territorial Cohesion*; European Commission: Brussels, Belgium, 2017.
5. Ranci, C.; Brandsen, T.; Sabatinelli, S. New Social Risks and the Role of Local Welfare: An Introduction. In *Social Vulnerability in European Cities. Work and Welfare in Europe*; Ranci, C., Brandsen, T., Sabatinelli, S., Eds.; Palgrave Macmillan: London, UK, 2014; pp. 3–30.
6. Kiss, M. *Vulnerable Social Groups before and after the Crisis*; European Parliament: Luxembourg, 2016.
7. Begg, I.; Mushövel, F.; Niblett, R. *The Welfare State in Europe. Visions for Reform*; Royal Institute of International Affairs: London, UK, 2015.

8. Dorling, D.; Ballas, D. Spatial Divisions of Poverty and Wealth. In *Understanding Poverty, Wealth and Inequality: Policies and Prospects*; Ridge, T., Wright, S., Eds.; Policy Press: Bristol, UK, 2008; pp. 103–134.

9. Lemoy, R.; Raux, C.; Jensen, P. *Where in Cities do Rich and Poor People Live? The Urban Economics Model Revisited*; Hal Archives Ouvertes: Paris, France, 2013.

10. Vives Miró, S. *L'espai Urbà del Capitalisme. La Construcció del Projecte Neoliberal de Palma*; Universitat Illes Balears: Palma de Mallorca, Spain, 2013.

11. Rullan Salamanca, O. Urbanismo expansivo en el Estado Español: De la utopía a la realidad. In *Geografía y Desafíos Territoriales en el Siglo XXI*; Gozálvez, V., Marco, J.A., Eds.; Asociación de Geógrafos Españoles & Universidad de Alicante: Alicante, Spain, 2012; pp. 165–209.

12. Burriel de Orueta, E. La década prodigiosa del urbanismo español (1997–2006). *Scr. Nova* **2008**, *270*, 64.

13. Lois González, R.C.; Piñeira Mantiñán, M.J. Urban development processes in Spain—From consolidated cities to urban regions with an overdensified housing market. In *Contemporary Problems of Urban and Regional Development*; Mierzejewsa, L., Wdowicka, M., Eds.; Bogucki: Poznan, Poland, 2011; pp. 61–71.

14. Lois González, R.; Piñeira Mantiñán, M.J.; Vives Miró, S. The urban bubble process in Spain: An interpretation from the theory of circuits of capital. *J. Urban Reg. Anal.* **2016**, *8*, 5–20.

15. Gaja i Díaz, F. El 'tsunami urbanizador' en el litoral mediterráneo. El ciclo de hiperproducción inmobiliaria 1996–2006. *Scr. Nova* **2008**, *270*, 1.

16. Jiménez Asensio, R. Las instituciones locales en tiempo de crisis: Reforma institucional y gestión de recursos humanos en los Gobiernos Locales. *Cuad. Derecho Soc.* **2011**, *25*, 57–77.

17. Buck, N.; Gordon, I.; Harding, A.; Turok, I. *Changing Cities: Re-Thinking Competitiveness, Cohesion and Governance*; Palgrave Publishers: New York, NY, USA, 2005.

18. Lois González, R.C.; Piñeira Mantiñán, M.J. The revival of urban social and neighbourhood movements in Spain: A geographical characterization. *Di Erde* **2015**, *146*, 127–138.

19. González Pérez, J.; Lois González, R.C.; Piñeira Mantiñán, M.J. The Economic Crisis and Vulnerability in the Spanish Cities: Urban Governance Challenges. *Soc. Behav. Sci.* **2016**, *223*, 160–166. [CrossRef]

20. Méndez, R.; Abad, L.D.; Echaves, C. *Atlas de la Crisis. Impactos Socioeconómicos y Territorios Vulnerables en España*; Tirant lo Blanch: Valencia, Spain, 2015.

21. Seopan. *Construcción e Infraestructuras: Estadísticas 2016 y Previsiones Para 2017*; Seopan: Madrid, Spain, 2016.

22. EPA. *Encuesta de Población Activa*; Instituto Nacional de Estadística: Madrid, Spain, 2013.

23. Durán Villa, F.R.; Piñeira Mantiñán, M.J. Evictions and the social crisis in Spanish cities. In *Urban Challenges in a Complex World: Resilience, Governance and Changing Urban Systems*; Moore, N., Ed.; University College Dublin: Dublin, Ireland, 2016; pp. 80–85.

24. Valiño, V. *Emergencia Habitacional en el Estado Español: La Crisis de Las Ejecuciones Hipotecarias y Los Desalojos Desde una Perspectiva de Derechos Humanos*; Observatorio OESC: Barcelona, Spain, 2013.

25. EPA. *Encuesta de Población Activa*; Instituto Nacional de Estadística: Madrid, Spain, 2016.

26. Fundación 1 de Mayo. *Mercado de Trabajo y Protección Por Desempleo*; Fundación 1 de Mayo: Madrid, Spain, 2016.

27. Caravaca, I.; González, G.; López, P. Crisis y empleo en las ciudades españolas. *Eure* **2017**, *43*, 31–54. [CrossRef]

28. European Commission. *Draft Joint Employment Report 2018*; European Commission: Brussels, Belgium, 2018.

29. Fundación BBVA. *Distribución de la Renta, Crisis Económica y Políticas Redistributivas*; Fundación BBVA: Bilbao, Spain, 2016.

30. Ministry of Development. *Análisis Urbanístico de Barrios Vulnerables*; Ministry of Development: Madrid, Spain, 2006.

31. González Pérez, J.M. Planificación y construcción de ciudades medias en el sistema urbano industrial: Los casos de Palma de Mallorca y Vigo. *Bol. AGE* **2005**, *40*, 449–471.

32. Albertos, J.M.; Sánchez, J.L. *Geografía de la Crisis Económica en España*; Universidad de Valencia: Valencia, Spain, 2014.

33. Subirats, J.; Martí-Costa, M. *Ciudades Vulnerables y Crisis en España*; Fundación Pública Andaluza Centro de Estudios Andaluces: Seville, Spain, 2014.

34. Casado, M.; Rodríguez, P.; Vilà, A. *Document on Ageing and Vulnerability*; Universidad de Barcelona: Barcelona, Spain, 2016.

35. Escudero Gómez, L.A.; Lois González, R.C.; Piñeira Mantiñán, M.J. The new shopping center bubble and its impact on urban dynamics: The case of A Coruña. *Geotema* **2016**, *51*, 83–89.
36. Méndez, R. Ciudades y metáforas: Sobre el concepto de resiliencia urbana. *Ciudad Territ.* **2012**, *44*, 215–231.

urban science

MDPI

Article

Counter Land-Grabbing by the Precariat: Housing Movements and Restorative Justice in Brazil

Clara Irazábal

Department of Architecture, Urban Planning + Design (AUP + D), University of Missouri—Kansas City,
5120 Rockhill Rd, Haag Hall 204D, Kansas City, MO 64110, USA; irazabalzuritac@umkc.edu;
Tel.: +1-917-539-9828

Received: 27 February 2018; Accepted: 5 June 2018; Published: 13 June 2018

Abstract: Social housing movements in Brazil, whose majority members are part of Brazil's precariat or lowest-income class, are courageously pressing for true urban reform in Brazil, whose old promise has been systematically delayed and subverted, even by some of those who were put in power to realize it. By occupying vacant and underutilized land and buildings, not only are these movements confronting neoliberalism in Brazil at a time of the model's highest level of hegemony in the country and the world, they are also unveiling the impossibility of the system to deliver sociospatial justice to the poor and are enacting an alternative. Through restorative justice practices, they go beyond critique and press for an alternate sociopolitical project that would allow millions of people in Brazil access to decent housing, and through it, to a myriad of other opportunities, including the right to the city. As shown in the experiences of those participating in housing struggles, restorative justice deserves further exploration as an alternative planning mode that can combine the strengths of advocacy planning and communicative action while reducing their drawbacks. These reflections focus on the *Movimento dos Trabalhadores Sen Teto* (MTST) and partially feed from team ethnographic and planning studio work on several building and land occupations in Rio de Janeiro and São Paulo in Brazil in 2016.

Keywords: land grabbing; precariat; social movements; housing; restorative justice; Brazil

---

1. Introduction

A large group of members of the Brazil's precariat or lowest income class, politically organized in social housing movements, are courageously pressing for a true urban reform in Brazil. The promise of the Brazilian urban reform movement of the 1980s delivered important accomplishments [1,2] among them, new progressive institutions, laws, and citizen participation mandates and mechanisms. However, the full realization of its aspirations—the right to the city for all in Brazil—has been systematically delayed and/or subverted, even by some of those who were put in power to realize it, such as elected officials from the *Partido dos Trabalhadores* (Workers' Party, PT).

By occupying vacant and underutilized land and buildings in and around Brazilian cities, not only are the social housing movements' unsung heroes/heroines confronting neoliberalism in Brazil at a time of the model's highest level of hegemony in the country and the world [3], the movements are also unveiling the impossibility of the neoliberal system to deliver sociospatial justice to the poor and enacting an alternative. Through restorative justice practices the movements triggered through land and building occupations, as well as through their internal dynamics and in their dealing with the state and other housing and land stakeholders, they go beyond critique of neoliberalism. They press for a substitute sociopolitical project that would allow millions of people in Brazil access to decent housing and to a myriad of other opportunities—including better access to education, health, jobs, decision making participation and autonomy, etc., i.e., the right to the city [4–7]. As shown in the experiences of those participating in the movements' housing struggles, restorative justice deserves further exploration as an alternative planning mode that can combine the strengths of advocacy planning and communicative action while reducing their drawbacks.

I argue that the way and scale by which low-income, roofless people are grabbing lands and buildings through these social housing movements in both central and peripheral areas of multiple Brazilian cities constitutes a restorative land grab that turns the national, urban land system upside down. They counter the land-grabbing phenomenon expanding as a key instrument of "accumulation by dispossession" [8,9], which is globally taking place as one of the latest waves of neoliberalism. Not only does the social housing movements' land grab resist the negative implications resulting from the land grabbing by the powerful, but also aims to reverse them.

The article expands these arguments through the following sections: the *Movimento dos Trabalhadores Sen Teto* (Roofless Workers' Movement, MTST) as a social housing movement, land grabbing turned on its head, the precariat as leaders of the struggle for land reform in Brazil, restorative justice as a path to authentic and lasting urban reform, core planning instruments that support the social housing movement MTST's *modus operandi*, and persistent obstacles faced by the movement.

2. A Note on Methodology

These reflections partially feed from team ethnographic and planning studio work on several building and land occupations by the MTST and other social housing movements in Rio de Janeiro and São Paulo in Brazil in 2016. A colleague and I cotaught a semester-long, international planning studio course with seven master students of planning at Columbia University in New York, USA, entitled, "Right to the City: Housing and Community Development in Brazil", in the spring of 2016 [10]. The MTST was our main interlocutor in São Paulo and Rio de Janeiro. We sustained conversations with leaders and members of the movement via Skype while in New York and in person during our two-week stay in Brazil. The studio also had a Columbia-Brazilian institutional partner, Studio-X Rio de Janeiro. We benefited from its research, contacts, and events on social housing movements in Rio de Janeiro and São Paulo, and performed our own participant observations, interviews, presentations, and focus group discussions with MTST members in its venue and in the localities of several occupations in both cities.

3. The *Movimento dos Trabalhadores Sen Teto*: A Social Housing Movement

This manuscript does not attempt to analyze the specificities of Rio de Janeiro's or São Paulo's occupations, but instead discuss the MTST movement from a broader perspective—its philosophy, strategies, and implications—situating it on larger political economy contexts in both Brazil and the world (i.e., neoliberalism and land-grabbing processes) and positioning its *modus operandi* as example of emancipatory politics, specifically, restorative justice.

I refer to the MTST as a social *housing* movement because it places housing at the center of its struggles. Yet, it conceives of housing as larger than physical shelter. Rather, it views it as the entry point to the right to the city, not solely in the sense of access to better education, health, jobs, etc., but to a different type of city altogether in which use value is prioritized over exchange value. Hence, the movement explicitly problematizes the capitalist order, proposing instead to open up urban land and decent housing to those in need independently of their purchasing power. MTST is a *social housing* movement because its conception of the right to housing is solely realized if housing is available to all. In its words:

> It is of no use getting houses if life continues in the same way, with capitalism imposing its rules. For this reason, [the strategy of] occupations has a greater meaning for us than the struggle for housing: it is a way of forming new militants for the struggle, of building reference in the urban periphery, and of showing workers that—with unity and organization—we have the power to confront this system. [11]

The movement engages in demonstrations (marches, blockading of major streets, picketing of political offices) demanding housing and a larger urban reform, yet those actions are done in support of their main strategy—occupations. In the movement's testimony:

> Our most important form of action is urban land occupations. With them we directly pressure the big landowners and the state, denounce the social problem of housing, and construct a process of autonomous organization of the workers. [12]

The MTST is a national movement with chapters in several metropolitan areas of Brazil. In addition, it has multiple movements and institutional "partners" with which it both collaborates and benefits from (for a list of MTST's partners, see http://www.mtst.org/parceiros/). Aside from the MTST, there are many other social housing movements in Brazil that differ in their aims, strategies, organization, and ways of engagement with the state. Apart from their individual aims and actions, movements frequently build coalitions and strive to collaborate with each other, including the MTST.

Unfortunately, information about how much vacant and underutilized land and idle housing has been grabbed by the MTST and how much housing was built as a result of its land-grabbing is not readily available. This is not information the movement keeps systematic track of or, at least, does not have it publicly available. It is understandable, since occupations are deemed illegal by the establishment and the movement and members of it can be accused, fined, and jailed due to their participation in occupations.

As a proxy to this information in the municipalities of São Paulo and ABC (metro region), the Removal Observatory [13], an action research group of Universidade de São Paulo (USP) and Universidade Federal do ABC Paulista (UFABC), maps, monitors, and develops collaborative actions with communities in territories threatened with evictions since 2010. According to the Observatory, at least 14,000 families have been evicted from their homes in the metro region since 2017. The great majority of evicted people relocate to favelas and occupations in the historical center of the capital—occupations of buildings—and peripheral fringes. The Observatory's data are collected from social media (WhatsApp) denunciations, the monitoring of news reports in the media, and contacts with the movements, leaders, and legal defense institutions. My own preliminary mapping of occupations in São Paulo (produced May–August 2016) used those sources and corroborated spatial information with Google Maps. It verified information about 30 occupied buildings (just one of which led by MTST), 10 occupied land lots by MTST, and 10 more by other social movements (see locations of MTST occupations according to the movement's reports on Figure 1).

I use the term social housing to denote housing constructed with public funding through the *Minha Casa-Minha Vida* (My House, My Life, MCMV), the federal housing program of Brazil. The majority of the MCMV projects, particularly in metro areas such as São Paulo's, are multifamily and owner-occupied (more on the program below). The exclusivity of owner-occupancy is one more way in which the MCMV program neither experiments with nor expand other housing tenure modes (e.g., rental and more progressive tenure modes such as community land trusts or cooperatives) that could make access to housing more affordable and versatile.

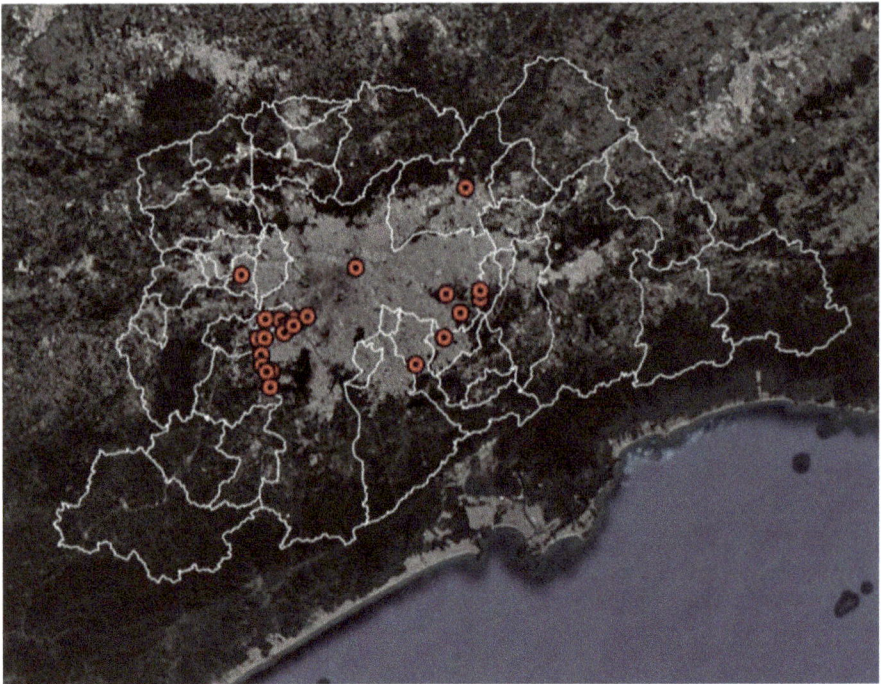

Figure 1. Occupations by the MTST in metropolitan São Paulo, 2016. Map elaborated by Luiza Lacerda, Daniela DiasRegis, and Renata Camarate.

4. Land Grabbing Turned on Its Head

Land grabbing has been defined as land "acquisitions or concessions that are one or more of the following: (i) in violation of human rights, particularly the equal rights of women; (ii) not based on free, prior and informed consent of the affected land users; (iii) not based on a thorough assessment, or are in disregard of social, economic and environmental impacts, including the way they are gendered; (iv) not based on transparent contracts that specify clear and binding commitments about activities, employment and benefits sharing, and; (v) not based on effective democratic planning, independent oversight and meaningful participation" [14].

Land grabbing is a term that is increasingly used in the development studies literature to refer to the contentious issue of large-scale land acquisitions: the buying or leasing of large tracts of land, mostly in developing or emerging countries by domestic or transnational companies (such as Monsanto, Nestlé, or Coca-Cola), governments (such as the UK, the US, China, and India) or individuals. It primarily refers to large-scale land acquisitions following the 2007–08 global food price crisis [15] and has also led to an associated trend of water grabbing [16]. The process has expanded globally under neoliberalism, as a key instrument of "accumulation by dispossession" [8,9].

These large-scale investments in land have been criticized by civil society organizations and scholars as having negative impacts on local communities because of their effects on land insecurity, poor or inexistent local consultation and compensation for land, development-induced displacement, unemployment and underemployment of local people, shady processes of negotiations between investors and governments, negative environmental and labor consequences of large-scale agriculture, and neocolonialism—a renewed economic imperialism of developed or rapidly developing countries over developing nations [17].

I distinguish three broad, historical periods of land grabbing in Brazil: colonial land grabbing, 1530 to late 19th century; modern land grabbing, late 19th century to mid-20th century; and neoliberal land grabbing, 1970s to the present.

With the Portuguese occupation of Brazil in 1530, the rules of occupation of urban and rural land were defined by the king, the church, and oftentimes the landowners to be, particularly belonging to or favored by the aforementioned institutions [18]. The law tried to regulate access to unoccupied areas and established a land registry to define the areas that would belong to the state. However, the acquisition of unoccupied areas was allowed, independently of their occupation by indigenous people, who were evicted or killed. Colonial land grabbing lasted for centuries. The Law of Lands in 1850 instituted private property. Landowners needed to demarcate and register their rural and urban properties, but without much supervision or proof of previous ownership. This condition enhanced fraud in the records in public registers. A scamming practice called *grilagem* was widely used by which property titles were put in boxes filled with crickets so that they made the papers look old and valid [18]. It is estimated that some 100 million hectares in Brazil were grabbed in this way.

Within the modern land grabbing period, Constantino [19] identifies the agricultural export stage (late 19th century to 1930s) and the industrialization stage (1930s to 1970s). The year of 1964 carried significant change in the agrarian scenario. The creation of the Land Statute ensured that rural propriety had to fulfill social functions, which involved a satisfactory level of land productivity. If a large propriety did not satisfy its social functions, it could be expropriated for agrarian reform [18]. Unfortunately, implementation of this law has been very poor.

Thus, the need and hopes of agrarian reform fueled the creation of one of the largest and longer-lasting social movement in the world—the Landless Workers' Movement (*Movimento dos Trabalhadores Sem Terra*, MST). The MST represents millions in rural Brazil that do not have access to decent livelihoods, given that according to 1996 census statistics, 3% of the population owns two-thirds of all arable land in Brazil. The movement legally justifies its occupations of unproductive land pointing to the Constitution of Brazil [20], which states that land should fulfill a social function (Article 5, XXIII).

With the advent of neoliberalism in Brazil (1970s until the present), land grabbing has been facilitated by changes made to land regulation for land belonging to foreigners. In 1995, Brazil's National Congress approved an amendment to the Brazilian Constitution eliminating article 171, which had previously made a distinction between national and foreign companies, effectively removing barriers to the amount of land foreign corporations were able to purchase in Brazil [21]. Since the global food crisis in 2008, there has been an increase in the purchase or lease of large portions of land in Brazil by foreign investors. More than half of the foreign capital invested in land in Brazil comes from just seven countries: Portugal, Japan, Italy, Lebanon, Spain, Germany, and the Netherlands. The lands are cultivated for various purposes—the so-called "flex crop" phenomenon [19,22]. The neoliberal reforms meant having land offered to the more lucrative activities, leaving aside important considerations about employment or food and nation-state sovereignty. Recent activities (mostly natural resource extraction) are often produced in highly automated industries with relative high profit and low employment. Some companies representing these lucrative activities are Cargill, Bunge and Born, PDVSA, and Petrobras [19].

This land grabbing phenomenon is not exclusive to Brazil. A global Land Portal database reports on about 50 billion hectares of land deals in the world, with about half of that been of transnational land acquisitions, mostly of investments in the production of palm oil and biofuels [23]. The largest destination country is Brazil with 11 percent by land area. In 2010, Brazil started enforcing a long-existing law that limits the size of farmland properties foreigners may purchase, halting a large part of projected foreign land purchases [24]. However, this trend may be reversing since the overturn of President Dilma Roussef in 2016.

As this brief historical account illustrates, land grabbing by individuals, institutions, and companies in Brazil is an integral part of its history and its present. Today, the inequality of rural land distribution in Brazil is one of the highest in the world and has not been able to be redressed by failed attempts to agrarian reform. Aside from indigenous resistance since the colonial period, more recently landless rural social movements that started in the 1960s and roofless urban social movements that started in the 1980s have been flipping land grabbing in Brazil on its head by performing restorative land occupation of their own. This has happened at a much more modest scale, but it is still of significance.

In the 1980s, an urban reform movement surged fueled by grassroots and multisectoral coalitional mobilization in Brazil [1,2]. It tried to redress the unjust land distribution in cities, realizing the right to housing and the right to the city [4–7]. The right to housing is recognized in the Universal Declaration of Human Rights and in many nation-state constitutions, including Brazil's. It is also broadly discussed in academic literature analyzing and advocating for the decommodification of housing. As such, it is tied to the right to the city as housing is conceived as a necessary, albeit insufficient entry point of access to the city's services and opportunities. The urban reform movement helped enthrone these rights in the new Brazilian constitution [20] and the ensuing federal and local laws—particularly the federal, 2001 City Statute. Since then, people have been organizing in urban social movements to collectively demand and press for the realization of their right to the city and to housing. One main strategy they use in their struggle is the grabbing of idle buildings and lands that are not serving their constitutionally mandated social function and could be relatively easily—mediating favorable political and judicial will—converted into decent social housing projects.

I argue that the low-income, roofless people grabbing lands and buildings at the scale that they are doing so through these housing movements in both central and peripheral areas of multiple Brazilian cities is nothing short of a counter, restorative land grab that turns the national, urban land system upside down. Not only is it a land occupation that resists the negative, aforementioned implications resulting from the land grabbing by the powerful, but also aims to reverse them. Instead, these land occupations create conditions conducive to land security, just local consultation and compensation for land, security of permanence and tenure and dignified employment for local people, just and transparent processes of negotiations between investors, governments, and communities, good stewardship of the environment and local agriculture, food sovereignty, and thus overall real conditions for overcoming neocolonial development and subjectivity formations.

5. The Precariat: Unsung Leaders of the Struggle for Land Reform in Brazil

In sociological and economic terms, the precariat is a social class formed by people suffering from precarity, a condition of living without security or predictability, affecting material and psychosocial wellbeing. Unlike the proletariat class of industrial workers in the 20th century, who lacked their own means of production and sold their labor to live, today's members of the precariat are only partially involved in labor. They are subjected to conditions of job insecurity, intermittent employment or underemployment, and the resultant precarious existence [25]. The emergence of this class has been ascribed to the entrenchment of neoliberal capitalism [26,27]. Standing [28] analyzed the precariat as an emerging social class. In his words, the precariat, consists of a multitude of insecure people, living bits-and-pieces lives, in and out of short-term jobs, without a narrative of occupational development, including millions of frustrated educated youth who do not like what they see before them, millions of women abused in oppressive labor, growing numbers of criminalized people tagged for life, millions being categorized as 'disabled', and migrants in their hundreds of millions around the world. They are denizens; they have a more restricted range of social, cultural, political, and economic rights than citizens around them.

In visiting occupations in Rio de Janeiro and São Paulo, Brazil I heard multiple stories of people unemployed, underemployed, and precariously working in an on-and-off basis. Their chronic challenges earning a living lead to persistent food insecurity and housing poverty. Ghillerme Boulos [29,30], member of the National Coordination of the Roofless Workers' Movement (*Movimento dos Trabalhadores Sen Teto*, MTST), corroborated that MTST members and members of a myriad of other social housing movements in Brazil are regularly people that are in one or more of these situations: homeless, unable to sustain current housing (rent or mortgage) costs without neglecting other needs; doubling up with relatives or friends as a favor; living in precarious housing; and people who lost their shelter to disasters or are at high risk of facing disasters where they reside.

Massive discontent can turn the precariat into "the new dangerous class", as Standing [25] called it. In Brazil, the precariat can indeed be considered 'dangerous', but not in the Marxian way in which the *lumpenproletariat* was considered dangerous, i.e., its lack of class consciousness, but precisely for its rebellious potential as destabilizer of the status quo (in this case a land and property regime destabilization purposely pursued by the MTST). Precarity does pose a great danger to the status quo because members of the social housing movements push for the Brazilian constitution and the urban reform to be truly realized, and not just remain as meaningless words on a piece of paper.

More importantly, the level of chronic poverty of the precariat should primarily be considered a danger to members within the class, because it subjugates them to subhuman conditions of living, threatening their well-being, their health, and ultimately their lives. Their precarity should also be deemed dangerous to society at large, because it compromises the wellbeing of members of the current labor class and future generations, with many of today's children facing limited opportunities to reach their full potential as productive and healthy adults.

To further explain the notion of the precariat, I invoke Agamben's [31] concept of the *homo sacer*. The *homo sacer* (Latin for "the accursed man") was a figure of ancient Roman law: a person who was banned and could be injured or killed by anybody with impunity. The idea of a person declared as unprotected by law who can consequently be hurt by anyone with immunity persisted throughout the Middle Ages, reproving the entire human intrinsic moral worth of the condemned outlaw, dehumanizing her literally as an animal—a "wolf" [32]. The notion was first revoked by the English Habeas Corpus Act of 1679, which declared that any person must be judged by a tribunal before being punished.

Agamben takes the concept of the *homo sacer* as a starting point in his work on "sovereign power and bare life". As a clear example of "bare life"—bodies stripped off their human and political dignity—and homo sacer, the precariat members of the housing movements in Brazil (not all members of the MTST and other housing social movements in Brazil are part of the precariat, as the movements have allied members, but the majority are) have been evicted from some of their building and land occupations with disproportionate, unchecked police and civil violence. Frequently, mysterious fires have destroyed their occupations, women have been abused and raped, and men have "disappeared" or been tortured, with no accountability for the perpetrators of these crimes. Bare life or a *homo sacer* is what the average member of the MTST and similar social movements is considered, in-and-of herself, by a large sector of Brazilian society and its legal apparatus: a non-fully human, non-fully political body: a noncitizen or, at best, a subcitizen. The mainstream media and politicians and landowners threatened by the values driving social housing movements' actions in Brazil portray them as criminals and even terrorists, which in turn put their members at higher risks and make their actions more difficult. The criminalization of social housing movements and their members performing land and building occupations has been a permanent challenge the MTST has faced, even under political regimes empathetic to their goals, such as the *Partido dos Trabalhadores* (PT). In the latter cases, criminalization has been low or nonexistent from the part of state authorities, but has come from the political opposition, landowners, and others philosophically or materially threatened by the movements' actions.

In order for a deemed noncitizen or subcitizen to be "dangerous", as Standing [25] called the precariat, she would need to become part of a social class, and even more so, a social movement with class consciousness. A powerless person cannot systemically transform anything on her own—she is not as dangerous. Her dignity as a human being is deemed so small or inexistent—a *homo sacer* or bare life—that it can be inconsequentially dismissed, i.e., its violation would hardly carry any moral or legal judgment or consequence. Yet, when many "powerless" human beings come together they accrue a collective dignity and power that is hard to dismiss any longer. They go from a powerless *homo sacer* to a collective "homo social", in the process acquiring a power that is dangerous, i.e., potentially transformative. In explaining this phenomenon, Saskia Sassen [33] speaks about the power of the powerless. Cities are places where the powerless can shape history, she claims. Thus, the Brazilian housing movements are going from "making life" dynamics—the reproduction of quotidian life—to "making history" ones—pushing for structural transformations [34,35]. As the work of Zibechi [36,37] on social movements in Bolivia has demonstrated, courageous and innovative social movements can succeed in transforming states with new forms of emancipatory politics that challenge neocolonialism and neoliberalism.

As an example of the array of Brazilian social housing movements, the MTST had 23 land occupations in Greater São Paulo in 2016, with 50–60,000 people participating in them, according to members' reports (see Figure 1). Just in the Nova Palestina occupation in the outskirts of São Paulo, MTST members claimed to have about 300,000 sq. mt. of land (see Figure 2). With these large land occupations, not only do they call the attention of other housing-poor people that end up joining the movement, they also force the attention of landowners and city officials that for whatever reason—often times greed, ideological opposition, and/or political indifference—had not been responsive to the movement's demands. So, this is a sizable and symbolically powerful urban land grab by which the precariat is pushing for restorative justice as both a central process and outcome in the struggle for Brazil's needed new urban land reform [38].

Figure 2. Partial view of MTST occupation Nova Palestina in the periphery of São Paulo. Photo: Clara Irazábal, 2016.

6. Restorative Justice as a Path to Authentic and Lasting Urban Reform

There is a vast historical social debt that Brazil, as many other countries around the world, has vis-à-vis its precariat. By claiming their constitutional rights to the city and to housing, Brazilian housing movements are inviting the power holders in Brazil—and with that all of us citizens of the world—to courageously embrace restorative justice as an approach to justice that could accomplish much in redeeming such debt.

Restorative justice focuses on the recovery of the victims, and not on the arrest and conviction of the offenders. The offender may get a punishment for acts s/he committed, if restorative and criminal justice operate concomitantly. More importantly, under a restorative justice approach, the offender will take responsibility for her/his actions and commit to redressing the existing injustice. In a dialogical process, which a facilitator may mediate, the victim would be able to understand why the crime has happened and the offender would be directed to the next steps intending to reduce the harm caused by her/his actions. Thus, the systemic social order in place that produced the injustice is acknowledged and explained, not ignored or justified. The stakeholders then explore and agree on how to collaborate to subvert the root causes of the injustice.

Distinct from the punitive approach of criminal justice in Brazil (and most countries, including the U.S.), restorative justice focuses on the needs of victims, offenders, and the involved community. The intent is for everybody to make progress as people build together a more just society. This is in contrast to punitive justice approaches where the main aim is to castigate the offender or satisfy abstract legal principles. The approach is based on a theory of justice that considers wrongdoing to be an offence against individuals and communities, rather than the state [39]. Restorative justice fosters dialogue and empathy, showing high rates of participants' satisfaction and accountability [40].

Bringing this concept to urban planning, both the substance—demands for the right to housing and to the city—and processes—participatory and consciousness-raising—of MTST and other social housing movements in Brazil are expressions of restorative justice. Regarding the substance, the social housing movements have built their rationale on Brazil's Federal Constitution of 1988 [20], which states that "property shall serve a social function" (Art. 170-III and Art. 5-XXIII). It also states, "[T]he state shall require from the owners of an under-used or vacant urban property the promotion of its proper utilization [...] under penalty of expropriation" (Art. 182). In addition, the federal Statute of the City (2001) enshrines the "right to decent housing" (I) and "the prevalence of common interests over individual property rights" (III).

The movements have also called attention to the quantitative and qualitative housing deficit in Brazil. According the the Fundação João Pinheiro [41], Brazil was lacking 6.06 million housing units, and in greater São Paulo the deficit was of 629,891 in 2014. About 80% of such deficits concentrated in people earning 0–3 minimum wages—the lowest-income bracket. Despite this concentration of need, people at this socioeconomic stratum are for the most part not served by the social housing program in Brazil. With no housing alternatives, they constitute the movements' majority membership. Restorative justice starts in this case with the act of urban residents claiming what is rightfully theirs by the constitution—such as the right to housing—through occupations and demonstrations in order to get the government's attention to its legal responsibilities and the urgency of the housing condition. In this manner, they also call the attention of land and property owners not fulfilling their legally mandated obligations.

Regarding processes, the MTST chooses very carefully the land it could occupy, trying for it to have the best conditions so it can serve a social function, as requested by the national constitution—particularly by being vacant or underutilized for a long time and delinquent in property taxes. The MTST prefers to occupy land in the urban periphery instead of buildings in central areas of the city (as other social housing movements do) for several reasons: land plots are larger in the urban periphery and can accommodate more people; the periphery is where the largest part of its constituent base lives, thus making it easier for them to attract current and new members to their movement and occupations; and, when the movement is successful in attaining social housing projects in occupied lands, it helps improve the underserved areas with new transit, utilities, and services needed.

Whether occupying vacant or underutilized land in the periphery or central areas, the movements incentivize (often absentee) landowners and the government to negotiate with each other and themselves. Such negotiations grant landowners the possibility of becoming compliant with the law by having their land perform a social function. This can be done by either building a project on it or by selling the land so that another entity (the state, a private, or non-for-profit agent) can develop it. In the process, original owners can be compensated for the land and the government can exonerate them of accumulated unpaid taxes. Negotiations also grant governments the opportunity to fulfill their mandate of realizing the social function of land and the right to housing as commanded in the national constitution and other laws. They also bring the state closer to a constituency that it has often been unable or unwilling to reach—that of individuals with the lowest or no income.

Overall, these negotiations bring participants face to face with each other, opening up the possibility of mutual understanding, compassion, and consensual agreements. If and when such negotiations are facilitated and conducted appropriately, the dialogue can get to the structural causes of the injustice been discussed (in this case the housing deficit and its effect on millions of Brazilians) and the acknowledgment of the different agents' and institutions' implications in both creating and solving it. I claim that, in the instances when the social housing movements' representatives are successful at making the collective rights (to housing) prevail over the relative individual rights (of private property), justice is restored (vacant or underutilized lands are converted into social housing or mix-use projects serving the underserved). All actors involved make sacrifices yet also gain something and can claim a fundamental contribution to solving conflict and promoting or restoring justice.

Restorative justice is not unknown in Brazil. In 2004, the Brazilian Ministry of Justice received a small United Nations Development Program's (UNDP) grant to launch the country's first official restorative justice (RJ) pilot projects. Dominic Barter [42] led projects in São Paulo and Porto Alegre, relying on the experience of the Center for Nonviolent Communication (CNVC), which studies how people use their power to create partnership and cooperation, "emphasizing compassion as the motivation for action rather than fear, guilt, blame, coercion, threat or the justification of punishment" [43]. Barter created "restorative circles" in favelas confronting violence, which involved three key participants: the author of a given act, the recipient of that act, and the local community. These terms (author, recipient) were preferred to the victim and offender labels, in recognition of the complex web of mutuality that much violence both involves and demands to be solved [44]. Despite these promising experiences, today restorative justice in Brazil mainly exists in order to assist the judicial process. Since the judiciary is not capable of keeping up with its demand, small cases are often directed into mediation through restorative justice, giving it an auxiliary role, which it has also had in the US and other countries.

As a planning mode, restorative justice can combine the strengths of advocacy planning and communicative action while reducing their drawbacks. On the one hand, restorative justice would correct a traditional weakness associated with the equity or advocacy planning approach:

> Traditionally invested in the promotion of outcomes of social equity, the advocacy model has less to say about the procedural aspects of the planning process itself. Through social learning, a more inclusive, participatory process would be able to accommodate varying viewpoints without losing sight of the goals of social equity. The practice of advocacy, currently carrying adversarial undertones, would be subsumed under a more general effort to cultivate trust and reciprocity between stakeholders. [45] (p. 132).

Thus, without relinquishing a clear benchmark of justice as a result of the planning process, restorative justice would press for a participatory and compassionate process of deliberation, which is not an emphasis of advocacy planning.

On the other hand, the crafting and nurturing of a participatory process in restorative justice approaches would not abandon the pursuit of more just tangible outcomes as a result of planning, as may be the case in communicative action processes [45]. In fact, communicative action has been criticized for its focus on process at the expense of a concern with outcomes [46]. Proponents argue that consensus building is not doomed to produce the lowest common denominator solutions to planning problems and can deliver outcomes that are more than the sum of the expectations that stakeholders come to the negotiating table with [47]. Yet, power differentials can be deterministic in decision-making processes and can result in a zero-sum game of winners and losers. Indeed, "[s]ome empirical research from planning practice has demonstrated that the ideals of communicative rationality and consensus-formation are difficult to achieve" [46] (p. 123). Actors may see no benefit in behaving communicatively when strategic, instrumental power plays and manipulation of information could result in more favorable outcomes for themselves [48]. "Skillful facilitation of the process and stakeholders that have both something to give to and something to gain from other stakeholders are key" for some tangible just outcomes to be attained [46] (p. 123). Restorative justice is predicated on such a process.

7. Planning Instruments

Aside from building the rationale for its housing struggles on the federal laws of the country (and in many instances congruent local laws), the social housing movements in Brazil have made use of progressive planning tools, programs, and professionals that can and have operationalized their demands. I briefly discuss and provide examples of four fundamental ones:

7.1. Zoning: Special Zones of Social Interest or ZEIS

Zoning is "inclusionary" when it is used to increase the supply of affordable housing or social housing in locations where pure market mechanisms would have the effect of deepening socio-spatially segregationist processes [49]. In that spirit, the Brazilian zoning instrument Special Zones of Social Interest (*Zonas Especiales de Interés Social*, ZEIS) is a form of both inclusionary zoning and land value capture in benefit of the community in the form of production of social housing.

Since the 1980s, ZEIS has been frequently used in Brazil to recognize and consolidate informal settlements (ZEIS of regularization). Yet, in its most recent and innovative uses, the instrument designates land for the promotion of social housing by public and private developers. There are five types of ZEIS: (1) Regularization of land occupied by informal settlements; (2) Vacant or underutilized lots with potential to be urbanized; (3) Vacant or underutilized building in urbanized areas; (4) Vacant or underutilized lots in protected areas with potential to be urbanized; and (5) Vacant or underutilized lots in an urbanized area. ZEIS is the most widely used instrument for recognition of land possession, protection of the right to housing, and prevention of forced evictions. Some municipalities have demarcated ZEIS in urban voids close to or surrounded by urbanized areas, with the intention of articulating housing needs with opportunities, such as underutilized land and surrounding urban infrastructure [50].

The Edith Garden ZEIS in the city of São Paulo is located in one of city's areas of real estate expansion. Given growing market pressures, the local low-income population at risk of eviction had to organize, build a coalition of supporters, and bring its case to court to be able to attain the ZEIS designation that protected its permanence in place. Similarly, through negotiations following occupation, the MTST was able to convert the land occupied by the encampment Nova Palestina from its original designation as protected area, in which only 10% of the land could be built, into a ZEIS 4, applied to natural areas in which 30% of land area is allowed to be built. In the process, MTST members also committed to become the stewards of the 70% of the remaining natural land.

7.2. Property Taxation: Urban Property and Land Tax or IPTU

The progressive Urban Property and Land Tax (*Imposto Predial e Territorial Urbano*, IPTU) increases the percentages of tax on each accumulated year of property idleness. It is the mechanism used by municipalities in Brazil to dincentivize both real estate idleness and speculation in areas with consolidated infrastructure. Vacant or underutilized structures and lots receive a notification by the government. Owners of the property have a year to present plans for using the building or land. After that period, the owner needs to start paying progressive taxes on the property while it remains idle. After five years of increased taxation, if there is no progress in using the property, it can be expropriated by the municipality. The mechanism is supported by the City Statute, a federal law that since 2001 regulates the use of property.

Implementation of the progressive IPTU has been very slow in Brazil. In addition to São Paulo, only seven other Brazilian cities have applied the IPTU so far, and in only two—Maringá (PR) and São Bernardo do Campo (SP)—the mechanism has not suffered discontinuity with the change of administrations. In the city of São Paulo, as of May 2018, 1098 idle real estate owners have ignored the warning of the city to use their property and, therefore, are subject to pay more expensive IPTU. The number represents 85% of the addresses notified by the government so far, yet the number of notifications is small in comparison with the number of idle lands and buildings that would qualify for it in the city [51].

In São Paulo, the progressive IPTU began to be charged in 2016. According to city records, until December 2017, only 94 properties notified had fulfilled the obligations—less than 10% of the total. There are fewer cases than hoped for in which the notification of idleness is reversed by the proper use of the property. The very logic of the real estate market represents an obstacle to make effective the use of empty real estate in the city, especially in the central region. Addresses in the city center concentrate the largest amount of vacant or underutilized real estate. Most are from commercial buildings that lost condominiums to more coveted addresses. With low demand, rental prices plummeted. In some cases, it was more economically advantageous for owners to keep their buildings closed or turn them into parking lots. Many owners also chose not to pay progressive taxes expecting instead compensation for expropriation by the public sector or amnesty of tax debt. In some cases, some owners concentrate a lot of real estate and it makes no difference to them if they get one or two of their properties closed [51].

Besides the low adhesion of empty real estate owners to use their property, the incentive to the social function of buildings provided for in the constitution suffered a setback in the mayoral administration of João Doria (PSDB), succeeded in April 2018 by Bruno Covas (PSDB). The number of idle addresses reported in 2017 (58) fell sharply compared to those in Fernando Haddad's administration (PT)—more than 500 in each of the last two years of the mandate. In 2018, only five new properties has been included in the list. Political will is lacking.

Despite these challenges, there are examples of how the application of progressive IPTU can be converted into housing. In addition to the conversion of individual properties, the potential of IPTU to address the social housing deficit can be scaled up. For instance, in Santo André (SP) in 2015, the city government created a land bank formed by notified owners who preferred to cede their idle real estate. The properties were allocated to the construction of housing by MCMV. This is a precedent that the MTST could help to emulate in other cities and metro areas.

7.3. Federal Social Housing Program My House My Life—Entidades (MCMV—E)

The My House My Life [52], is Brazil's first effort at large-scale public housing, a nationwide program tasked with constructing 3.4 million homes as part of a broader effort to both tackle the housing deficit and expand economic growth. Initiated by President Lula and expanded by President Rousseff, MCMV was instituted in 2009 to provide improved housing for an estimated seven million Brazilians residing in suboptimal living conditions. The first phase of the program received a budget of R$34 billion (USD $17.55 billion) to construct one million homes. The second phase of MCMV was established in 2011 with a budget of R$72 billion (USD $35.1 billion) to build an additional two million homes by 2016. Participants of the program are offered financing options either to buy a home constructed by the government or to renovate an existing one. Families with monthly incomes of less than R$5000 are invited to apply, with priority given to families who earn less than R$1600 per month [53], an income still too high for most MTST members. In 2016, the Minister of Cities was preparing the launch of a third stage of MCMV but, given Brazil's crisis, could not establish goals or procure funding.

Despite the commendable resources and political will invested on MCMV, the program has been justly criticized as representing a reversal of the spirit of the urban reform or even an anti-reform, incrementing the commodification, the sociospatial segregation, and the unsustainability of Brazilian cities [54]. Indeed, through this program, an enormous transfer of public land has been put in the hands of large private companies that have profited while making terribly small, poorly built, and badly located housing for some in the upper brackets of the poor. Such transference of public subsidy to private companies has not trickled down to the poorest of the poor, who Brazil categorizes as people earning 0–3 minimum wages per month (minimum wage in Brazil was 954 BRL/Month in February 2018 = US$294.46/month [55].

There is, however, a small fraction of the MCMV Program called Entidades, implemented in 2009. It is an alternative affordable housing program made for families with incomes lower than R$1600 (Stratum 1) organized in housing cooperatives, social movements, associations, and nonprofit private agencies. Families have active participation in the design, management, and construction processes. Beneficiaries of the project are responsible for the management of resources and monitoring of projects, not developers. In this manner, people have more control and are able to make more efficient use of resources in accordance to their needs [56] (Portal Brasil, 2016). The average square footage of apartments produced by large developers is around 40 m^2, while Entidades units' is 63 m^2 [57]. Another advantage of Entidades is that it has produced some mix-use developments, integrating into housing projects some cooperative production spaces. Unfortunately, the percentage of funding from MCMV that has been allocated to the program Entidades has been minuscule (1–4%, varying by state and city), another way in which the MCMV program has disproportionately favored large and wealthy private developers to the detriment of small entrepreneurs, professional firms, non-for-profit housing organizations, and community groups. Since 2009, only about 7800 Entidades units have been delivered in Brazil. Another 12,500 have had projects approved and are in the construction or building permit phase. The amount of capital dedicated to this has been R$2.5 billion [56] (Portal Brasil, 2016). The best housing projects attained by the MTST have been produced by MCMV—E with significant involvement of the movement's members.

7.4. Socially Committed Professionals

As stated above, small development entrepreneurs, professional architecture and planning firms, non-for-profit housing organizations, and community groups can apply for MCMV—Entidades funds to build social housing developments. Communities can develop projects and use Entidades funding to contract architecture, planning, and/or development firms to work for them. Given the reduced scope and profitability of these projects (each is unique and is done one at a time) in contrast with the large, one-size-fits-all, cookie-cutter approach of the rest of MCMV projects, it is usually socially committed professionals that take these projects on.

One exemplary firm that has been doing this type of work in Brazil since before Entidades started is USINA CTAH (Usina is Portuguese for factory); and CTAH stands for *Centro de Trabalhos para o Ambiente Habitado* [58] based in São Paulo. Founded in 1990 by multidisciplinary professionals to offer technical assistance to social movements, the USINA CTAH articulates processes to plan, design, and build by/with the members of the social housing movements themselves. It mobilizes public funds and support in the context of the urban and agrarian reforms in Brazil. USINA has participated in the conception and execution of more than 5000 housing units, as well as community centers, schools, and childcare centers in various cities and rural settlements, mainly in the states of São Paulo, Minas Gerais, and Paraná. USINA engages in urban planning, favela urbanization projects, and the organization of work cooperatives. This group of professionals purposely problematizes the single-authored production of architecture and urbanism and generate alternative processes to the logic of capital through social, spatial, technical, and aesthetic anti-hegemonic experiences. USINA uses the social housing movements' occupations of land within the city as opportunities to carry out their projects as contributions to the struggle for the democratization of land and the right to the city. They do so by synergistically promoting the use of *mingas* (traditional communal work), self-management, and the government's programs and economic contributions (e.g., MCMV—Entidades). Each member in the community contributes according to his/her abilities [54,58].

Scaling up the contributions of socially committed professionals would make a much needed, positive impact in ameliorating the scale of the housing deficit in Brazil and the challenges identified with the housing production of the standard MCMV program. These professionals operate under the assumption of housing as a human right, i.e., valuing housing primarily by its use value as home and a bundle of rights, including the right to the city, towards which we all need to contribute to restore justice. This sense of social commitment and responsibility can be purposely instilled in higher education, and trained through internships programs for students and apprenticeship programs for new professionals.

8. Persistent Obstacles

Despite their persistent mobilization via occupations and their sporadic successes in converting them into permanent social housing projects, the MTST and other social housing movements face some chronic and new challenges in their struggle for the right to housing. Most importantly, these are:

8.1. Brazil's Current Political and Economic Crisis

Brazilian President Rousseff (Workers' Party) was suspended in May 2016 after the senate voted to initiate an impeachment process, deciding in favor of it in September that same year. Rousseff was accused of moving funds between government budgets, which is illegal under Brazilian law. Yet, given the magnitude and widespread level of corruption by government officials in Brazil, including and most particularly some of Rousseff's most prominent accusers, many believe the impeachment was politically motivated—a legalized coup [59]. In parallel, the massive corruption scheme associated with the oil company Petrobras, together with other negative political-economic factors, subsumed Brazil into a political-economic crisis. The MCMV housing program has been paralyzed since mid-2015 due to a lack of public funds, and was suspended following President Rousseff's removal from office and under interim President Michel Temer's administration.

Popular support for the MCMV program stalled initial attempts by the Temer administration to suspend it for good, and it resumed in June 2016 with the construction of 4200 paralyzed units under stratum 1, destined for families with a monthly income of up to R$1800. In August of 2017, MCMV construction continued for units within the stratum 1.5 of the program, destined for families with a monthly income between R$1800 and R$2350–50,100 units at a cost of R$1.2 billion. These timid actions suggest that while many changes under Temer's administration represent a drastic departure from the Workers' Party's social policy priorities, the elimination of high-profile social programs such as MCMV may further question the shaking legitimacy of the interim administration [60].

8.2. The Assiduous Political Disenfranchisement of the Precariat

Members of the social housing movements participating in street demonstrations and vacant land/building occupations have chronically been subjected to aggressive, and often times physically violent, police, para-police, and even private forces in Brazil. Some of the movements' leaders and lay members have been persecuted, attacked, raped, imprisoned, tortured, and even "disappeared" (the disappeared are presumed dead). Some of their encampments and belongings have been vandalized, burned, confiscated, or robbed; aside from the many evicted. In addition, mainstream media have often portrayed the movements and their members as criminals, anti-socials, and even terrorists. This social and physical harassment and negative stereotyping have intensified since Temer took office.

When the Workers' Party was in power, the social housing movements' progress was partially buttressed by support from some political allies in government positions. Even so, there were conflictive relations between the Workers' Party, which was pressed to sustain "order" while in power, and the movements, which were challenging the status quo. Now, intent on rapidly restituting a neoliberal regime in Brazil, the Temer administration is ideologically and politically against the agenda of the precariat in general, and the social housing movements' in particular.

8.3. The de Facto Primacy of the Notions of Land and Housing as Commodities

Although *de jure* the right to housing and the right to the city as collective rights should have legal primacy over individual rights in Brazil, the judicial system, police, and common subjectivity of many Brazilian citizens favor a *de facto* primacy of the notion of land as a commodity. Thus, private property is usually assumed to be, and treated as if it were, an absolute right, as opposed to a relative right subjected to a social function, as instituted by Brazilian law.

Land and property (housing) need to be partially considered and legally dealt with according to their use value, in addition to and in prevalence over their market exchange value. Unless and until this is accomplished, the social housing movements in Brazil will continue to face overwhelming challenges to successfully convert their organizing campaigns—and particularly their land and building occupations—into permanent housing projects for the people. This would also be the case for social housing movements in other contexts under similar political-economic circumstances to those in Brazil.

9. Conclusions

This paper reflects on Brazilian social housing movements' courageous response to the grave and growing land and housing crisis in the country. More than merely representing a progressive resistance, it presents the movements' agenda as a proactive crusade that shows us a way forward out of the straightjacket of neoliberal urbanism. Effectively showing us a path to contest TINA "There is no alternative" [61], it carries lessons for countries around the world, both in the so-called developing and developed worlds, given the ubiquitous spread of the housing crisis.

In Brazil, the challenges ahead to protect and expand the right to housing and the right to the city are daunting. Social housing movements are mustering greater courage, determination, strategic planning, and effort in the midst of a more hostile political and economic environment. These movements would also need more resolute support from allies in order to cooperate with them to protect and claim constitutional rights; placing the existing public planning tools into action; reinstating and expanding MCMV—E; empowering social movements through social and legal recognition, capacity building, and programmatic financial support; and promoting and demanding solidarity and reconciliation so that a social contract and ethos is strengthened in the country. The latter is essential grounding for restorative justice to be practiced.

As allies, planners could expand research and advocacy at the intersection of social, affordable, and inclusionary housing; social movements, codesign, and cooperative building/management; and innovative and progressive legal and planning instruments. Planning could also reform professional education to promote social solidarity and commitment, through the mainstreaming of service-learning and internship components into the curriculum in ways that create opportunities for all students to directly experience and develop a sense of responsibility for addressing the housing (and other planning) needs of society's most disenfranchised.

The example of Brazilian social housing movements' strategies and actions also helps us move beyond the process vs. outcomes debates in planning theory, proposing restorative justice as a way of overcoming the biases and weaknesses of communicative action and advocacy planning on the two poles of this continuum, respectively. Adopting and mainstreaming restorative justice as a planning model can help planning deliver on its emancipatory promise—to be a discipline whose practice leads to outcomes that liberate communities from oppressive socio-spatial conditions [44]. Restorative justice can be instrumental in tackling structural poverty and inequality, making visible the invisible, incentivizing all stakeholders to participate and become responsible for restoring justice, and demanding justice in both processes and outcomes.

Successful restorative justice precedents in Brazil (and elsewhere) can be scaled up and used to strengthen the ways *Movimento dos Trabalhadores Sen Teto* and other social housing movements are operating to restore justice in Brazil. Calling attention to urban land and housing injustices and pressing, not in this case for law reform, given Brazil's progressive laws, but rather for radical law implementation, Brazilian social housing movements courageously show us a way to a more just and sustainable urban world we should aspire for and contribute to build. Let us heed their call and respond creatively and responsibly.

Funding: Funding for the international planning studio was provided by the Graduate School of Architecture, Planning, and Preservation (GSAPP) at Columbia University in New York.

Acknowledgments: I thank the leaders and members of the MTST and other social housing movements in Rio de Janeiro and São Paulo for their generosity in hosting us in their occupations and sharing their insights with us. I also thank Studio-X Rio, the participants in the international planning studio, and Brazilian research assistants Luiza Lacerda, Daniela Dias Regis, and Renata Camarate.

Conflicts of Interest: The author declares no conflict of interest. The founding sponsor had no role in the design of the study; in the collection, analyses, or interpretation of data; in the writing of the manuscript, and in the decision to publish the results.

References and Notes

1. Friendly, A. Urban Policy, Social Movements, and the Right to the City in Brazil. *Latin Am. Perspect.* **2017**, *44*, 132–148. [CrossRef]
2. Maricato, E. The Future of Global Peripheral Cities. *Latin Am. Perspect.* **2017**, *44*, 18–37. [CrossRef]
3. Rolnik, R. *Guerra dos Lugares: A Colonização da Terra e da Moradia na era das Finanças*; Boitempo: São Paulo, Brazil, 2017.
4. Lefebvre, H. *Le Droit à La Ville*; Anthropos: Paris, France, 1968.
5. Harvey, D. The right to the city. *New Left Rev. II* **2008**, *53*, 23–40.
6. Irazábal, C. Citizenship, Democracy, and Public Space in Latin America. In *Ordinary Places, Extraordinary Events: Citizenship, Democracy, and Public Space in Latin America*, 2nd ed.; Series: Planning, History and Environment; Routledge/Taylor & Francis Group: New York, NY, USA; London, UK, 2008.
7. Mayer, M. The "right to the city" in urban social movements. In *Cities for People not for Profit: Critical Urban Theory & The Right to the City*; Brenner, N., Marcuse, P., Mayer, M., Eds.; Routledge: New York, NY, USA, 2012; pp. 63–85.
8. Harvey, D. *The New Imperialism*; Oxford University Press: Oxford, UK, 2003; p. 158.
9. Harvey, D. The 'new' imperialism: Accumulation by dispossession. *Soc. Regist.* **2004**, *40*, 63–87.
10. Class, S.; Irazábal, C.; de Castro, A. *Right to the City: Housing and Community Development in Brazil*; Columbia University: Columbia, MO, USA, 2016; p. 49.
11. MTST. NDa. A Organização do MTST. Available online: http://www.mtst.org/quem-somos/a-organizacao-do-mtst/ (accessed on 1 May 2018).
12. MTST. NDb. As Linhas Políticas do MTST. Available online: http://www.mtst.org/quem-somos/as-linhas-politicas-do-mtst/ (accessed on 1 May 2018).
13. Observatório de Remoções, O. 2018. Available online: https://www.observatorioderemocoes.fau.usp.br/ (accessed on 1 May 2018).
14. D'Odorico, P.; Rulli, M. International Land Grabbing. *Oxf. Bibliogr. Environ. Sci.* **2014**. [CrossRef]
15. Borras, S.M., Jr.; Hall, R.; Scoones, I.; White, B.; Wolford, W. Towards a better understanding of global land grabbing: An editorial introduction. *J. Peasant Stud.* **2011**, *38*, 209. [CrossRef]
16. Rullia, C.M.; Savioria, A.; D'Odorico, P. Global Land and Water Grabbing. *Proc. Natl. Acad. Sci. USA* **2013**, *110*, 892–897.
17. Vidal, J. *Fears for The World's Poor Countries as the Rich Grab Land to Grow Food*; The Guardian: Kings Place, London, 2009.
18. Reydon, B.P. A Questão Agrária Brasileira Requer Solução no Século XXI. Retrieved 16 June 2016. Available online: http://gestaodaterra.com.br/arquivos/A_questao_agraria_brasileira_requer_solucao_no_seculo_XXI_Prof_Bastiaan_Philip_Reydon.pdf (accessed on 1 May 2018). (In Portuguese)

19. Constantino, A. Land Grabbing in Latin America: Another Natural Resource Curse? *Agrar. South J. Political Econ.* **2014**. [CrossRef]

20. Constituição Federal. 1988. Available online: http://www.planalto.gov.br/ccivil_03/Constituicao/Constituicao.htm (accessed on 1 May 2018).

21. Oliveira, A.U. *A Questão da Aquisição de Terras Por Estrangeiros no Brasil: Um Retorno aos Dossiês*; Agrária: São Paulo, Brazil, 2010; pp. 3–113.

22. Sauer, S.; Leite, S.P. Expansão agrícola, preços e apropriação de terra por estrangeiros no Brasil. *Rev. de Econ. e Sociol. Rural* **2012**, *50*, 503–524. (In Portuguese) [CrossRef]

23. Holden, J.; Pagel, M. Transnational land acquisitions, Economic and Private Sector Professional Evidence and Applied Knowledge Services. January 2013, p. 49. Available online: http://partnerplatform.org/?azrv33t9 (accessed on 3 May 2018).

24. Peer Voss, a Farmland Brokerage. Retrieved 30 November 2011. "Restrictions Now Limiting the Size of Farm Land...". 2011. Available online: http://www.rawfarmlandinvestmentsforsale.com/ (accessed on 3 May 2018).

25. Standing, G. *The Precariat: The New Dangerous Class*; Bloomsbury Academic: New York, NY, USA, 2011.

26. Lorna, F.O.; O'Mahony, D.; Hickey, R. (Eds.) *Moral Rhetoric and the Criminalisation of Squatting: Vulnerable Demons?* Routledge: London, UK, 2014.

27. Wacquant, L. Marginality, ethnicity and penality in the neo-liberal city: An analytic cartography. *Ethn. Racial Stud.* **2014**, *37*, 1687–1711. [CrossRef]

28. Standing, Guy. 2011. Available online: http://www.policy-network.net/pno_detail.aspx?ID=4004&title=+The+Precariat+%E2%80%93+The+new+dangerous+class (accessed on 3 May2018).

29. Boulos, G. *Por que Ocupamos? Uma Introdução á Luta dos Sem-Teto*; Autonomia Literária: São Paulo, Brazil, 2014.

30. Boulos, Ghillerme. Interviewed by Clara Irazábal, on 20 February 2016.

31. Agamben, G. *Homo Sacer: Sovereign Power and Bare Life*; Trans. Daniel Heller-Roazen; Stanford University Press: Stanford, CA, USA, 1998.

32. Gerstein, M.R. Germanic Warg: The Outlaw as Werwolf. In *Myth in Indo-European Antiquity*; Larson, G.J., Ed.; University of California Press: Berkeley, CA, USA, 1974; p. 132.

33. Sassen, S. *Expulsions: Brutality and Complexity in the Global Economy*; Belknap Press of Harvard University Press: Cambridge, MA, USA, 2014.

34. Flacks, R. *Making History: The Radical Tradition in American Life*; Columbia University Press: New York, NY, USA, 1988.

35. Irazábal, C. (Ed.) *Ordinary Places, Extraordinary Events: Citizenship, Democracy, and Public Space in Latin America*, 2nd ed.; Routledge, Taylor & Francis Group: New York, NY, USA; London, UK, 2008.

36. Zibechi, R. *Dispersing Powers: Social Movements as Anti-State Forces*; AK Press: Oakland, CA, USA, 2010.

37. Zibechi, R. *Territories in Resistance. A Cartography of Latin American Social Movements*; AK Press: Oakland, CA, USA, 2012.

38. Irazábal, C. One Size Does Not Fit All: Land Markets and Property Rights for the Construction of the Just City. (A Debate Regarding Anne Haila's Article 'The Market as the New Emperor'). *Int. J. Urban Reg. Res.* **2009**, *33*, 558–563. [CrossRef]

39. Price, M. Personalizing Crime. *Disput. Resolut. Mag.* **2000**, *7*, 8–11.

40. Sherman, L.W.; Strang, H. *Restorative Justice: The Evidence*; University of Pennsylvania: Philadelphia, PA, USA, 2007.

41. Fundação João Pinheiro (2016). Available online: http://www.fjp.mg.gov.br/index.php/fjp-na-midia/3785-1-3-2017-deficit-habitacional-aumenta-com-a-recessao (accessed on 3 May 2018).

42. Restorative Circles, n.d. Available online: https://www.restorativecircles.org/ (accessed on 3 May 2018).

43. Bouvier Szczepanik, S. Available online: http://www.cnvc.org/ProfileInformation/2013/11/25/sylvia-bouvier-szczepanik (accessed on 3 May 2018).

44. Wachtel, J. *Toward Peace and Justice in Brazil: Dominic Barter and Restorative Circles*; International Institute for Restorative Practices: Bethlehem, PA, USA, 2009.

45. Irazábal, C. Realizing Planning's Emancipatory Promise: Learning from Regime Theory to Strengthen Communicative Action. *Plan. Theory* **2009**, *8*, 115–139. [CrossRef]

46. Fainstein, S. New Directions in Planning Theory. *Urban Affairs Rev.* **2000**, *3*, 51–78.

47. Innes, J. Consensus Building: Clarifications for the Critics. *Plan. Theory* **2004**, *3*, 5. [CrossRef]

48. Hillier, J. Agonizing over Consensus: Why Habermasian Ideals Cannot Be "Real". *Plan. Theory* **2003**, *2*, 37. [CrossRef]

49. Calavita, N.; Mallach, A. Inclusionary Housing, Incentives, and Land Value Recapture; Lincoln Institute of Land Policy. January 2009. Available online: http://www.lincolninst.edu/sites/default/pubfiles/1552_777_Article%203.pdf (accessed on 3 May 2018).

50. Rolnik, R.Y.P.S. Zonas Especiales de Interés Social (ZEIS) en ciudades brasileñas: Trayectoria reciente de implementación de un instrumento de política de suelo. In *Documento presentado en el Foro Latinoamericano sobre Instrumentos Notables de Intervención Urbana*; Instituto Lincoln de Políticas de Suelo y Banco del Estado de Ecuador, con apoyo del Ministerio de las Ciudades de Brasil: Quito, Ecuador, 2013. (In Spanish)

51. Zylberkan, M. 1.098 Imóveis Ociosos em SP Ignoram Alerta e Ficam Sujeitos a IPTU Mais Caro. Número Representa 85% dos Endereços Vazios já Notificados Pela Prefeitura. Folha de São Paulo. 15 May 2018. Available online: https://www1.folha.uol.com.br/cotidiano/2018/05/1098-imoveis-ociosos-em-sp-ignoram-alerta-e-ficam-sujeitos-a-iptu-mais-caro.shtml?utm_source=twitter&utm_medium=social&utm_campaign=comptw (accessed on 5 May 2018). (In Portuguese)

52. Governo do Brasil. Como funciona o Minha Casa Minha Vida Entidades. Last Modified 6 May 2016. Available online: http://www.brasil.gov.br/cidadania-e-justica/2016/05/perguntas-e-respostas-sobre-o-minha-casa-minha-vida-entidades (accessed on 8 July 2016).

53. Healy, M. Minha Casa Minha Vida: An overview of public housing in Rio. Rio on Watch. 5 June 2014. Available online: http://www.rioonwatch.org/?p=14887 (accessed on 4 February 2018).

54. Usina. Bienal Panamericana de Arquitectura de Quito; Quito, Ecuador, 2018. Available online: http://baq-cae.ec/usina/ (accessed on 5 May 2018).

55. Institute for Applied Economic Research (IPEA): Brazil. Available online: http://ipea.gov.br (accessed on 7 May 2018). (In Portuguese)

56. Portal Brasil, 2016. Available online: http://www.portalbrasil.net/ (accessed on 7 May 2018). (In Portuguese)

57. Vieira, I. Prefeitura e Famílias de Ocupação no RJ Discutem Moradias Populares. EBC Agência Brasil. Last Modified 5 November 2014. Available online: http://agenciabrasil.ebc.com.br/direitos-humanos/noticia/2014-11/prefeitura-e-familias-de-ocupacao-no-rj-discutem-moradia-populares (accessed on 8 July 2016).

58. Flávio, H.H.; Guerreiro, I.; Arantes, P.F. Sandro Barbosa de Oliveira (Colectivo USINA). Reforma Urbana y Autogestión en la Producción de la Ciudad: Historia de un Ciclo de Luchas y Desafíos para la Renovación de su Teoría y Práctica. En María Mercedes di Virgilio y María Carla Rodríguez (comp.). In *Producción social del Hábitat: Abordajes Conceptuales Prácticas de Investigación y Experiencias en las Principales Ciudades del Cono Sur*; De las Ciudades, C., Ed.; Editorial Café de las Ciudades: Buenos Aires, Argentina, 2013. (In Spanish)

59. McInerny, P. What's behind Brazil's Economic and Political Crises? UCLA Experts Weigh in on Turmoil the Country is Facing on Multiple Fronts. UCLA Newsroom. 16 May 2016. Available online: http://newsroom.ucla.edu/stories/what-s-behind-brazil-s-economic-and-political-crises (accessed on 3 February 2018).

60. Healy, M. Minha Casa Minha Vida Housing Construction to Be Resumed in August. Rio on Watch. 23 July 2016. Available online: http://www.rioonwatch.org/?p=30841 (accessed on 4 February 2018).

61. Letelier, F.; Irazábal, C. Contesting TINA: Community Planning Alternatives for Disaster Reconstruction in Chile. *J. Plan. Educ. Res. JPER* **2017**, *38*, 1–19. [CrossRef]

MDPI

St. Alban-Anlage 66

4052 Basel

Switzerland

Tel. +41 61 683 77 34

Fax +41 61 302 89 18

www.mdpi.com

Urban Science Editorial Office

E-mail: urbansci@mdpi.com

www.mdpi.com/journal/urbansci

www.ingramcontent.com/pod-product-compliance
Lightning Source LLC
Chambersburg PA
CBHW051315020426
42333CB00028B/3354